Modality: studies in form and function

Modality

Studies in form and function

Edited by
Alex Klinge
and
Henrik Høeg Müller

Published by
Equinox Publishing Ltd.
UK: 1 Chelsea Manor Studios, Flood Street, London SW3 5SR
USA: DBBC, 28 Main Street, Oakville, CT 06779
www.equinoxpub.com

First published 2005
Reprinted 2006
This paperback edition published 2010

British Library Cataloguing-in-Publication Data
A catalogue record for this book is available from the British Library.

ISBN 978 1 84553 910 8 (paperback)

Library of Congress Cataloging-in-Publication Data

Modality : studies in form and function / edited by Alex Klinge and
Henrik Høeg Müller.
        p. cm.
  Includes bibliographical references and index.
  ISBN 1-904768-97-0 (hb)
  1. Modality (Linguistics) I. Klinge, Alex. II. Müller, Henrik Høeg.
  P299.M6M646 2005
  415'.6--dc22

                                2004017481

Typeset by Catchline, Milton Keynes (www.catchline.com)

Printed and bound in the UK by Lightning Source UK. Ltd., Milton Keynes
and in the USA by Lightning Source Inc., La Vergne, TN

Contents

Contributors

Andreas Ammann
University of Antwerp, Belgium

Per Durst-Andersen
Copenhagen Business School, Denmark

John Ole Askedal
University of Oslo, Norway

Johan van der Auwera
University of Antwerp, Belgium

Kasper Boye
University of Copenhagen, Denmark

Lars Fant
University of Stockholm, Sweden

Lars Heltoft
University of Roskilde, Denmark

Michael Herslund
Copenhagen Business School, Denmark

Saskia Kindt
University of Antwerp, Belgium

Alex Klinge
Copenhagen Business School, Denmark

Iørn Korzen
Copenhagen Business School, Denmark

Henrik Høeg Müller
Copenhagen Business School, Denmark

Jan Nuyts
University of Antwerp, Belgium

Introduction

Alex Klinge and Henrik Høeg Müller

Modality: intrigue and inspiration

Modality is one of the areas of study which continue to intrigue and inspire logicians, philosophers and linguists. Since the pioneering work in philosophical logic by von Wright in the 1950s, the kinds and degrees of modality relevant to linguistic study, the subject of this volume, have been scrutinised and interpreted in countless ways in countless languages. A cursory scan of a sample of salient studies also reveals that the area of modality has served as one of the testing grounds of the linguistic models of the day, e.g. the semantic features of Marino (1973), the speech acts of Boyd and Thorne (1969) and, more recently, the relevance theory of Papafragou (2000). In linguistics many descriptive concerns have limited staying power, but modality does not seem to fall out of fashion.

What is it about modality that makes it so resilient? One very attractive feature is that to capture its essence, it seems to be necessary to cut across the boundaries of morphology, syntax, semantics and pragmatics and all dimensions from cognition to communication are involved. It follows that studies in modality hold challenges at all levels of linguistic description. Another remarkable fact is that most often modality is not directly coded in linguistic expressions but arises through interpretation in a context of utterance, be that through conventional indirectness, metaphorical mapping, enrichment procedures, non-demonstrative inference or other context-bound mechanisms. Modality thus poses a challenge to any theory which claims to retrace the path from linguistic form to utterance interpretation. Finally, the elusive nature of the concept of modality is in itself a motivating factor to anyone who sees his job as a linguist as primarily one of providing conceptual clarification. As Nuyts succinctly points out in this volume:

> 'Modality' is one of the 'golden oldies' among the basic notions in the semantic analysis of language. But in spite of this, it also remains one of the most problematic and controversial notions: there is no consensus on how to define and characterise it, let alone on how to apply definitions in the empirical analysis of data.

The eleven studies of modality included in this volume[1] address formal and functional aspects of modality. The volume falls into three main parts roughly reflecting three main perspectives on modality:

- Part I contains five articles which essentially take a top-down perspective in that their main concern is one of conceptual clarification of modal categories and modal functions;

- Part II contains four articles which essentially take a bottom-up perspective in that their main concern is to trace the path from linguistic form to utterance functions;

- Part III contains two articles which essentially take a lateral perspective in that their main concern is to account for the functional domain of modality across language types.

In Part I, Nuyts questions the felicity of trying to operate with a single-level notion of modality that has to accommodate a plethora of functionally diverse phenomena. Nuyts argues in favour of a supercategory of modality with several universally motivated hierarchical subcategories which correlate with some basic dimensions of perception and conceptual processing. According to Nuyts it is not fruitful to look for modality as a category in language because only the basic-level notions of epistemic, deontic, evidential, etc. are on a par with other linguistic categories such as tense. Like Nuyts, Boye also calls for conceptual clarification of the notions involved under the general heading of modality. Boye's own approach is cast in the framework of force dynamics, which offers a set of independently motivated notions which are ideal for capturing modal intensities. Boye introduces the complex notion of force-dynamic potential to describe the meaning of Germanic modals and goes on to discuss the interplay between modality and evidentiality.

Herslund convincingly shows that the dimensions of subjective and objective modality need to be taken seriously. Since Lyons (1977) introduced the distinction into the study of modality, too little has been done to clarify the notions of objectivity and subjectivity. The centrality of the distinction is illustrated by Herslund in specific and non-specific readings of the indefinite article, in the function of the two Danish passives, in some peculiar uses of *will*-verbs and in the use of Danish hearsay *skulle*. On the basis of the data discussed Herslund extracts some of the features that must be elements in the definition of objective modality. In the next chapter Heltoft sets himself the task to explain how levels of linguistic expressions in an illocutionary and predicational hierarchy turn into speaker subjectivity. Heltoft discusses speaker subjectivity on the basis of data drawn from sentence topology, subjunctive mood, modal auxiliaries, particles and sentence adverbials. Going into the act of communication Fant's approach to modality is concerned with how discourse management is achieved through the use of modality. Fant favours a particularly broad notional category which includes communicative needs of rapport management, e.g. mitigation or aggravation devices and intersubjectivity and own-speech management.

In Part II, four contributors take their point of departure in linguistic form. It is noteworthy that only two contributors in this volume choose the semantics of modal auxiliaries as their central object of study, viz. Müller, who discusses the interplay of the Spanish modals *deber*, *tener que* and *poder* and tense in various domains of interpretation, using categoricality as the fundamental descriptive tool; and Klinge, who provides arguments in favour of treating English *will* as a modal auxiliary on a par with the other central modals with a point of departure in potentiality as the semantic field shared by the modal auxiliaries. Korzen has a similarly narrow focus on the expression category of the Italian tense system, more specifically the past perfect form *trapassato prossimo*. He investigates how the meaning of 'distance from present reality' inherent in past tense translates into a meaning potential which spreads well into modal territory and how this may be explored in discoursal backgrounding. The perspective of these three writers is clearly bottom up, going from linguistic form to contextually conditioned functions. In the fourth contribution in Part II Askedal investigates linearisation patterns in German verb chains containing modal verbs or predicates, which is a central concern to anyone assuming iconic form-function correlations. Askedal shows that in fact such correlations may be identified, though they do not appear to be perfect.

In Part III, Durst-Andersen introduces a new cognitively-oriented approach to typology. His typology organises languages into speaker-oriented languages, where mood is the determinant category, reality-oriented languages, where aspect is the determinant category and hearer-oriented languages where tense is the determinant category. It is argued that the determinant category of the TAM-system will have a tendency to take over functions which are peripheral to its own inherent semantic territory, 'squeezing' the other verbal categories, which means that a study of the modal system of a given language requires a study of the full interplay of the TAM-system. In their typological study of modal polyfunctionality in 237 languages, van der Auwera et al. operate with a narrow possibility-necessity pair as the object of focus, a dimension easily traceable through a substantial number of languages. Since they have no preconceived formal category to look for, a priori verbal categories, non-verbal affixes, particles and adverbs all qualify as data on an equal footing. Interestingly, on the basis of their findings they hint at the possibility that the close association of modality with verbal categories might be a phenomenon prevalent in languages which belong to a particular European *Sprachbund*.

In the process of working as editors with the writers and their contributions to this volume it became increasingly clear to us that finer internal distinctions in a super-category of modality are urgently called for, preferably with the empirical support of typological studies. These finer distinctions probably need to be pegged to an illocutionary and predicational hierarchy, most likely one reflecting basic cognitive categories involved in utterance processing. Those cognitive categories include the dimensions of perceived objectivity and subjectivity, which seem to be of central importance to our understanding of modality as a super-category. Studies going from form to function are also essential to uncovering central elements to the formulation of more adequately delineated categories. This volume offers suggestions for clarification of the notional framework involved in the study of modal forms and modal functions and it offers analyses of a wide range of data illustrating the scope of modality in language. It is our hope that both the suggestions made and the data analysed will intrigue and inspire linguists to strive for further conceptual clarification.

Note

1   The initiative to compile this volume was taken by the participants at the Copenhagen Modality Symposium at the Faculty of Language, Communication and Cultural Studies of the Copenhagen Business School in August 2002. As editors we would like to thank all the contributors for their unwavering support in this endeavour; we would like to thank the Danish Research Council for the Humanities and the Copenhagen Business School for granting the resources that made both the Symposium and this publication possible. We would also like to thank Susanne Schmidt for helping us to sort out intricacies of layout that lie beyond our modest command of new technology.

References

Boyd, J. and Thorne, J. (1969) The Semantics of Modal Verbs. *Journal of Linguistics* 5: 57–74.
Lyons, J. (1977) *Semantics. Vol. 2*. Cambridge: Cambridge University Press.
Marino, M. (1973) A feature analysis of the modal system of English. *Lingua* 32: 309–23.
Papafragou, A. (2000) *Modality: issues in the semantics-pragmatics interface*. Oxford: Elsevier Science.

1 The modal confusion: on terminology and the concepts behind it

Jan Nuyts

1 Introduction[1]

'Modality' is one of the 'golden oldies' among the basic notions in the semantic analysis of language. But, in spite of this, it also remains one of the most problematic and controversial notions: there is no consensus on how to define and characterise it, let alone on how to apply definitions in the empirical analysis of data. And there are no signs that the debates are heading in the direction of a final solution. Palmer (2001: 1) posits that 'it has come to be recognized in recent years that modality is a valid cross-language grammatical category that can be the subject of a typological study [and no doubt any other kind of study]'. As such, Palmer argues, modality is comparable to the categories of tense and aspect. Bybee et al. (1994: 176), however, already suggested that, unlike for the domains of tense and aspect, 'it may be impossible to come up with a succinct characterization of the notional domain of modality'. Still, they too expressed the belief, in line with Bybee's (1985) forecast, that 'a real understanding of modality would emerge from a study of [...] diachronic relations'. However, if – as is abundantly clear by now – the notion is so hard to grasp, the question imposes itself whether it is really a felicitous one, in terms of its basic conception.

In this chapter, then, I will take a no doubt highly controversial position and argue that the current notion of 'modality' is not a very fortunate one[2], for basic conceptual reasons. First of all, it should not be considered a notion at the same level of analysis as tense (or time marking more generally) and aspect: it rather constitutes a 'higher order category'. But as such, it conflates and separates semantic dimensions in ways in which it ought not to. It would be best if the (current) notion were 'disassembled' in favour of a number of more specific semantic concepts, each of which (or at least most of which) should be treated as basic and should be studied in its/their own right, on an equal par with time and (types of) aspect. Some (but not all) of these more specific 'modal' categories may still be grouped together (more loosely and probably with the inclusion of yet other categories) in a wider 'supercategory' on the basis of certain semantic criteria (though different ones from those commonly assumed to underlie the notion of modality) – but something similar applies to notions such as time and aspect as well.

Of course, this discussion also crucially hinges on the question which semantic (sub)categories ought to be distinguished within the traditional domain of modality and how they ought to be defined. Part of the ongoing controversy about the notion of modality is precisely about this issue – in fact, disputes about the subcategories are no doubt in part fed by the 'pressure' to enforce a uniformity among them which at once legitimises the global notion of modality. So a considerable part of this chapter will be devoted to an argument for one specific way of dividing the inheritance of the traditional category of modality.

Discussions regarding terminology and its conceptual foundations are unavoidably always inspired by one's theoretical perspective on language. The view underlying the present analysis – what I have called a cognitive-functional one – is set out in some detail in Nuyts (1992; 2001a). Relevant aspects of it will be introduced in the course of the discussions in this chapter.

This chapter is organised as follows. The next section is devoted to a discussion of the different (sub)notions which figure centrally in the 'traditional' analysis of the concept of modality, viz. the triplet dynamic modality, deontic modality and epistemic modality (the latter plus or minus the notion of 'evidentiality'), as well as a few notions which involve a regrouping of these. Section 3 critically reviews a number of arguments which are/might be put forward in favour of grouping these different notions or meanings together in one supercategory of modality. And Section 4 presents a wider perspective on the semantic position of these three (or four) modal notions, also in relation to the notions of time and aspect and other relevant ones, in an attempt to demonstrate in which ways they do (and do not) hang together.

2   Defining modality-cum-modal subcategories

Definitions of categories such as 'tense' and 'aspect' usually involve a straightforward and coherent semantic characterisation of the domain. Tense, for example, would by many be defined as the grammatical expression of the temporal situation of the event or the state of affairs expressed in the clause (see e.g. Comrie, 1985). Aspect would be defined (at least) as the grammatical expression of the internal temporal constituency of the state of affairs (see e.g. Comrie, 1976)[3]. However, as already implied in the quote from Bybee et al. (1994) in the introduction, it is practically impossible to come up with a comparable basic definition of the domain of modality. We virtually have no choice but to cast a definition explicitly in terms of a set of more specific semantic categories, each of which needs to be defined separately. And the definition of 'modality' as such is then very often no more than the listing of those categories, or it involves a reference to certain features which these more specific categories would share[4].

As suggested in the introduction, there is no unanimity regarding what the list of participating categories should look like, but in one version there are three dimensions: dynamic, deontic and epistemic modality. The meanings at issue in these three are also to be found in other views regarding the composition of the list, but are then 'hidden' behind other labels which organise the semantic fields involved somewhat differently – I return to such alternative views at the end of this section[5]. There is, of course, also no unanimity about how each of these three notions should be characterised in detail. The definitional matter is all too often glossed over rapidly (definitions of the relevant notions in the literature often take up no more than one or two lines). Since having a clear concept of what one means by these notions is crucial to the debates, however, let me first spend a few pages defining and characterising them, specifically in terms of how they will be used in this chapter[6].

2.1   Dynamic modality

First, there is a category which has been labelled 'dynamic modality' (Palmer, 1979; 1983; 2001; Perkins, 1983), or 'facultative modality' (de Schutter, 1983; Goossens, 1985) or 'inherent modality' (Hengeveld, 1988) – I will use the term 'dynamic modality' here. In the traditional definition (e.g. Goossens, 1985), this is usually characterised as an ascription of a capacity/ability to the subject-participant in the clause (the subject is able to perform the action expressed by the main verb in the clause), of the kind expressed in the modal auxiliary in (1a) or the predicative adjective in (1b). It would be better to speak about a capacity of the first argument of the predicate, or of the 'controlling' participant in the state of affairs, though, since in passives such as (1c) it is this (implicit) participant rather than the grammatical subject who/which 'carries' the capacity[7].

(1) (a)   John can cook fabulously.
     (b)   John is able to come to the party tomorrow after all.
     (c)   The table has been dismantled, so that it can be transported more easily.

But the category of dynamic modality should probably be caught wider than is sometimes suggested, in a number of ways.

First of all, to the extent that it concerns the notion of capacity/ability, this needs to be defined broadly: the ability can be entirely inherent to the first-argument participant, as in (1a) (at least in its most obvious reading), or it can be a capacity of that participant determined by the circumstances explicitly expressed in the clause, as in (1c), or implicit in the context, as in (1b). (1a) can actually get this reading too, if used in the appropriate context, e.g. when one adds: 'provided his wife gives him the necessary instructions'. (Similarly, *be able to* can also be used in a strictly participant-internal way.)

Second, the category is not restricted to ability alone, but also covers an expression of needs of the first-argument participant (as is also observed by Palmer, 1979: 91ff). One can thereby again distinguish between a need which is entirely inherent to the first-argument participant, as expressed by the modal auxiliary in (2a) and the auxiliary-like predicate in (2b), and one which is determined by the circumstances, as in the modal auxiliary in (2c) and the auxiliary-like predicate in (2d)[8].

(2) (a) I must eat something now, or I'll starve.
     (b) I have to clean up this room, I can't stand the chaos.
     (c) To get into the garden you must pass through the kitchen (there's no
          other way).
     (d) You need to clean your paintbrush before you can start painting again.

Coates (1983), e.g., does not (within her category of 'root modality', see below) mention this 'inherent necessity' meaning of *must*, as distinct from what in the present context would be called the deontic use of this modal (unlike for *can*, for which she does distinguish between 'ability', 'possibility' and 'permission'). Yet the meaning of *must* in (2a) and (2c) can clearly not be grasped under the label of 'moral necessity'.

Third, the category probably needs to be extended even further to cover cases which go beyond abilities or needs of any participant in the state of affairs in particular and rather characterise a potential or an inevitability inherent in the situation described in the clause as a whole (i.e. what van der Auwera and Plungian, 1998 label 'participant-external modality'). The clearest instances of this appear in expressions in which there simply is no participant, as in (3a), but it can also appear in cases with inanimate first participants such as (3b) and it is even possible with animate (including human) first participants, as in (3c), or in (3d) in which the first participant is left implicit (all these examples involve a potential, but one can easily imagine similar ones involving a necessity).

(3) (a) It can snow in winter.
     (b) The book you're looking for can either be in the library or on my desk(but
          nowhere else).
     (c) Little Stevie cannot have broken the vase since he was not around.
     (d) It is possible to open the door now, I've cleaned up the rubbish behind it.

One might want to question whether it is adequate to still call such cases 'dynamic modal'. In any case, they are not (yet)[9] epistemic since they do not involve an estimation of the chances that the state of affairs applies in reality or not. In a (slightly metaphorical) way they may be characterised as expressing an 'ability/need of a situation' and as such they are arguably still fairly close to the definition of dynamic modality [10].

2.2   Deontic modality

Deontic modality is traditionally often defined in terms of the notions of 'permission' and 'obligation' (cf. e.g. Kratzer, 1978: 111; Palmer, 1986: 96–7), but again, this characterisation is too narrow and in this case even somewhat unfortunate. In more general and more appropriate terms, it may be defined as an indication of the degree of moral desirability of the state of affairs expressed in the utterance, typically but not necessarily on behalf of the speaker[11]. As the notion of 'degree' already indicates, this may be taken to involve a gradual scale going from absolute moral necessity via the intermediary stages of (on the positive side of the scale) desirability, acceptability and (on the negative side of the scale) undesirability, to absolute moral unacceptability. (This analysis implies that the category also includes a dimension of polarity.) The notion of 'morality' involved should actually be defined widely: this can relate to 'societal norms', but likewise to strictly personal 'ethical' criteria of the person responsible for the deontic assessment[12]. This semantic category is rendered in the most direct or straightforward way by expressions such as the modal auxiliary in (4a), here expressing moral necessity[13], and the predicative adjective in (4b), expressing moral desirability; it is represented in a more complex way by expressions of permission, obligation or interdiction for the first-argument participant in the clause to realise the state of affairs expressed in the utterance, as involved in the modal auxiliary in (4c) and the speech act verb in (4d).

(4) (a) We cannot afford to lose face, so we must resolve this problem
           before it gets public.
     (b) (It is) Good that you have solved that problem before it got into the papers.
     (c) You may go now.
     (d) I insist that you leave the room immediately.

Expressions of permission, obligation and interdiction are more complex because they do not only involve an assessment of the degree of moral acceptability of a state of affairs, but also a 'translation' of this assessment into (non-verbal) 'action terms'. Specifically they also involve an intention to instigate or to (not) hinder another person's actions or positions (usually the addressee's, who also figures as the first-argument participant in the clause) pertaining to the state of affairs, in view of the judgment of its degree of acceptability.

A matter of dispute is whether the notions of volition and intention, as expressed by the auxiliary-like predicate in (5a) and by the auxiliary in (5b) respectively, also belong to the domain of deontic modality.

(5) (a) I want you to leave me alone.
     (b) Alright, I will leave you alone.

Some authors do count these notions as subcategories of deontic modality (e.g., Palmer, 1986 tends in that direction regarding volition), others do not and rather include them in the category of dynamic modality (e.g., Goossens, 1983; Palmer, 2001, explicitly do so again regarding the notion of volition). Yet, if permission and obligation are considered deontic, to the extent that the notion of 'intention' equally relates to action terms – the difference being that in this case it relates to the actions of the assesser him/herself – it should be considered deontic as well [14]. Volition is more problematic: on the one hand, it is less clearly related to action plans; and on the other hand, it first and foremost appears to refer to desires and the question is whether that still counts as a deontic notion. I will return to this issue later (see the discussion of the notion of 'boulomaic attitude' in Section 4).

2.3   Epistemic modality – plus or minus evidentiality

The third 'subcategory of modality' is epistemic modality. The 'core definition' of this category is relatively non-controversial: it concerns an indication of the estimation, (again) typically but not necessarily by the speaker, of the chances that the state of affairs expressed in the clause applies in the world or not, or, in other words, of the degree of probability of the state of affairs, as expressed by the modal auxiliary in (6a) or the modal adverb in (6b).

(6) (a) John will have gotten home by now.
     (b) John isn't home yet – well, maybe he missed the bus.

Since this type of assessment is a matter of degree, as in the case of deontic modality, we are again dealing with a scale, going from absolute certainty that the state of affairs is real, via intermediary stages of (on the positive side) probability, possibility and (on the negative side) improbability, to absolute certainty that it is not real (so this dimension, too, involves a component of polarity).

This 'scalar' view of epistemic modality (and deontic modality, for that matter) is not generally accepted, of course. It is probably quite non-controversial in functional linguistic circles. But particularly in formal semantic approaches (cf. e.g. Kratzer, 1978) there is a strong trend to consider modality (epistemic and other) a matter of discrete categories, usually only possibility and necessity [15]. (This is no doubt closely related to attempts to find a common set of basic notions applying to all 'subtypes' of modality, see Section 3.) From a cognitive perspective, however, the latter approach appears implausible: there is little doubt that humans do think and speak about this dimension in terms of a scale, even if for most purposes they will probably only distinguish rough positions on it. Thus, in English (like in many other languages) the most precise basic terminology for the category is provided by the system of modal adverbs and adjectives and this allows a direct expression of the positions of certainty, probability, possibility, improbability and impossibility. But speakers can and do further scalarise these positions by means of grading expressions (*very probable*, *rather certain*, *almost certain*, etc.). And ultimately, if needed, they can even quantify likelihood (e.g., *a 90 per cent chance*). So, if one accepts the position that a linguistic analysis ought to be cognitively (and functionally) plausible, accepting a scalar account seems unavoidable.

Another matter of dispute is whether/where to draw the borderline between epistemic modality and evidentiality. Evidentiality is usually defined in terms of 'sources of information' (cf. Chafe and Nichols, 1986; Willett, 1988), or, in slightly more general terms, as an indication of the reasons (again usually but not necessarily for the speaker) to assume or accept the existence of the state of affairs expressed in the clause. That is, it involves a characterisation of the perceptual origins of the state of affairs and/or of its compatibility with the general epistemological background of the 'issuer'. This is actually a fairly heterogeneous category, usually taken to cover the marking of information as being:

- directly perceived through the issuer's own sense organs (often called 'experiential'), as expressed by the main predicate in (7a);
- indirectly deduced on the basis of other, directly perceived information ('inferential'), as expressed in the auxiliary-like predicate in (7b);
- derived from or compatible with other general background knowledge ('reasoned') 16, as expressed by the predicative adjective in (7c); or
- received from others ('hearsay' or 'reportative'), as expressed by the main predicate in (7d) [17].

(7) (a) I've noticed that he has changed his office hours.
     (b) His car is parked here and the lights are on in the house, so he appears to have gotten home.
     (c) That story sounds very plausible.
     (d) I hear he's got a new job.

Some authors do include evidentiality in the category of epistemic modality (e.g. Bybee, 1985; Palmer, 1986), others do not directly do so, but do closely associate the two categories by adjoining them under one modal 'supercategory' (cf. Hengeveld's 1989 category of 'epistemological modality', or Palmer's 2001 category of 'propositional modality'), yet others simply exclude evidentials from the set of modal categories (e.g. Bybee et al., 1994). It is beyond doubt (and the discussion later in this chapter will further underscore) that there are close relations between the two dimensions (much closer than between epistemic, deontic and dynamic modality, actually): epistemic judgments are based on evidence and evidentials refer to types of the latter. Hence it is no surprise to find that evidential categories often suggest or imply a certain degree of probability of the state of affairs. For example, hearsay evidence tends to be considered less reliable than direct visual perception. Hence the former often suggests lower probability of the state of affairs than the latter, which normally implies certainty. (See also Givón, 1982 on relations between epistemic values and the use of evidential markers.) Still, these observations do not change the fact that the two categories can be defined in clearly distinct terms, corresponding to the fact that they express different aspects of the 'existential' status of knowledge. In fact, the epistemic implications of the evidentials are not necessary ingredients of their meaning, as is evident from the fact that they are cancellable: although a hearsay marker will often suggest that one does not trust the information entirely, it can also have the opposite effect if used in the appropriate context (e.g. when one is reporting on the opinion of experts) [18]. For these reasons, the present position will be that it is better not to lump epistemic modality and evidentiality together on an *a priori* basis and to treat them as separate categories even if one may expect intricate interactions between them. This still leaves open the question whether evidentiality should be included among the modal notions, of course. But since the bottom line of this chapter is that the notion of modality should be abandoned anyway, there is no point in taking issue with this now.

2.4   Alternative views of the modal subcategories

As indicated above, not everyone accepts or uses these three (or four) notions in defining the category of modality. There is at least one other somewhat different way of looking at the semantic domains involved. The difference usually does not concern the question which meanings are actually involved in the category of modality, however, but only the question how those meanings ought to be organised in (sub)categories. Thus, in the Anglo-American literature one frequently encounters the notion of 'root modality' as the only counterpart for the notion of epistemic modality. This notion is sometimes explicitly related to the notion of deontic modality, among others by Steele (1975), Talmy (1988) and Sweetser (1990), but at least Sweetser's and probably also Talmy's actual use of it turns out to be wider, also including (at least part of) dynamic modality. And Hofmann (1976) and Coates (1983), for example, even explicitly use it as a cover term for deontic and dynamic modality. In the same vein, Palmer (2001) covers deontic and dynamic modality under the label of 'event modality' (as opposed to 'propositional modality', covering epistemic modality and evidentiality). And Bybee and colleagues (cf. Bybee, 1985; Bybee et al., 1994; Bybee and Fleischman, 1995) introduce the label of 'agent-oriented' modality for precisely the same purpose (again opposing it to epistemic modality). In addition, the latter also discern a category of 'speaker-oriented' modality, however, which is meant to cover (markers for) 'directive' speech acts (imperative, permissive, optative, etc.) – i.e. a category which is closely related (at least)[19] to the deontic notions of obligation and permission (which as such form part of the category of 'agent-oriented' modality, though).

Conjoining deontic and dynamic modality into one modal subnotion, which is then contrasted with the notion of epistemic modality, seems unfortunate, however. For, as the above definitions may already show, dynamic and deontic modality are no less different from each other than they are from epistemic modality. In fact, as I will try to demonstrate in Section 4, deontic modality shares much more with epistemic modality than with dynamic modality. This is true particularly also for the matter of agent vs. speaker orientation. Dynamic modality is indeed fully agent-oriented, or better, 'first-argument-participant-oriented'[20]. But deontic modality is in principle fully speaker-oriented, exactly like epistemic modality: it involves an assessment of a state of affairs on the part of the speaker (at least in the default situation)[21]. In the 'basic' subtype involving acceptability and necessity, there appears to be no particular (additional) orientation towards the first-argument participant at all. Only in the subtype involving permission and obligation, there is also a tie to the first-argument participant, in that it is that participant – most typically the second person, referring to the hearer – who is the receiver of the permission or obligation. (So the nature of this relation to the first-argument participant is entirely different from that in the case of dynamic modality anyway, since in the latter that participant is the source of the ability or the need, but not so in deontic modality.) But even this subtype involves as much speaker-orientation as first-argument-participant-orientation, exactly like the categories which Bybee et al. label 'speaker-oriented modality', actually[22]. In fact, as already suggested, the 'directive speech act meanings' covered by the latter notion appear identical to the traditional deontic meanings of obligation and permission and more or less related meanings such as volition and desire, so from a purely semantic perspective it is also hard to see why they should constitute a category separate from other deontic notions[23][24].

Rather than elaborating further on the foregoing dispute in particular, however, let us now turn to the different arguments for and against including these different meanings (irrespective of how they should be subdivided) in a covering category of modality. For many of the elements of the latter discussion automatically carry over to the more 'local' dispute regarding the relationship between dynamic and deontic modality.

3   Arguments for a 'supercategory' of modality

As mentioned, the notion of modality can hardly be defined without explicitly offering a listing of member categories of the kind discussed in Section 2. What are the arguments, then, for handling this list as a coherent set of notions such that their grouping into a distinctive 'supercategory' is warranted? They appear to fall into two types.

One type of argument – no doubt the major one for most functionalist linguists – draws on a combination of two facts. The first is that there is a significant cross-linguistic trend for languages to have a category of grammatical expression forms – the 'modal' auxiliaries – which expresses precisely this set of meanings. The second fact (and related to the previous one) is that there is, again cross-linguistically, a systematic developmental relationship between these meanings: they evolve along a quite fixed path which runs from dynamic via deontic to epistemic. This path applies in diachrony (cf. e.g. Goossens, 1982; Shepherd, 1982; Bybee and Pagliuca, 1985)[25] and apparently also in ontogenesis (cf. Stephany, 1986; 1993; Shepherd, 1993).

The question is, however, whether these – obviously undeniable and theoretically significant – observations constitute a sufficient reason to group these three meanings together in one 'supercategory'[26]. This kind of argument – and to a large extent the 'supercategory' of modality in general – is clearly the product of one specific kind of empirical approach, which is absolutely dominant in current functionalist linguistics, viz. what may be called a 'form-to-function'[27] approach. In such an approach, the issue of the relationship between forms and meanings or functions is addressed from the perspective of the forms (i.e. the modal auxiliaries); meanings are handled as they impose themselves in the course of one's concern with forms and exclusively in function of the analysis of the forms. While there is obviously nothing wrong with this approach *per se*, it potentially leads to a biased view of the 'matching' problem in language – hence of the way language 'functions' – unless it is systematically complemented by a 'function-to-form' approach, i.e. one in which one takes the perspective of the meaning categories expressed in language and looks at the range of possibilities to realise them formally in the language.

In this perspective, then, it is important to observe that each of the 'modal' meanings is also expressed by several other expression forms besides the modal auxiliaries, as may already have become apparent from the examples in Section 2. In fact, there is a strong trend – no less systematic and cross-linguistic than the above observations – for these meaning categories (and many comparable ones – together to be called 'qualifications', see below – including time and aspect) to have a range of form types available for their expression in any language, belonging to different major 'parts of speech' and (most of them) featuring a considerable variety of individual lemmas (often wider than the set of modal auxiliaries). Thus, in English, for one, the modal categories can be expressed, not only by means of the grammatical category of the modal auxiliaries (and related auxiliary-like categories which are however not traditionally considered part of the modals, such as *have to* or *need to*, or – if evidentials are included in the modal category – *seem* or *appear*), but also by means of the following:

- adverbs, such as (dynamic) *possibly* or *necessarily*, (deontic) *better* (as in *you better leave now*) or *unfortunately*, or (epistemic) *maybe* or *certainly* (or evidential *apparently* or *supposedly*);
- predicative adjectives, including (dynamic) *be able*, (deontic) *be compulsory* or *be advisable*, or (epistemic) *be probable* or *be certain* (or evidential *be obvious* or *be plausible*)[28]; and
- main verbs, such as (deontic) *hope* and *deplore*, or (epistemic) *think* or *believe* (or evidential *gather* or *figure*) – there do not appear to be any dynamic modal main verbs, however.

(See Nuyts, 2001a, for an analysis of the range of epistemic alternatives.) Now the large majority of forms in these alternative categories do not feature the same range of meanings as the modal auxiliaries do: most of them express just one modal meaning (with a few exceptions, such as the adjective/adverb *possible/possibly* which can be used dynamically or epistemically). Moreover, many or most of them have diachronically acquired their modal meaning along paths which are quite different from those observed in the modal auxiliaries and often even without them involving any other modal meaning at all. Assuming that these other expression forms are not less relevant for understanding the meaning categories underlying all of them, this considerably weakens the argument for grouping the modal meanings together in one supercategory[29].

But even the set of modal auxiliaries as such casts some doubts. For they also feature several meanings beyond the three traditional modal meanings. In view of the discussion regarding the status of evidentiality *vis-à-vis* epistemic modality, one may or may not still assign a 'modal' status to evidential meanings such as the inferential meaning of *must*, as in (8a)[30], or the hearsay meaning of, e.g., German *sollen*, as in (8b) (German *wollen* and Dutch *zullen* can receive a comparable hearsay meaning). But some modals also have temporal meanings, such as English *will*, as in (8c) (the same meaning is present in Dutch *zullen* and in Middle Dutch even *moeten* 'must' and *mogen* 'may' could occasionally receive this same future meaning), or aspectual meanings, such as the iterative or habitual reading of Dutch *kunnen* exemplified in (8d).

(8) (a) The door is unlocked and the lights are on, so somebody must be in here
          somewhere.

     (b) *Der Pfarrer soll diesen Mord begangen haben.*
          They say the priest has committed this murder.

     (c) John will come home around 10 tonight.

     (d) *Jan kan knap vervelend zijn.*
          John can be damned irritating. (i.e., he sometimes/regularly is)

In the diachronic development of these forms, these meanings, too, clearly fit
into the natural semantic processes in which also the modal meanings participate. Time and aspect are clearly beyond what are commonly called 'modal'
categories. But why should they be, if the above argument for the supercategory
were appropriate?[31]

A second type of argument often – explicitly or implicitly – adduced in support of the category of modality is the assumption that there is some fundamental
semantic property or characteristic which all three (or four) semantic dimensions
involved in it share. If such a shared property exists, this could of course be used
to define the category of modality as a whole[32]. There are a few different (but
not necessarily mutually exclusive) variants of this line of reasoning.

One variant of this kind of argument – typically associated with those who
think of these domains in terms of discrete values (see Section 2) – involves
the claim that all the modal categories can be characterised in terms of the
notions of 'possibility' and 'necessity' (cf. e.g. Kratzer, 1978; van der Auwera
and Plungian, 1998). A problem for this assumption, however, is that – even
if we disregard the issue of polarity – the notions of deontic and of epistemic
modality (and, if one includes evidentiality in the category of modal meanings,
then also of inferentiality and reasoning) clearly cover more than those two
values. As indicated in the discussion of the scalar view of these semantic
notions in Section 2, many languages also have 'basic' terms (though often
not modal auxiliaries) for the intermediary value of 'desirability' (and, with
an additional 'action perspective', of 'advice') in the deontic range and of
'probability' in the epistemic range (and of 'appearance' in the inferential
range and of 'plausibility' in the reasoning range), and speakers can express
(and think in terms of) much more fine-grained intermediary values if they need
to. Only dynamic modality appears to be exhaustively definable in terms of
the two notions of possibility and necessity – in fact, unlike for the two other
'modal' categories, this category is arguably not scalar, but just contains those
two values[33]. (Evidential categories such as experiential and hearsay cannot
be characterised in these terms at all, of course, so if they are to be included
among the modal categories, they offer a problem for this argument, too.)

But even apart from this, one can obviously only claim in strongly metaphorical terms that the three modal categories share the notions of possibility and necessity, for these notions cum 'values' in fact denote something quite different in the dynamic, the deontic and the epistemic range (and in the range of inferencing and reasoning). For example, without invoking a metaphorical use of these terms, 'possibility' can hardly be said to mean the same thing as (dynamic) 'ability', or as (deontic) 'acceptability' or 'permission' (let alone evidential 'seeming') – thus, the notion is 'literally' only applicable to participant-external dynamic modality and to epistemic modality, because, trivially, these are precisely the two meanings which the lexical item *possibility* can have. And even then, the two meanings are not identical, of course. Similarly for the notion of 'necessity': this predominantly deontic term is obviously only metaphorically 'synonymous' to (dynamic) 'need' or (epistemic) 'certainty' (or evidential 'obviousness'). This may sound trivial, but it is not: it means that these three (or four) categories are essentially different and that at best they can be said to share (at a very abstract level) the property that they feature (at least) two values which in some ways can be said to function as opposites (a feature which no doubt contributes substantially to their potential to relate diachronically or developmentally), while they also have several properties which they do not share (including what these two values precisely are or mean). In fact, there are yet other semantic categories which have this property, too, even if it would be stretching the metaphorical usage of the labels of possibility and necessity too far to also use them in these cases: in a way, past and future time are similar opposites and spatial closeness vs. distance are so, too (both are actually also scales, but then of a different kind from those involved in deontic and epistemic modality, viz. without involving a dimension of polarity). And there are probably yet other categories (cf. e.g. 'boulomaic attitude' to be introduced in Section 4).

There are yet other semantic correspondences between the modal categories brought up in the literature which one might try to use as a motive to maintain the supercategory of modality. But without success. Talmy (1988), for example, has argued that one can describe each of these categories in terms of 'force-dynamics'. But he has also shown that this element of force-dynamics can be used to characterise a fairly wide range of very different linguistic categories and so it does not warrant a grouping of these three categories in particular. Kratzer (1978), or Perkins (1983), among others, characterise the modalities as resulting from relating a state of affairs to specific domains of knowledge (*Redehintergründe*, as Kratzer calls them): (in Perkins' terms) about natural laws, about social rules and conventions, or about rational principles. But, as I will argue in the next section, this characterisation can, first of all, again also be used for many other semantic categories and, secondly, it actually does not fit all modal categories equally well: dynamic modality in particular is only marginally characterisable in these terms.

So, none of the motives for postulating the supercategory of modality appears fully convincing. On the contrary, if one takes a wider perspective on the issues involved, there turn out to be good reasons to 'partition' the semantic domains involved in different ways. Let me show how.

4   Modal notions in the context of the system of qualifications of states of affairs

The modal categories, quite like tense or (more generally) time marking and aspect, obviously form part of a wider set of categories of (what I will henceforth call) 'qualifications' which speakers can express with respect to the states of affairs they are talking about, i.e. categories by means of which the state of affairs can be modified, situated or evaluated. This set is far from just an arbitrary and unorganised collection of dimensions, however. Let me briefly explain how, before I get back to our present discussion.

For one thing, the growing functionalist and typological literature on these categories strongly suggests that their basic inventory is universal, in the sense that all languages offer one means or another for expressing all of them[34]. This should actually not come as a surprise if one reflects a bit further on the nature of these dimensions. Clearly, they are not just relevant for grasping the meaning of certain linguistic expressions. They actually constitute basic features of the way humans handle the 'world', perceptually and behaviourally. This is probably most obvious for the dimensions of space and time: all our actions (walking, doing the dishes, travelling and whatever else you have) require careful planning both in terms of timing and in terms of the spatial coordination of the different motor components of the action, at different levels of complexity. Similarly, epistemic modality as expressed in language appears to be no more than a reflection of a profound dimension of our functioning in the world: (nearly) all planning of future activities includes a component of estimating the chances that certain actions will or will not contribute to achieving certain goals and that certain intermediary goals will contribute to achieving wider goals (at different levels of generality). When you cross the street, you'll estimate the chances that you will reach the other side before any cars can reach you. When you decide to enter a BA program, you do so on the basis of an estimation of the chances that you will manage to obtain the degree and that the degree will bring you in life where you want to get (e.g. in terms of liking the job and having a decent income). The same reasoning applies for all the other qualificational dimensions (the modal ones and others alike). In this perspective, then, this set of categories appears to be a basic functional part of our system for conceptualising the world and, presumably, the basic elements of that system are the same in humans anywhere on earth, as biologically given[35].

For another thing, the system of qualificational categories also turns out to be internally structured. In language, this structuring is most directly manifest in the relative 'extension' of the semantic scope of these categories, which is reflected in the possibilities for interpreting them if they are combined in an utterance[36]. Here are some illustrations of this principle.

(9) (a) <u>Evidentiality</u> and <u>time</u>:
He is <u>apparently</u> planning to go to some party <u>tomorrow.</u>

(b) <u>Epistemic modality</u> and <u>time</u>:
He'll <u>probably</u> leave <u>shortly after lunch.</u>

(c) <u>Deontic modality</u> and <u>time</u>:
You <u>have to</u> deliver the report <u>tomorrow.</u>

(d) <u>Time</u> and <u>space</u>:
<u>Yesterday around this time</u> I was still <u>in Paris.</u>

(e) <u>Time</u> and <u>quantificational aspect</u>:
Your mother called <u>more than 20 times</u> <u>last week</u>.

(f) <u>Space</u> and <u>quantificational aspect:</u>
<u>In Frankfurt</u> they have a book fair <u>each year.</u>

(g) <u>Quantificational</u> and <u>qualificational aspect</u>:
During the ceremony he <u>started</u> crying <u>several times</u>.

In (9a), the inferential marker *apparently* is clearly not covered by the time marker *tomorrow*: the inference is valid at the moment of speech, it is not situated tomorrow. But the opposite does apply: the time marker is part of the information which is said to be inferred. In other words, the time adverbial is within the semantic scope of the evidential adverbial, but not vice versa. In (9b), the speaker's judgment of the probability of the state of affairs is clearly not restricted by the time marker *shortly after lunch*: again, the judgment is situated at the moment of speech. But vice versa does apply: the temporal situation of 'his leaving' is part of the information which is being judged epistemically. (9c) does not mean that the hearer will have the obligation tomorrow to hand in the report, it means that the hearer has the obligation (at least) from the moment of the utterance onwards to hand in the report tomorrow. So the deontic form has the temporal one within its scope, but not vice versa. It is not difficult to see that the same principle applies in all the other examples in (9): each time, the meaning category with single underlining has scope over the category with double underlining, but not vice versa.

Again, it appears that these semantic relations among categories are not accidental (in the sense that they would just vary depending on the individual example), but systematic, within any language and across languages [37]. Hence the different qualificational categories can be hierarchically ordered in these (purely semantic) terms, more or less as in the – in many respects tentative, no doubt incomplete and highly informal – schema in (10)[38].

(10)   > evidentiality
           > epistemic modality
             > deontic modality
               > time
                 > space
                   > quantificational aspect [frequency]
                     > qualificational aspect [internal phases]
                       > (parts of the) STATE OF AFFAIRS

Returning to the core of our discussion, then, in this schema, evidentiality, epistemic modality and deontic modality figure separately at the same level of analysis as time, space and the two types of aspect. In fact, as rendered in (10), there appears to be a hierarchical relation between them quite like between the other categories in the qualificational system. This is less easy to demonstrate than for the different combinations given in (9). The reason is that straightforward combinations of (any two of) these three categories in one clause appear to be difficult to achieve, a fact which is no doubt related to their specific status (I briefly return to this at the end of this section). But the hierarchical relations can be construed 'logically', as follows: one needs (types of) evidence regarding some state of affairs before one can even start thinking about its likelihood, but the opposite is obviously nonsensical, so evidentiality logically precedes epistemic modality; and one needs to have assumptions about the possible exist-ence or non-existence of some state of affairs before one can start thinking about its desirability, but again the opposite is obviously nonsensical, so epistemic modality logically precedes deontic modality. This observation regarding the scope relations between these categories obviously perfectly corresponds to the observation in Section 3 that these categories are really substantially different from each other, no less so than categories such as time, space and aspect are.

Dynamic modality does not figure separately in (10), however, and the reason is – as already suggested in Section 3 – that actually it should be viewed as a subcategory of quantificational aspect (this is so independently of the question whether it should be considered scalar or not). In fact, notions such as 'ability/potential' and 'need' are clearly semantically akin to notions such as 'iterative', 'habitual' or 'generic', in the sense that they are all concerned with the 'appearance' of the state of affairs in the world. Thus, like the dynamic modal notions, quantificational aspect notions typically also relate to the first-argument participant in the clause: it is this participant who is said to regularly do something (*John happened to take a walk in the park every Sunday afternoon*), or who is said to have a property with a 'law like' character (*men will be men*). Interestingly, like the dynamic modal notions, the quantificational aspect notions also appear to have a 'participant-external' variant: one can also say of situations that they are, e.g., habitual (*it happens to rain here on Christmas day*)[39]. This observation is further underscored if one considers the scope readings of dynamic modal notions *vis-á-vis* other qualificational categories, as e.g. in example (11):

(11)   [Since the circumstances will be optimal] Armstrong will probably be able to break the world record in Mexico tomorrow.

Armstrong's ability to realise the state of affairs is not only caught within the confines of the probability statement, but is also clearly confined by the temporal and spatial characterisation in the example, while it appears impossible to construe the meaning the other way around. This is perfectly in line with expectations if dynamic modality is actually quantificational aspect (cf. also example (9e) above).

As already suggested, the foregoing observations do not preclude that at some higher level of organisation some of the modal categories nevertheless do form a group. In fact, although the system in (10) is gradual, it does appear possible to 'partition' it, and in this partitioning, deontic modality, epistemic modality and evidentiality do indeed form a group (probably jointly with at least one other category), while – as might be expected on the basis of the foregoing discussion – dynamic modality does not belong to it. This grouping is not motivated by any of the criteria discussed in Section 3, however, but draws on completely different factors. To see how this works, let us first turn to some further observations about the nature of the system in (10).

This system has been developed on the basis of observations regarding the semantic scope of qualificational expressions in language. But, in line with our earlier observation that the categories in the system are actually basic conceptual dimensions, the system as a whole also appears to reflect (a combination of) a few basic dimensions of human perception and conceptual processing, which probably offer a fundamental explanation for the scope issues. Thus, climbing up this hierarchy involves a gradual extension of the perspective on the state of affairs and thus of the role of information external to the state of affairs in assessing its status. Correlated with this, there appears to be a decreasing role for actual perception of the 'whereabouts' of the state of affairs in assessing its status and an increasing role for abstractness and generalisation, hence for interpretation and involvement on behalf of the qualifying subject. Let us compare a few qualificational categories at different levels in the system in these terms (but the reasoning applies to the other categories as well)[40].

Qualificational aspect specifies aspects of the internal constitution of the state of affairs. Making this kind of assessment in principle only requires the immediate perception of the state of affairs and the observation of its state of deployment; it requires no or hardly any knowledge or information beyond the state of affairs. And there is fairly little room for personal interpretation in these terms.

Quantificational aspect already requires the repeated perception of states of affairs and the detection of similarities between them (as stored in memory) in order to assess a type behind the tokens, which can then be quantified (semelfactive, iterative, habitual, etc.), or granted the status of a 'law' (generic) (or of an ability/potential or a need/necessity – again, the dynamic modal notions perfectly fit the properties of this category). And this obviously leaves some room for interpretation. Still, little information is required beyond the (memory of the) relevant states of affairs.

If we jump to time, however (but the situation is comparable for space), assessing the situation of a state of affairs in those terms requires assessing its relation to a complex set of other facts about the world and more specifically about the cycles of the sun and the moon and about patterns and subpatterns in them which – because of their complexity and abstractness – are strongly subject to culturally defined conventionalised generalisation, among others (at the most complex level) in terms of 'calendars'. Moreover, this assessment can be with or without the positioning of the state of affairs relative to some other state(s) of affairs, which is/are obviously equally situated in terms of the 'temporal conventions' just mentioned (cf. *John left for France two weeks ago* vs. *John left for France immediately after he got his highschool degree*). No question that there is a fair amount of flexibility in how a speaking subject can interpret/present the situation of a state of affairs in these terms.

Making an epistemic judgment in terms of the degree of probability of a state of affairs, however, in principle does not involve the perception of the state of affairs anymore (if there is direct perception, there is no need for an epistemic judgment, of course), but is purely a matter of relating and comparing other bits and pieces of information about the world, including concrete facts as well as abstract generalisations about the 'logic' presumably at work in them, to achieve an estimation of the chances that some purely hypothetical state of affairs applies in the world or not. This kind of assessment is obviously much less based on conventionalised patterns of information than (e.g.) situation in time is, because there is much more variability – in fact, in principle an endless variability – in the kinds of information which play a role in it. And correspondingly there is, of course, even more room for interpretation on the part of the speaking subject[41].

Now, although these dimensions are gradual (in line with the graduality of the system in (10)), they nevertheless appear to cause a few real 'leaps' in the hierarchy. A first leap is situated between qualificational and quantificational aspect: dimensions below it are concerned with the internal status of the state of affairs[42], dimensions above it are not anymore (cf. the definition of the borderline between the predicate layer and the predication layer in the analysis of the qualificational hierarchy in functional grammar: see e.g. Dik, 1997: 63–5). A second leap – the relevant one for our discussion – is between time and deontic modality: dimensions below it (and above the previous leap) are concerned with the situation of the state of affairs in the world (hence time and one type of aspect also form a 'supercategory', jointly with space, viz. the group of 'situating' qualifications), but dimensions above it are not anymore. In the latter, the role of 'interpretation' becomes primordial – in a way it even becomes the 'subject matter' of the qualificational dimensions.

In fact, from deontic modality upwards, the categories are all explicitly concerned with the issue of the commitment of the speaking subject (or another, reported person – see below) to the state of affairs. Or, in yet other words, these categories involve (different types of) speaker attitudes towards the state of affairs. For deontic and epistemic modality, this characterisation is probably self-evident. Deontic modality concerns an explicitation of the degree of moral commitment of the speaker to a real or possible state of affairs, i.e. the extent to which (s)he can approve of the state of affairs in terms of his/her personal and/or societal norms. And epistemic modality involves an explicitation of the degree of 'existential' commitment of the speaker to the state of affairs, i.e. the extent to which (s)he believes the state of affairs has been or will be realised in the 'real world'. The 'commitment' status of evidential categories may be less obvious: at first sight, they involve no more than the naming of a type of informational source regarding the existence of the state of affairs. But (at least certain types of) evidentials do more than that, of course: by bringing up the issue of the sources, they signal that the existential status of the state of affairs is not obvious. The fact that the categories of inference and reasoning even involve an indication of the degree of confidence with which the existence of the state of affairs can be concluded from the evidence (see Section 2) is perfectly in line with this analysis, of course[43].

This kind of characterisation obviously does not apply to categories from time downwards. One can hardly claim that the adverb *tomorrow* in an utterance such as *John is coming tomorrow* explicates some kind of commitment of the speaker to the state of affairs – it merely situates the state of affairs, without any further 'comments' on the part of the speaker. Or, in yet other words: it does not make sense to call time marking a kind of 'attitude' towards the state of affairs. The same is true for all lower qualifications, including dynamic modality, as part of quantificational aspect.

The list of attitudinal categories actually may not be restricted to these three. There appears to be at least one further category – only sporadically mentioned in the literature (but see Hengeveld, 1989), and hardly ever considered (but see Kratzer, 1978) let alone thoroughly analysed in studies of the modal categories, probably because most authors would not consider it a modal category at all – which should be included in it, viz. what (by the authors just mentioned) has been called 'boulomaic' attitude. This concerns an indication of the speaker's (or someone else's) liking or disliking (emotionally) of the state of affairs, of the kind expressed by the predicative adjective in (12a), by the adverb in (12b), or by the main verb in (12c).

(12) (a)   (It is) Great that you are coming to my party tonight.
      (b)   Unfortunately, I cannot come to your party tonight.
      (c)   I hate it that I cannot come to your party tonight.

This category appears to be scalar again, with a positive and a negative pole (like deontic and epistemic modality). As was already suggested in Section 2 (cf. the discussion of deontic modality), the category of 'volition' may actually also belong under this label. It is no doubt often difficult to draw a precise borderline between this category and deontic modality – and this extends beyond the issue of the status of volition – but the core of both categories really does seem to be semantically different, hence to warrant a separate category. Thus (referring back to the discussion in Section 3 regarding the notions of 'possibility' and 'necessity'), the weak deontic notion of 'acceptability' is only metaphorically applicable to the weak boulomaic notion of 'agreeability' ('possibility' is not applicable at all, of course) and the strong deontic notion of 'necessity' hardly seems applicable at all, not even metaphorically, to the strong value of the present category, which may be characterised as 'delightfulness'[44]. The reason why this category is hardly ever mentioned or analysed in the modality literature is no doubt that (pace Kratzer's 1978 assumption) it does not belong to the meanings expressed by the classical set of modal auxiliaries (with the exception of volition, if it is a subtype of this category – but that is not how the literature has handled volition, of course). However, there appears to be a considerable number of lexical (adverbial, adjectival and verbal) forms expressing this semantic notion and it is far from rare in everyday language use. In any case, there can be little doubt that expressions of the kind in (12) are attitudinal, i.e. that they explicitly mark a specific type of commitment to the state of affairs. In the system in (10), then, this category probably belongs just above or just below deontic modality, but its precise position (and internal structure) is in need of further investigation.

There are at least two more 'behavioural features' which appear to be characteristic for this set of four categories, which are no doubt related to the attitudinal character of these categories and which thus also further underscore the status of these as a group within the system in (10). First of all, all these categories feature a structural distinction (which has been hinted at several times above) between performative and descriptive uses. In a performative use (which is the default), the qualificational expression marks an attitude of any of these types held by the speaker him/herself at the moment of speech – i.e., the speaker is fully committed to the attitude. In a descriptive use, the speaker is only reporting on an attitude regarding some state of affairs held by someone else, or by him/herself but at some point in time other than the moment of speech (usually: sometime in the past), or (s)he is only throwing up an attitude as a hypothetical possibility, without there being any (indication of a) commitment to that attitude on his/her own part at the time of speech. (So note: this distinction really concerns the issue of the speaker's commitment to an attitude or (degree of) commitment to the state of affairs.) As demonstrated in Nuyts (2001a), this distinction is structurally present in the system of epistemic modal expressions (some expression types – the predicative ones – allow one to make this distinction in a very direct way) and at first glance the same is true in the system of expressions of the other categories mentioned. (13) illustrates the descriptive uses of these different categories.

(13) (a) Evidentiality:
> In those days it seemed obvious that there would be eternal economical growth.

  (b) Epistemic modality:
> John doubts that this will happen.

  (c) Deontic modality:
> John insists that you drop the plan.

  (d) Boulomaic attitude:
> John absolutely hates the idea that he'll have to do the dishes.

This kind of distinction appears to be largely absent in all the qualifications from time downwards. One can, of course, also report on someone else's view of e.g. the temporal situation of some state of affairs without suggesting that one shares that view, but to do so one needs to introduce a fully independent reportative marker in the clause (e.g. *John says that...*), i.e. it is not the temporal marker itself which allows the speaker to make the distinction. (In line with the above discussion, the same is clearly true for dynamic modal expressions.) The reason for the difference in this regard between attitudinal and other categories seems obvious: if one is talking about commitments, it is important to be able to make it very clear, in an immediate way, who is making them.

Secondly, the four 'attitudinal' categories feature a structural distinction between what may be called 'subjective' and 'intersubjective' uses. In the subjective use, the speaker[45] indicates that the attitude is strictly his/her own, while in the intersubjective use (s)he indicates that the attitude is shared by a wider group of people (including the speaker him/herself – this is thus not to be confused with a descriptive use of the forms), hence, possibly, or at least in many cases, that it is also common ground between speaker and hearer[46]. As was the case with the descriptivity issue, the investigation in Nuyts (2001a) has revealed that this dimension is structurally present in the system of epistemic expressions (again, the predicative expression types do feature either or both of these values, while the other expression types are inherently neutral in these terms) – and again it looks like the same is true for the other attitudinal categories. In the epistemic system, this meaning is among others realised by choosing a form type which allows an impersonal subject (indicating inter-subjectivity) or a first person subject (indicating subjectivity), as in (14a) – the same patterns can be found in the system of expressive devices for the other attitudinal categories, as shown in (14b) to (d).

(14) (a) Epistemic modality:
      It is improbable that the maffia is behind this killing. (intersubjective)
      I am sure the mafia did it. (subjective)

   (b) Evidentiality:
      It is obvious that the sheriff helped them. (intersubjective)
      I gather he didn't do it. (subjective)

   (c) Deontic modality:
      It is advisable that you stay out of this business. (intersubjective)
      I insist that you investigate this case to the bone. (subjective)

   (d) Boulomaic attitude:
      Your help in this investigation is highly welcome. (intersubjective)
      I'd love it if you could help us out with this problem. (subjective)

Again, this distinction appears hardly relevant for the categories in the system in (10) from time downwards (including dynamic modality, of course). And the reason why there should be such a difference between the two sets of categories is similar as for the performativity vs. descriptivity issue: if one is concerned with attitudes, it is again often essential to be able to make it clear whether one is alone in one's views, or whether one has 'backing' for them. For 'situating' dimensions such as time or space or (quantificational) aspect, however, this seems hardly applicable[47].

5 Conclusion

In sum, this chapter has tried to make the following points.

i)   The traditional notion of modality (or any successor of it) cannot be equated or contrasted with notions such as tense/time marking or the two types of aspect since it does not belong at the same level of analysis. Only the more specific notions of deontic modality, epistemic modality and evidentiality are – individually – comparable to these other notions[48]. The notion of dynamic modality probably does not even apply at that level of analysis, however, since it is best regarded as a subtype of the category of quantificational aspect.

ii) Even as a supercategory, the traditional notion of modality is unfortunate, since it groups a number of categories which – if their wider semantic embedding is considered – turn out to be substantially different from each other (in spite of the fact that these categories do share at least one abstract property which enables developmental meaning transitions between them). Specifically, the notion of dynamic modality is the odd one out.

iii) It is possible to group deontic modality, epistemic modality and evidentiality together in one supercategory, though jointly with at least one other category, which may be called 'boulomaic attitude'. The criteria for this grouping are different from those usually brought up in the context of the traditional category of modality, however: what groups these categories is their 'attitudinal' character, i.e. the fact that they are all about types of commitments to states of affairs. As such, this group can be compared with a few other groupings of qualifications of states of affairs, including the 'situating group', which includes time and quantificational aspect, next to space. In other words, if qualificational categories are to be compared or contrasted (also in terms of the precision of their definitions – see the introduction above), then it is according to the levels of analysis as rendered in (15) (which for the sake of simplicity is confined to the two groupings just mentioned).

(15)   superordinate level:

            attitudinal   vs.   situating

            basic level:

            evidential, epistemic, deontic,   vs.   time, space, quant. aspect
            boulomaic

The question is, of course, whether in this perspective we should maintain the notion of modality as such. The 'cleanest' solution would no doubt be to simply abandon it altogether so as to avoid any confusion with the traditional characterisation of it, and to replace it by the label 'attitude'. We would then have to start talking, not only about a boulomaic attitude (see above), but also about an evidential attitude and epistemic attitude and a deontic attitude (but not about a dynamic attitude, of course). Realistically speaking, however, it seems highly unlikely that the notion of modality will disappear, since it is so deeply entrenched in our scientific discursive habits and practices. But if so, it would have to be used as a synonym for 'attitudinal'. And then one should hope that at least the notion of 'dynamic modality' will soon disappear and that the different remaining 'modal' categories will each receive full attention in their own right – much as the categories of time and (types of) aspect are studied in their own right, even if with due respect for their mutual relations.

Notes

1   This research has been sponsored by a collaborative project funded by the Fund for Scientific Research – Flanders (VNC-project G.0470.03), as well as by a collaborative project (*Geconcerteerde Onderzoeksactie*) funded by the Research Council of the University of Antwerp (GOA 2003/4). Thanks to Johan van der Auwera, Andreas Ammann and several other members of the Center for Grammar, Cognition and Typology at the University of Antwerp for critical feedback.

2   This is not to say that the notions of aspect and tense are beyond dispute. There are good reasons, e.g. to split up the notion of aspect into two dimensions: 'phasal aspect' (or 'qualificational aspect', as it is sometimes called, e.g. by Dik, 1997) and 'quantificational aspect' (see below). Still, the problems with these categories are minimal as compared to those facing the notion of 'modality' and few people will want to dispute their basic identity and integrity.

3   If one accepts the distinction mentioned earlier between two types of aspect, this definition only applies to the category of phasal or qualificational aspect. For the category of quantificational aspect, the definition would be something like 'the grammatical expression of the frequency of the state of affairs'.

4   The term 'modality' is occasionally also used to cover any kind of speaker modification of a state of affairs (i.e., even including tense and aspect). This use is most common in philosophy (see Perkins, 1983: 6ff; Palmer, 1986: 9ff for references), but occasionally also occurs in linguistics (e.g. Ransom, 1977; 1986; Dietrich, 1992). So used, the term is synonymous with what I will call 'qualifications' of states of affairs later in this chapter.

5   There is one modal notion which I will not consider any further in this chapter, viz. the notion of 'alethic modality', which has been proposed in the context of modal logic (see von Wright, 1951; Lyons, 1977: 791f; Palmer, 1979: 2–3; 1986: 10–11). According to this tradition, alethic modality would concern the

necessary or contingent truth of propositions (i.e. 'modes of truth'), as opposed to epistemic modality which would concern the state of a proposition in terms of knowledge and belief (i.e. 'modes of knowing'). The status of alethic modality in an 'empirical' semantic theory is not clear, however. One possibility is that it is actually another word for what in linguistic semantics is usually called 'dynamic modality': it cannot be equated with the 'prototypical' dynamic modal sub-categories of ability and need, but it does show some similarities to what I will call 'participant-external dynamic modality' below. Another possibility is that the distinction between alethic and epistemic modality relates to that between subjective and objective epistemic modality often made in linguistic semantics (on this link, see Lyons, 1977). If so, I can refer to the discussion of the latter further below in this chapter. If, however, the distinction between 'alethic' and 'epistemic' should distinguish between types of likelihood in terms of something like 'truth in the world' vs. 'truth in an individual's mind' (as is suggested by the definition), it has no role in an analysis of the cognitive status of epistemic modality. As Palmer (1986: 11) states, 'there is no distinction between [...] what is logically true and what the speaker believes, as a matter of fact, to be true'. As far as the semantics of natural language goes, 'truth' is always truth for the language user, hence truth in his/her knowledge of the world (see Nuyts, 1992: 47ff). Thus, it is not surprising to find that 'there is no formal grammatical dis-tinction in English and, perhaps, in no other language either, between alethic and epistemic modality' (Palmer, 1986: 11). In fact, Nuyts (2001a) has not uncovered any linguistic signs whatsoever for such a distinction, in any of the Germanic languages, either.

6   If the 'supercategory' of modality is to be abandoned, it might be better to drop the label 'modality' in each of these more specific categories as well. For reasons of recognisability, I will maintain the traditional names for the more specific categories in the course of this chapter – but see the conclusion.

7   One may wonder, though, whether the capacity is as clearly tied to the implicit actor in (1c) as it is to the explicit actor in (1a) and whether (1c) is not rather tend-ing towards the 'participant-external' dynamic reading to be discussed below. In this connection, also observe that *John is able to transport the table* is fine, but *the table is able to be transported* is not. This obviously raises interesting questions pertaining to the role of the syntactic structure in the meaning of (the dynamic uses of) these auxiliary verbs. This issue is certainly in need of further investigation.

8   Both *need to* and *have to* can also be used with the alternative meaning nuance, though. A similar observation applies repeatedly in other examples below, so I will not mention it again.

9   There is little doubt, though, that this meaning diachronically constitutes a step from the 'core' dynamic modal meaning to the epistemic modal meaning.

10 Van der Auwera and Plungian (1998) actually consider this a separate modal category, yet one which is very close to deontic modality – in fact, they consider deontic modality a special case of participant-external modality. (A comparable position is taken in Goossens (1983). This position is probably not the same as

that in Bybee et al. (1994), however, in which also (participant-internal) dynamic modality is included in the same category as participant-external and deontic modality. See further below for discussion of the latter.) However, unlike deontic modality, this category has nothing to do whatsoever with 'moral judgments'. On the contrary, as argued above, it is a matter of inherent potential/necessity, exactly like participant-internal dynamic modality, the only difference with the latter being in terms of what/who 'carries' this potential/necessity, viz. an animate individual or a situation. The discussion below will suggest further arguments for this: cf. e.g. the fact that deontic modality (and epistemic modality, for that matter) does, but dynamic modality does not constitute an 'attitudinal' category (cf. Section 4) – the participant-external variant is clearly on the same side as participant-internal dynamic modality.

11   Speakers can report on others' deontic assessments. See the discussion of performativity vs. descriptivity in Section 4 below.

12   A gangster can deontically assess some state of affairs in quite positive terms while the average civilian would assess the same state of affairs as morally unacceptable (and the gangster can obviously be perfectly aware of this clash).

13   The deontic modals are typically described as expressing permission or obligation (this fact is no doubt also the cause for the fact that deontic modality as such is usually defined in these terms), yet at least for some of them this is only part of the story. To confine this to English: It may be true that deontic *may* can only express permission, but deontic *must* can clearly also be used to express mere moral necessity, without it involving an expression of an obligation to do something. One might even argue that in the case of *must* the 'moral necessity' reading is the basic one and the obligation reading is only triggered in certain specific contexts, viz. when the first-argument participant is the hearer. But I will not pursue this matter any further here.

14   Another option, which I will not pursue any further since it is not crucial for the remainder of this chapter, would be to consider obligation, permission and interdiction together with intention as a completely separate category, which actually belongs at a different 'level' in a semantic analysis from notions such as dynamic or deontic modality, precisely because it involves not only an assessment of the status of a state of affairs, but also an action plan.

15   This trend is not limited to formal semantic approaches, though: e.g., van der Auwera and Plungian (1998) adopt this perspective, too. (Van der Auwera and Plungian, 1998: 82–3 admit that one could make further refinements in this division, though. But even then, none of their suggestions for what such refinements could involve actually affect their basic division of the field in two values.)

16   Willett (1988) actually includes the latter in the category of inferentiality.

17   The category of evidentiality traditionally has been defined to cover grammatical expressions of these meanings. As I will argue in more detail below, however, there is no reason to limit the linguistic analysis of a semantic category such as this one – or any of the others discussed in this chapter, for that matter – to gram-

matical markers only, to the exclusion of predicative or adverbial markers. In fact, in the West European languages evidentiality in particular is seldom expressed by grammatical means, but predominantly by predicative and adverbial devices. The precise delimitation of forms expressing this category is far from simple, however, especially for the categories 'experiential' and 'hearsay'. Does the normal use of the perception predicates – not only the 'vague' one in (7a), but also more specific ones such as *see, hear, feel*, etc., as used in expressions such as *I've seen him jump in that car over there*, or *I've heard how he shouted at his wife the evening before the murder* – belong to the category of experientials? And does the normal use of markers of direct or indirect speech reporting – often simple speech act verbs, e.g. as used in 'vivid' narration, as in *and he said: 'don't be so silly'. 'I'm not silly' she answered. 'Oh yes you are' he replied.* – belong in the range of hearsay markers? And what about the prepositional phrase in *according to the financial experts this government should be declared bankrupt*? Is this hearsay? These matters are beyond the present scope, but they definitely require further consideration in order to clear up the status of the category of 'evidentiality'.

18   There appears to be a difference, though, between different subcategories of evidentiality in terms of how close they are to the category of epistemic modality: inferentiality and reasoning, for example, are clearly much closer to it than hearsay or experientiality (cf. also Palmer, 2001: 8–9 about the status of the evidential category 'deductive', i.e. inferential). Thus, like epistemic modality, inferentiality and reasoning appear to involve degrees (hence, probably, a scale of values). There are strong forms (e.g. *must, clearly, obviously, logical*), there are moderate forms (e.g. *appear, plausible, presumably*) and there are rather weak forms (e.g. *seem*), while this is not the case for hearsay or experientiality (in the latter, languages may mark differences between types of sense organs – visual, acoustic, tactile, etc., cf. Willett, 1988 – but that is obviously not a matter of degrees of experientiality). And cancelling the epistemic implications of degrees of inferentiality appears more difficult than cancelling those of e.g. hearsay (even if it is not entirely impossible). This underscores the observation that evidentiality is actually a much more heterogeneous category than epistemic or deontic or dynamic modality, an observation which will be repeated a few times later in this chapter. Nevertheless, even inferentiality and reasoning should be kept distinct from epistemic modality, since they do not express degrees of probability that the state of affairs exists, but degrees of strength of the available (indirect) evidence. The fact that it is sometimes difficult to decide whether a form should be considered epistemic or inferential (as is the case in *must*; see also Palmer, 2001: 8–9) does not alter this.

19   Some of the dimensions involved (e.g. the optative) relate to the notions of volition and desire and the question is whether those are still deontic – see the discussion above. But this issue is not essential for the gist of the following discussion.

20   This is true at least for the most basic subtype of dynamic modality, involving the notions of ability and need. For participant-external dynamic modality as defined above this characterisation is not entirely accurate – but a characterisation in terms of speaker orientation would not be adequate either.

21   This is true, at least, for what further below I will call the 'performative' variant
     of these meanings, which is the default use. It does not apply to the 'special'
     descriptive variant. But that is of no special relevance for the present discussion
     – in fact, it applies to the deontic and the epistemic meanings alike.

22   The latter term is unfortunate, too, since epistemic modality is even more
     extremely speaker-oriented (first-argument-participant-orientation is entirely
     lacking), yet is not covered by it.

23   This is, of course, true unless one takes the option already suggested above to split
     off all 'action-related' notions from the more basic deontic notions. But then this
     should involve the entire concepts of obligation and permission and related ones
     and not only these notions as expressed by the relevant directive speech act types.

24   Bybee et al. motivate their terminology on the basis of the observation that cross-
     linguistically, (their) speaker-oriented modality, as well as epistemic modality,
     show a strong trend to be expressed inflectionally, while (their) agent-oriented
     modality is most often expressed periphrastically, e.g. by means of auxiliaries.
     This implies that they radically adopt the perspective of the forms and use them as
     the prime criterion for making semantic distinctions. But if one takes the perspec-
     tive of the meanings, then Bybee et al.'s observations have a completely different
     interpretation: since the semantic notions of permission and obligation are present
     both in the set of 'speaker-oriented' modal notions and in the set of 'agent-ori-
     ented' modal notions, Bybee et al.'s observations actually mean that these catego-
     ries (unlike the dynamic and the epistemic ones) do get expressed in both ways
     cross-linguistically. That fact as such can then not be used to question the notion of
     deontic modality (as Bybee et al. do), it only leads to the conclusion that there must
     be reasons for this formal variability, which require further investigation. (Unless
     the inflectional markers coding the directive speech act categories should not actu-
     ally be considered the 'carriers' of these meanings, of course, but should rather
     be considered purely formal markers of the sentence types involved. But if so,
     then these forms obviously do not warrant the introduction of a separate semantic
     subcategory of modality anyway.) A similar reasoning applies to Bybee et al.'s
     argument for conflating the categories of deontic modality and dynamic modality.
     See the discussion regarding form-function mappings in the next section.

25   There are actually reasons to question the universality of the strictly linear char-
     acter of this diachronic path in the modals – see Nuyts (2001a: 232–3). Bybee et
     al. (see e.g. Bybee and Fleischman, 1995: 5) again use observations in this regard
     to bring deontic and dynamic modality under one cover notion – but again there
     are other ways to look at this matter. I cannot elaborate on this here, however.

26   It stands beyond any doubt that these observations cannot be accidental and thus
     require an explanation. Probably, there are some (very abstract) correspondences
     between these meaning categories which have made the diachronic transition
     between them, hence their systematic co-occurrence in one form category, pos-
     sible (see below). But such an explanation is not in conflict with the claim that
     otherwise these categories are semantically no less different from each other
     than from categories such as time or aspect, hence should not be lumped together
     into one supercategory.

27 Bybee et al.'s modal notions – see above – are obviously also the product of a radical version of this approach. The following discussion can be carried over easily to their arguments.

28 I will not bother with the tricky question whether adverbs and adjectives actually should be considered separate parts of speech or not and on the basis of what kind of criteria a specific form can be called an adverb or an adjective. I will simply differentiate between them in terms of their grammatical status: at the sentence level, adjectives are used predicatively (i.e. as a non-verbal clausal predicate) and adverbs are used adverbially (i.e. as an 'optional' clausal constituent).

29 The (modal) auxiliaries and grammatical markers in general, are often considered to have a special status among the expression types. In some respects this is no doubt correct, but this does not imply that they should also receive a preferential status in the analysis of the semantic dimensions at stake here. See Nuyts (2001a: 268ff; 2002) for a more elaborate discussion of this issue.

30 The status of this meaning of *must* is controversial: Coates (1983: 41ff), e.g., calls it epistemic but admits that it also has an inferential meaning component, Palmer (2001: 8–9) calls it 'deductive' (i.e. inferential) but handles it together with the epistemic forms, Bybee et al. (1994: 180) list it under the epistemic meanings but label it as expressing 'inferred certainty'. In the present view, this form expresses that the speaker infers a conclusion (a state of affairs) from information available to him/her, with a very high degree of reliability. As such, this form nearly automatically implies that the speaker is also nearly certain that the concluded state of affairs is true. Still, this is an implication, hence the form is really inferential, not epistemic. This is precisely how *must* in this usage differs from the epistemic use of *will*.

31 One might draw the consequence from this that *will* should not be considered a modal auxiliary at all. This kind of discussion loses its relevance, however, if – in line with the dissolution of the general notion of modality – the modal auxiliaries are no longer considered a separate form type, but if the forms at stake are simply considered an integral part of the system of auxiliaries in general, which as a whole constitutes one specific type of linguistic device for expressing all the major categories of what will be called 'qualificational' meanings in Section 4 below. See Nuyts (2001a: 268ff).

32 Obviously, related to this are attempts to find single core meanings for the individual modal auxiliaries (e.g., Kratzer, 1978; Perkins, 1982; Silva-Corvalán, 1995; Papafragou, 2000). Since the latter discussion extends into questions which are not at issue here (matters such as the nature of ambiguity or vagueness, the status of lexical items in a model, etc.), however, I will not go into it here. See Nuyts (2001a: 184ff) for some critical reflections.

33 One could actually contest this and claim that there **is** something like a scale going from 'being able/having the potential to do X' via 'doing X occasionally/habitually' to 'needing to do/necessarily doing X'. Note, however, that the intermediary stage(s) then belong(s) to what is generally called (quantificational)

aspect, a semantic category which is by all definitions of concern in this chapter clearly outside the scope of the category of modality. So, accepting such a scalar view of dynamic modality, which would be a possibility to maintain uniformity among the three modal categories, would at the same time 'blow up' the border-lines of the category as a whole, hence would again jeopardise its identity. But in fact, even irrespective of this issue of scalarity, there clearly is a close semantic tie between the dynamic modal meanings and quantificational aspectual meanings, hence it seems appropriate anyway to consider the former part of the latter. See Section 4.

34   This claim in no way belies the enormous variation among languages in this system: the individual categories are clearly not equally prominent in each language (cf. e.g. Bhat, 1999) and their 'implementation' differs considerably across languages, both in terms of the semantics – which (types of) subcategories are realised and which 'values' can be expressed within each (sub)category – and in terms of their structural realisation – which grammatical and/or lexical devices are available for their expression.

35   This is in no way a plea for a universalist view of human conceptualisation, let alone for an innatist view of it. All this is meant to mean is that the basic properties of the building blocs of the conceptual system are the same in all humans – but the 'buildings' made with them can vary wildly. See Nuyts (2001a: 364ff).

36   These differences in scope are also reflected linguistically, at least in certain cases and to some extent, viz. in the possibilities for ordering the qualificational expression forms if they cooccur in one clause. These are tendencies rather than absolute rules, however (cf. e.g. Bybee, 1985, Bhat, 1999) and they apply more clearly to morphological markers than to lexical markers such as adverbials. This is not surprising since the surface of linguistic expressions is not only determined by the basic conceptual semantic status of the categories but also by factors such as informational prominence, and the 'needs' of those alternative factors may be different.

37   There are factors which complicate the seemingly simple picture offered in (9), however, including the factor of performativity vs. descriptivity in certain categories in the system (see further below for a definition). The schema in (10) below essentially only applies to the performative 'version' of such categories. This is the wrong place to go any further into these matters however – see e.g. Nuyts (2001a).

38   More strongly formalised proposals for implementing such a hierarchical or 'layered' system have been made in the framework of a few functionalist grammar theories. The first such proposal was Foley and Van Valin's (1984), in the context of role and reference grammar, which in later versions of the model has been modified considerably (see Van Valin, 1993; 2003). The idea has also been adopted in the context of functional grammar (Hengeveld, 1989; Dik, 1997) and is continued in the most recent variant of it called 'functional discourse grammar' (Mackenzie and Gomez, 2003). If one familiarises oneself with these proposals, however, one soon realises that there are substantial differences between

them and this observation is indicative for the fact that we are still far removed from stable insights in this matter. Major open issues concern not only the precise format or organisation of the system, but especially also the position of such a system in a theoretical model (i.e., at which level(s) in a grammar it should be 'implemented'). See Nuyts (2001a) for discussion.

39   This is obviously an additional argument in favour of considering the 'participant-internal' and 'participant-external' variants of the dynamic modal notions – see Section 2 – part of one category.

40   Not all the evidential categories fit this pattern equally well, however. While the categories 'reasoning' and 'inference' do so perfectly, the categories 'experiential' and 'hearsay' do not: 'experiential' automatically implies that there is no external information required at all and 'hearsay' only requires the words of some other person and no interpretation at all. This again underscores the observation made in Section 2 that evidentiality is actually a heterogeneous category – and the question is whether it can be maintained as one notion.

41   The above discussion clearly underscores the argument in Section 3 that 'relating the state of affairs to some type of background knowledge' cannot be used to define modality as a category: time and space do so as well and dynamic modality/quantificational aspect does not really do so.

42   Qualificational aspect is probably not the only category in the lowest 'group': another category not mentioned in (10) but probably belonging there is 'directionality' – cf. e.g. Van Valin (1993: 7ff).

43   At least for some (what might appear to be) hearsay markers, this analysis is less obvious, however: it seems difficult to call the mere naming of a cited person (as in *according to John, Paul doesn't live there anymore*) a speaker attitude. If so, this is yet another illustration of the special status of hearsay.

44   The boulomaic notions used here are tentative, though: this category is in need of further exploration.

45   Or also, in descriptive cases: the issuer of the attitude. However, for the sake of simplicity of presentation, I will cast the following in terms of the speaker (i.e., of performative cases) only.

46   This dimension is actually meant as an alternative for the old distinction between subjective and objective (epistemic and deontic) modality. See Nuyts (2001a: 33ff and passim, 2001b) for arguments against the old and in favour of the present analysis. In those places, I have actually argued that this category of (inter)subjectivity belongs in the set of evidential meanings. However, even though it does in a way also concern the issue of background information pertaining to an attitudinal expression, the present category appears to be of a different nature as compared to the traditional evidential categories. In fact, the present category is clearly akin to the category of 'mirativity' as discussed in DeLancey (1997). DeLancey also argues that, in spite of the similarities and relations, his category should be kept distinct from pure evidentiality. (One of his arguments is that the two are combin-

able in one clause – this is clearly also true for the present category.) So I withdraw from my earlier position: (inter)subjectivity – like mirativity, for that matter – is better considered a separate semantic category and one which probably does not even belong in the system in (10) as such, but should be handled at a different level. How this might work is a subject for further investigation, though.

47   Related to the special character of this group of qualificational categories is also the observation already alluded to earlier in this section, that (unlike other combinations of qualifications) 'members' of this group do not straightforwardly combine with each other in one clause. (Again, dynamic modality is not part of this.) In fact, if one tries to do so, one either gets semantically anomalous expressions (such as *he is likely to hopefully get here in time* or *it appears he is probably going to be too late*), or one of the two qualifications turns descriptive (as in *you probably may go later today* or *it appears you must do this*), or one of the expressive devices receives a special meaning (as in *you might want to go to that meeting*, which overall expresses a deontic, not an epistemic evaluation and the epistemic modal only serves to mitigate the deontic verb). This may again be ascribed to the attitudinal character of these qualifications: issuing two different attitudes (performatively) in one clause appears hard to do, hence there exists something like a 'one-commitment-per-clause' principle. This fact may have an even more fundamental explanation in terms of the basic principles underlying the system in (10), but I cannot go further into these matters here. See Nuyts (2001a: 336ff) for further elaboration.

48   All of these categories (may) have yet further subdivisions, of course.

References

van der Auwera, J. and Plungian, V. A. (1998) Modality's semantic map. *Linguistic Typology* 2: 79–124.

Bhat, D. N. S. (1999) *The Prominence of Tense, Aspect and Mood*. Amsterdam: Benjamins.

Bybee, J. L. (1985) *Morphology*. Amsterdam: Benjamins.

Bybee, J. L. and Pagliuca, W. (1985) Cross-linguistic comparison and the development of grammatical meaning. In J. Fisiak (ed.) *Historical Semantics – Historical Word-formation* 59–83. Berlin: Mouton.

Bybee, J. L. and Fleischman, S. (eds) (1995) *Modality in Grammar and Discourse*. Amsterdam: Benjamins.

Bybee, J. L., Perkins, R. D. and Pagliuca, W. (1994) *The Evolution of Grammar: tense, aspect and modality in the languages of the world*. Chicago: University of Chicago Press.

Chafe, W. and Nichols, J. (eds) (1986) *Evidentiality*. Norwood: Ablex.

Coates, J. (1983) *The Semantics of the Modal Auxiliaries*. London: Croom Helm.

Comrie, B. (1976) *Aspect*. Cambridge: Cambridge University Press.

Comrie, B. (1985) *Tense*. Cambridge: Cambridge University Press.

DeLancey, S. (1997) Mirativity: the grammatical marking of unexpected information. *Linguistic Typology* 1: 33–52.

Dietrich, R. (1992) *Modalität im Deutschen*. Opladen: Westdeutscher Verlag.

Dik, S. C. (1997a) *The Theory of Functional Grammar*. Berlin: De Gruyter.

Foley, W. A. and Van Valin, R. D. (1984) *Functional Syntax and Universal Grammar*. Cambridge: Cambridge University Press.

Givón, T. (1982) Evidentiality and epistemic space. *Studies in Language* 6: 23–49.

Goossens, L. (1982) On the development of the modals and of the epistemic function in English. In A. Ahlqvist (ed.) *Papers from the Fifth International Conference on Historical Linguistics* 74–84. Amsterdam: Benjamins.

Goossens, L. (1983) 'Can' and 'kunnen': Dutch and English potential compared. In F. Daems and L. Goossens (eds) *Een spyeghel voor G. Jo Steenbergen* 147–58. Leuven: Acco.

Goossens, L. (1985) Modality and the modals. In M. Bolkestein, C. De Groot and L. Mackenzie (eds) *Predicates and Terms in Functional Grammar* 203–17. Dordrecht: Foris.

Hengeveld, K. (1988) Illocution, mood and modality in a functional grammar of Spanish. *Journal of Semantics* 6: 227–69.

Hengeveld, K. (1989) Layers and operators in functional grammar. *Journal of Linguistics* 25: 127–57.

Hofmann, T. R. (1976) Past tense replacement and the modal system. In J. McCawley (ed.) *Syntax and Semantics Vol. 7: notes from the linguistic underground* 85–100. New York: Academic Press.

Kratzer, A. (1978) *Semantik der Rede*. Königstein: Scriptor.

Lyons, J. (1977) *Semantics*. Cambridge: Cambridge University Press.

Mackenzie, L. M. and Gómez Gonzáles, M. A. (eds) (2003) *A New Architecture for Functional Grammar*. Berlin: Mouton.

Nuyts, J. (1992) *Aspects of a Cognitive-pragmatic Theory of Language*. Amsterdam: Benjamins.

Nuyts, J. (2001a) *Epistemic Modality, Language and Conceptualization*. Amsterdam: Benjamins.

Nuyts, J. (2001b) Subjectivity as an evidential dimension in epistemic modal expressions. *Journal of Pragmatics* 33: 383–400.

Nuyts, J. (2002) Grounding and the system of epistemic expressions in Dutch: a cognitive-functional view. In F. Brisard (ed.) *Grounding* 433–66. Berlin: Mouton.

Palmer, F. R. (1979) *Modality and the English Modals*. London: Longman.

Palmer, F. R. (1983) Semantic explanations for the syntax of the English modals. In F. Heny and B. Richards (eds) *Linguistic Categories Vol. 2.* 205–17. Dordrecht: Reidel.

Palmer, F. R. (1986) *Mood and Modality*. Cambridge: Cambridge University Press.

Palmer, F. R. (2001) *Mood and Modality*. Second edition. Cambridge: Cambridge University Press.

Papafragou, A. (2000) *Modality*. Amsterdam: Elsevier.

Perkins, M. R. (1982) The core meanings of the English modals. *Journal of Linguistics* 18: 245–73.

Perkins, M. R. (1983) *Modal Expressions in English*. London: Pinter.

Ransom, E. (1977) On the representation of modality. *Linguistics and Philosophy* 1: 357–79.

Ransom, E. (1986) *Complementation: its meanings and forms*. Amsterdam: Benjamins.

de Schutter, G. (1983) Modaliteit en andere modificaties in de Nederlandse grammatica. In F. Daems and L. Goossens (eds) *Een spyeghel voor G. Jo Steenbergen* 277–91. Leuven: Acco.

Shepherd, S. C. (1982) From deontic to epistemic. In A. Ahlqvist (ed.) *Papers from the Fifth International Conference on Historical Linguistics* 316–23. Amsterdam: Benjamins.

Shepherd, S. C. (1993) The acquisition of modality in Antiguan Creole. In N. Dittmar and A. Reich (eds) *Modality in Language Acquisition* 171–84. Berlin: De Gruyter.

Silva-Corvalán, C. (1995) Contextual conditions for the interpretation of poder and deber in Spanish. In J. Bybee and S. Fleischman (eds) *Modality in Grammar and Discourse* 67–105. Amsterdam: Benjamins.

Steele, S. (1975) Is it possible? *Working Papers on Language Universals* 18: 35–58.

Stephany, U. (1986) Modality. In P. Fletcher and M. Garman (eds) *Language Acquisition* 375–400. Cambridge: Cambridge University Press.

Stephany, U. (1993) Modality in first language acquisition: the state of the art. In N. Dittman and A. Reich (eds) *Modality in Language Acquisition* 133–44. Berlin: De Gruyter.

Sweetser, E. (1990) *From Etymology to Pragmatics*. Cambridge: Cambridge University Press.

Talmy, L. (1988) Force dynamics in language and cognition. *Cognitive Science* 12: 49–100.

Van Valin, R. D. (1993) A synopsis of role and reference grammar. In R. Van Valin (ed.) *Advances in Role and Reference Grammar* 1–164. Amsterdam: Benjamins.

Van Valin, R. D. (2003) *An Introduction to Role and Reference Grammar*. Cambridge: Cambridge University Press.

Willett, T. (1988) A cross-linguistic survey of the grammaticalization of evidentiality. *Studies in Language* 12: 51–97.

von Wright, G. H. (1951) *An Essay in Modal Logic*. Amsterdam: North-Holland.

2 Subjective and objective modality

Michael Herslund

1 Introduction

If modality is the linguistic manifestation of the speaker's attitude towards the propositional content of his utterance, it follows that a good deal of the field of modality can be subsumed under the label of 'subjectivity', cf. Palmer (1986: 16), Traugott (1989). Some scholars, however, draw a distinction between subjective and objective modality, a distinction which is far from clear in all cases. Others, e.g. standard treatments such as Palmer (1986), seem to treat such a distinction as a matter of more or less speaker commitment to the truth of the proposition. The basic discussion of the distinction seems to be that of Lyons (1977: 797ff). According to Lyons the subjective-objective distinction concerns the status of the speaker's evidence for an epistemic evaluation (cf. Nuyts, 2001b: 393): it is a distinction between formally reliable evidence and more intuitive guessing. On this view the distinction pertains exclusively to epistemic modality. But for all its wealth of observations and subtle points, Lyons' discussion is far from a model of clarity and does not lead to a thorough understanding of the differences involved. And it only treats cases with an explicit modal element such as a modal verb or adverb.

The distinction has been examined within the field of epistemicity in a number of works by Nuyts, e.g. (1992; 2001a; 2001b). It appears that subjectivity cannot be equated with speaker commitment, but that it is rather an evidential qualification which can be construed as an opposition between evidence known to the speaker alone and more or less shared or public evidence. Nuyts accordingly prefers to interpret the objective pole of the scale as intersubjectivity. Another systematic treatment of the distinction is that of Le Querler (1996: 63ff). This study draws a threefold distinction between subjective, intersubjective and objective modality. The subjective corresponds more or less to an epistemic reading, the intersubjective to a deontic reading and the objective to what she calls an implicational reading, as in:

(1)   *Pour grandir, il faut manger.*
        In order to grow (one) must eat.

Limiting the objective modality to such cases does not seem necessary, however and Le Querler also admits some larger interpretation, viz. the fact that the speaker implicitly subordinates his proposition to some other proposition as in:

(2)   *Il faut qu'une porte soit ouverte ou fermée.*
        A door must be open or closed.

where an implicit proposition such as 'everything has a right place' can be reconstructed. This subordination to some implicit assumption is, in my view, the essential feature of objective modality, hence its maxim-like nature.

A fourth interpretation is found in Hansen and Heltoft (1999: 5–122). These authors restrain the subjective modality (or 'subjective function', as they call it) to first person utterances and either neustic or tropic modification whereas other cases are seen as belonging to the objective function.

The four concepts of the subjective/objective distinction are really very different, but I shall try to pick from each of them what seems most immediately useful for my purpose here. What I want to suggest is that the subjective-objective distinction is a general distinction which runs through the whole field of categoricity-modality, thereby dividing all declarative sentences into two groups: those representing objective statements and those representing subjective statements.

2   Modality as tonality

In order to understand the field of modality, one can use different metaphors. I have earlier used myself the camera metaphor: the use of different objectives and lenses give different views of the same objective situation (Herslund, 1989: 8). I have come to the conclusion however that the distinction I wish to draw between subjective and objective modality is better grasped by its resemblance with the musical distinction between major and minor keys. This distinction runs straight across the system of musical keys and divides them into a number (actually 12) pairs of major and minor: the same melody can be played in a major or a minor key, you hear the same tune, but the difference is unmistakable. The further attractiveness of this metaphor is the following observation: Lyons suggests 'that the main difference between subjectively and objectively modalised utterances is that the latter, but not the former, contain an unqualified, or categorical, I-say-so component' (1977: 799). What he suggests is a simple difference at one particular point: there is a basic opposition between a qualified (subjective) vs. unqualified neustic (objective), just as the difference between major and minor is based upon the simple opposition between a major third first interval (major key) vs. a minor third first interval (minor key). Lyons' proposal is cast in the tripartition of the sentence into a neustic ('I-say-so'), a tropic ('it-is-the-case') and a phrastic component (the propositional content) proposed by Hare (1971). The notation used by Lyons is the following:

(3)   Subjective: poss . *p*
       Objective: . poss *p*

where the epistemic element 'poss' occupies the neustic component in the subjective, but the tropic component in the objective version. I shall however modify Lyons' analysis because he seems to overlook what could be called the 'source of modality': in a subjective epistemic utterance the speaker assumes full responsibility for the evaluation of the state of affairs reported, he is the only source of knowledge considered; in an objective epistemic utterance, on the other hand, the speaker just reports someone else's evaluation as in general statements, generic sentences, maxims and the like. I have in fact argued elsewhere (Herslund, 2003) that the different kinds of modality can be understood as differently located in Hare's three components. According to that analysis, dynamic modality is located in the phrastic, epistemic in the tropic and deontic modality in both, whereas the neustic component is responsible for the overall distinction between subjective and objective, cf. Herslund (2001b). The analysis of a subjective epistemic sentence accordingly will be the following:

(4)   *Peter kan komme hvert øjeblik.*
       Peter may come any moment.

       I say so   *it is possible*   *Peter come any moment*
       Neustic   Tropic   Phrastic

The objective epistemic, however, will contain some modification of the neustic (notice that this is the opposite of Lyons' original proposal!), cf. the assumption of an implicit proposition introduced above, or one might even suggest that this modification of the neustic turns this 'I-say-so' component into a 'It-is-said-so' component:

(4')   *Alkohol kan fryse ved lave kuldegrader.*
       Alcohol may freeze at low temperatures.
       I say so   *it is possible*   *alcohol freeze at low temperatures*
       Neustic   Tropic   Phrastic
       ↑
       Some proposition pertaining to the laws of physics

In what follows, I shall discuss some cases I believe can be understood and explained in terms of the subjective/objective distinction. Cases, that is, which exhibit clear linguistic differences between the two kinds of modality, something often lacking in discussions of the distinction, cf. Nuyts (2001b).

2.1   The indefinite article

As is well known, the indefinite article – or more generally, indefinite descriptions – permits different readings as in (5):

(5) (a) A musician entered the room.
     (b) A musician is wanted for the job.
     (c) A musician always sleeps late.

The reading in (a) is the 'ordinary' specific-referential reading: an instance of the concept 'musician' is picked out and something is predicated about this instance. Not so in (b), the so-called non-specific reading, where nothing is picked out: it is only stated that something matching the description 'musician' is needed, but the speaker doesn't assert that such a something exists. In previous work, Herslund (2001a; 2001b), I have proposed to interpret this reading, the non-specific, as an instance of the more general descriptive (or attributive, cf. Donnellan, 1966) use of indefinite noun phrases along with the reading in (c): this is the generic interpretation, whereby it is stated that (at least) the prototypical instance of the concept 'musician' has certain habits which, as it were, contribute to define the entire species (or 'genus').

Since the non-specific and the generic readings both manifest the descriptive use and since they seem to contrast in subject position – postverbally the contrast between the two readings seems to be neutralised, cf. Herslund (2001a; 2001b) – there must be some factor which explains this contrast, the indefinite phrase itself being the same each time. Otherwise stated, the difference between the two readings cannot be located in the indefinite noun phrase, so it must be somewhere else. In the work mentioned I propose that this factor is of a modal kind and more specifically the difference between subjective and objective modality: a descriptively used indefinite description is interpreted as non-specific in a subjectively modalised utterance and as generic in an objectively modalised utterance although sentences like these do not contain any overt modality marker such as a modal verb or adverb. They are thus categorical, or what I would call instances of 'neutral modality'.

As shown in Herslund (2001a; 2001b), the distribution of non-specific and generic readings correlates with other linguistic features which accompany the two kinds of modality. The objective modality is expressed by the simple present tense, i.e. the tense form which most readily conveys a general (atemporal), gnomic or even generic meaning whether accompanied by adverbs such as 'always', 'never' or explicit modality markers such as modal verbs or adverbs.

So the generic reading and the objective modality which authorises it, is only possible in sentences whose predicate allows a generic interpretation:

(6) (a) A heron hedges three times a year.
     (b) A heron is circling above our heads.

Whereas (a) has a generic reading – regardless of the obvious ornithological falseness of the statement – (b) can only be read referentially (non-descriptively): nothing in the sentence reflects objective modality.

The other syntactic corollary of the distinction between subjective and objective modality is the existence of two passives in certain languages (see Section 2.3 below) as convincingly demonstrated for Danish by Heltoft and Jakobsen (1996 and cf. Heltoft, this volume). At this juncture it is sufficient to point out that the combination of an indefinite description and the Danish -*s*-passive normally induces a generic reading, i.e. the descriptive use under objective modality:

(7) (a) *En togrejsende **udsættes** for lidt af hvert.*
          A train passenger expose-PASS to all sorts of things.

     (b) *En Alfa Romeo **leveres** ikke med automatgear.*
          An Alfa Romeo does not deliver-PASS with an automatic gear box.

The subjective modality, on the other hand, is expressed by an explicit or implicit modal element, by a hypothetical or an interrogative construction (cf. Lyons, 1977: 792ff). And in such contexts it is, as expected, the non-specific reading which appears:

(8) (a) *En messingskrue ville passe fint her.*
          A brass screw would fit in nicely here.

     (b) *Hvad ville du gøre hvis en kvinde blev generalsekretær for FN?*
          What would you do if a woman was to be elected secretary general
             of the UN?

Also the presentational *there*-construction is a sign of subjective modality and accordingly only the non-specific reading – or of course the referential reading, which is irrelevant for our purposes – is found in such contexts, even together with and overruling the -*s*-passive (cf. Heltof and Jakobsen, 1996):

(9)   *Der dør/bliver født/fødes en kineser hvert minut.*
          There dies/is born/bear-PASS a Chinese every minute.

2.2   Peculiar uses of the verb 'will'

The status as a genuine modal of verbs corresponding to English 'will' is debatable in many languages. Since it is traditionally counted among the modal verbs in languages which distinguish such a class – and that is especially, or even only, the Germanic languages – and since the uses I want to discuss are clearly modal, I assume that 'will' is a modal verb. Hansen and Heltoft (1999: 5–118ff) call Danish *ville* 'will' a 'broken modal verb'. The uses I want to discuss – so-called deontic uses of 'will' – are illustrated by the following examples:

(10)   Early Modern Danish:
      Her vil ties, her vil bies (Brorson, eighteenth century)
      Here 'will' be kept silence, here 'will' be waited.
      Her er et barn, som vil døbes (Blicher, nineteenth century, from Hansen and
         Heltoft, 1999: 5–121)
      Here is an infant who 'will' be baptised.

      German:
      Die Granitstufen wollen mit Vorsicht betreten sein (H. Knobloch, *Herr*
         Moses in Berlin 266)
      The granite steps 'will' be stepped upon with caution.

      Mexican Spanish (Chiapas):
      Este carro quiere lavado.
      This car needs to be washed.
      Quiere que vayas tú mismo.
      You have to go yourself (Gast, 2001)

The 'normal' use of 'will' is as a root modal (dynamic modality): the source of modality is located in the subject. But examples such as these clearly have a deontic meaning, one of necessity and the modal source is just as clearly not the subject of 'will': impersonal expressions, infants, granite steps and cars do not want anything. The explanation could be that they are examples of objective modal uses of the root modal 'will'. This interpretation is further enhanced by the tendency to form impersonal expressions with the verb 'will' as exemplified by both Danish *ville* and Chiapas Mexican Spanish *querer*, a use also present in Italian in the impersonal expression *ci vuole* 'there will-3sg', i.e. 'is needed'.

2.3   Two passives

In certain languages the existence of two passives seems to correlate rather systematically with the modal opposition between subjective and objective. This has been convincingly demonstrated for Danish by Heltoft and Jakobsen (1996 and cf. Heltoft, this volume): in Danish the analytic *blive*-passive conveys subjective modality (or indeed mood as they put it) whereas the synthetic -*s*-passive conveys objective modality (or mood), see the examples in (7) above in Section 2.1. This becomes especially clear in combinations with modal verbs. As already suggested, the objective modality has its modal source in some superordinate proposition, not in the speaker himself. Hence its maxim- and law-like character and hence its relationship with deontic modality. Modal verbs – which in Danish practically all can have epistemic as well as deontic meanings – are thus disambiguated by a following infinitive in either the analytic or the synthetic passive form (examples, adapted, from Hansen and Heltoft, 1999: 5–107):

(11)   *Kan kaninerne **blive spist** af ræven?* (subjective, epistemic)
         Can the rabbits be eaten by the fox?
         *Kan kaniner **spises**?* (objective, epistemic)
         Can rabbits eat-PASS?

         *Den lille sorte høne må ikke **blive spist*** (subjective, deontic)
         The little black hen must not be eaten.
         *Den lille sorte høne må ikke **spises*** (objective, deontic)
         The little black hen must not eat-PASS.

The same point can be illustrated for other languages as well, as in the following from French (cf. Herslund, 2000):

(12) (a) *La pierre **est soulevée*** (subjective)
         The stone is lifted.
         *La pierre **se soulève*** (objective)
         The stone is lifted/liftable.

    (b) *La pierre peut **être soulevée*** (subjective, epistemic or deontic)
         The stone can be lifted.
         *La pierre peut **se soulever*** (objective, epistemic, dynamic or deontic)
         The stone can be lifted.

The French reflexive passive in many respects resembles the Danish -*s*-passive, which is of course also etymologically a reflexive passive. And the obvious common ground of the two is the concept of objective modality. Much the same can be demonstrated for Spanish, whose reflexive passive however has a broader use than that of French. It seems, though, that maxims and other generalisations use the reflexive and not the periphrastic passive, which in a sense is the marked option in Spanish insofar as it only can be used in subjectively modalised utterances:

(13)   *¡Esto no se hace!*
         That is not done!

2.4   Epistemic *skulle* 'shall'

The Danish modal *skulle* 'shall, must' has several uses, just like its fellow modals. One of these, however, seems to depart from the normal distributional pattern observed with these modals, cf. Brandt (1999), Hansen and Heltoft (1999), Herslund (2002, forthcoming). This peculiar use is exemplified in (14):

(14) (a) *Han skal slå plænen.*
          He must mow the lawn.

   (b) *Han skal slå plænen.*
          He is alleged/said to mow the lawn.

The difference from the usual pattern, where the same modal has both a deontic and an epistemic use, is that *skulle* does not convey a 'simple' epistemic value of possibility, but rather as in (14b) an evidential-epistemic reading, the report of what has been told, a 'hearsay' according to Palmer (1986: 51ff). This use, which is also found with cognate forms of *skulle*, viz. German *sollen* and Old English *sculan* (cf. Traugott, 1989: 41f), can be explained as the objective epistemic version of this verb. In that way, the expression of epistemic possibility can be seen as shared between the two verbs *kunne* 'can' and *skulle* 'shall, must' as follows. In general, the epistemic meaning becomes clearer in the perfect, cf. Palmer (1986: 37f), Brandt (1999: 96ff), Herslund (2003):

(15) (a) *Han kan have slået plænen.*
          He may have mown the lawn. (subjective evaluation)

   (b) *Han skal have slået plænen.*
          He is said to have mown the lawn. (objective, report)

This area is of course one of the many where epistemicity and evidentiality meet, cf. Nuyts (1992; 2001a; 2001b).

3   Conclusion

Just as the delineation of the field of modality is a matter of some controversy, the frontiers between the different kinds of modality identified is hardly a matter of broad consensus either. The proposed distinction between subjective and objective modality thus has to find its place in this mess. But in order to know where to look for such a place we must recapitulate and try to define more precisely – 'exactly' would be hazardous and probably premature – the content of the distinction. The elements retained so far for the definition of objective modality – the subjective counterpart seems to be the unmarked case where most people would agree and which is indeed in many cases indistinguishable from plain categorical utterances – are the following:

- The objective modality is characterised by a modified neustic (I-say-so) component, a possible explicit modal element being located in the tropic and/or the phrastic component.
- The modal source is something else than the speaker's subjectivity which qualifies the tropic either with quantifiable degrees of certainty or by reference to some, mostly unexpressed, proposition. This corresponds with Le Querler's opinion and her concept of 'implicational modality' and Nuyts' concept of 'intersubjectivity'.

The objectively modalised utterance thus meets and in some cases almost merges with other kinds of modality:

- The objective epistemic may be indistinguishable from alethic modality.
- The objective epistemic may also resemble and indeed be indistinguishable from root or dynamic modality.
- The objective modality's reference to a proposition, whence its maxim- and law-like flavour, makes it resemble the deontic modality because as a maxim it prescribes rather than describes.

The overall picture is represented in Table 1 below:

	Subjective (major)	Objective (minor)
Neutral	description (= categorical)	norm, principle
Epistemic	evaluation, conjecture	law, report
Deontic	(personal) obligation	(social) prescription

Table 1: An overview of the subjective/objective

We have seen above that the difference between subjective and objective modality may be grammaticalised to a certain degree, e.g. in Danish. Such data lend some substance to the proposal that it is indeed justified to draw a distinction within the field of modality between subjective and objective modality, just as major and minor keys in music.

References

Brandt, S. (1999) *Modal Verbs in Danish*. Travaux du Cercle Linguistique de Copenhague XXX. Copenhagen: Reitzel.

Donnellan, K. (1966) Reference and definite descriptions. In D. Steinberg and L. Jakobovits (eds) *Semantics. An Interdisciplinary Reader in Philosophy, Linguistics and Psychology* 100–114. Cambridge: The University Press.

Gast, V. (2001) Deontic 'will'. Internet discussion. 6 August 2001. LINGTYP-discussion list.

Hansen, E. and Heltoft, L. (1999) *Grammatik over det danske sprog*. Preliminary version. Roskilde Universitetscenter.

Heltoft, L. and Falster Jakobsen, L. (1996) Danish passives and subject positions as a mood system. In E. Engberg-Pedersen et al. (eds) *Content, Expression and Structure. Studies in Danish Functional Grammar* 199–234. Amsterdam: John Benjamins.

Herslund, M. (1989) Modality. A presentation. In M. Herslund (ed.) *Modality*. Travaux du Cercle Linguistique de Copenhague XXIII 7–15. Copenhagen: Reitzel.

Herslund, M. (2000) Les deux passifs du français. In L. Schøsler (ed.) *Le passif*. Etudes Romanes 45: 71–81. Copenhagen: Museum Tusculanum.

Herslund, M. (2001a) Généricité, spécificité et article indéfini. In H. Kronning et al. (eds) *Langage et référence. Mélanges offerts à Kerstin Jonasson à l'occasion de ses soixante ans. Acta Universitatis Upsaliensis*. Studia Romanica Upsaliensia 63: 265–73. Uppsala University.

Herslund, M. (2001b) Modality and the indefinite article. In H. H. Müller (ed.) *Reflections on Modality*. Copenhagen Studies in Language 26: 67–80.

Herslund, M. (2002) *Danish*. Languages of the world. Materials 382. Munich: LINCOM EUROPA.

Herslund, M. (2003) Sur la modalité en danois et la tripartition de la phrase. In A. Rousseau (ed.) *La modalité dans tous ses états*. Revue belge de philologie et d'histoire 81: 867–82.

Le Querler, N. (1996) *Typologie des modalités*. Caen: Presses Universitaires de Caen.

Lyons, J. (1977) *Semantics*. Cambridge: The University Press.

Nuyts, J. (1992) Subjective vs. objective modality: what is the difference? In M. Fortescue et al. (eds) *Layered Structure and Reference in a Functional Perspective* 73–98. Amsterdam: John Benjamins.

Nuyts, J. (2001a) *Epistemic Modality, Language and Conceptualization*. Amsterdam/Philadelphia: John Benjamins.

Nuyts, J. (2001b) Subjectivity as an evidential dimension in epistemic modal expressions. *Journal of Pragmatics* 33: 383–400.

Palmer, F. (1986) *Mood and Modality*. Cambridge: The University Press.

Traugott, E. (1989) On the rise of epistemic meanings in English: an example of subjectification in semantic change. *Language* 65: 31–55.

3   Modality and the concept of force-dynamic potential[1]

Kasper Boye

1 Introduction

Three problems characterise contemporary linguistic research on modality:

i)   There is no consensus as regards the application of the term modality. In many cases, it is applied to a heterogeneous area of linguistic phenomena.

ii) In cases where it is applied to a more homogeneous area of linguistic phenomena, no convincing (i.e. precise and adequate) conceptual definition of this area exists. In other words, it seems we are still far from grasping the essence of the area(s) of linguistic phenomena to which the term modality is applied.

iii) There is no consensus as regards the delimitation of modality from related areas of interest. In particular, no convincing delimitation of modality from the related area of evidentiality exists.

Below, I shall address these three problems. In Section 2, I try to demonstrate that one of the reasons for the problems mentioned above is the chimerical nature of the term modality. Subsequently, I argue for a restricted use of the term, and propose that we reserve it for the range of meanings that are often paraphrased with 'necessity' and 'possibility'. In Section 3, I go through a few of the existing definitions of this meaning domain. In doing so, I try to demonstrate that another of the reasons for the problems mentioned above is the intriguing nature of the meaning domain. It is hard to define the domain conceptually and, thus, it is hard to grasp the essence of it. Nevertheless, in Section 4, I present the concept of force-dynamic potential and argue that the domain should be defined with reference to this concept. Taking this conceptual definition as my point of departure, in Section 5 I finally try to delimit from each other, and relate to each other, modal and evidential meaning.

2   The term modality

One of the reasons for the problems characterising contemporary linguistic research on modality is the term modality itself. On the one hand, the etymology of the term indicates a close relation to the phenomena of modification, modulation and mood, and – via some of these – to phenomena such as speaker attitude and subjectivity. Traditionally, on the other hand, the term modality has often been used in connection with research in the meaning domain of modal intensities, i.e. meanings such as those that are often paraphrased with the terms 'necessity' and 'possibility'. Together, the etymology and the use of the term modality, within linguistics, suggest the existence of a large and complex area of linguistic phenomena. This area would involve not only the epistemic and non-epistemic meaning variants of the meaning domain of modal intensities, but also phenomena such as modification, speaker modulation and mood.

Clearly, however, such an area does not exist as a well-defined and definable domain. Some linguistic items, of course, do seem to be modal in the broad sense outlined above. Consider the Turkish suffixes highlighted in (1) and (2) (adapted from Kornfilt, 1997: 373–7).

(1)   *Hasan orada ol   –malı.*
        Hasan there be   NEC
        Hasan must be there.

(2)   *Hasan orada ol   –abil -ir.*
        Hasan there be   POSS   AORIST.
        Hasan may be there.

Arguably, these suffixes express 'necessity' and 'possibility' because they are suffixes and not 'core predicational items' such as nouns or verbs, they may be said to have a modifying function. They may be said to be modifying in the sense that they do not express a primary autonomous semantic core (an entity, a relation or a predicational content), but, rather, are conceptually dependent on such a primary autonomous semantic core to which they add a secondary meaning nuance, e.g. a specification. It can be argued that in (1) and (2) the modal suffixes add a secondary meaning nuance to the primary autonomous predicational content *Hasan be there*. Moreover, in (1) and (2), the two suffixes have epistemic meaning, expressing the speaker's evaluation of the predicational content *Hasan be there* with respect to its truth. In this respect they may be said to have a modulating function (cf. Brandt, 1999: 20). They may be said to signal the speaker's modulation of or attitude to the predicational content and thus to be subjective. Finally, the two suffixes are verbal suffixes and thus, perhaps, characterisable as mood forms.

However, the meaning domain of modal intensities is not inherently bound up with mood, modification, speaker modulation or subjectivity. First of all, it is not inherently bound up with mood. On the one hand, necessity-possibility systems are often independent of mood systems. For instance, Jensen has pointed out that Italian modal verbs, although they encode the meaning domain of modal intensities, like other Italian verbs 'may appear in different moods' (Jensen, 1997: 109). On the other hand, examples of mood forms of which no necessity or possibility meaning can be postulated are abundant. The indicative mood form of the Germanic languages, for instance, does not encode these meanings (even though, of course, it may indeed have epistemic meaning).

Second, the meaning domain of modal intensities is not inherently bound up with modulation and thus with the concepts of speaker attitude and subjectivity. It does not inherently 'signal the presence of man in language' (Herslund, 1989: 7). On the one hand, a substantial number of linguistic items are capable of signalling speaker modulation without expressing necessity or possibility. In (3), for instance, the adverb *frankly* modulates the speech act of asserting the predication *Kristian is a bad guy* and thus signals the speaker's attitude towards the predicational content. But clearly, it is far-fetched to postulate that it does so by expressing necessity or possibility.

(3)   Frankly, Kristian is a bad guy.

On the other hand, a linguistic item may express necessity or possibility without signaling speaker modulation. To be sure, the Danish modal verb *skulle*, expressing necessity, in (4) may, on the face of it, seem to involve an element of modulation, speaker attitude or subjectivity if it is read deontically. With a deontic reading of *skulle*, the indicative clause may be used as a directive speech act, an order. Since the person eliciting this order necessarily must be identified with the speaker, it seems, at first sight, reasonable to claim that the clause meaning involves an element of speaker attitude. However, the only reason why (4) may be said to involve an element of speaker attitude is exactly that, for an immediate reading, it must be understood as a directive speech act. And the reason for that resides not in the modal verb but in the second person subject (cf. Boye, 2002: note 4, for a more full-fledged account of the interplay between the pragmatic interpretations and the dynamic and deontic core meanings of modal linguistic items).

(4)   *Du skal   gå   nu.*
         You must go   now.
         You have to leave now.

(5)   *Kristian skal   gå nu.*
         Kristian must   go now.
         Kristian has to leave now.

In (5), a third person subject has replaced the second person subject and this makes it harder to use and understand the clause as an order. The modal verb *skulle* still expresses deontic necessity, but, for an immediate reading, the utterance of (5) must be understood as an assertive speech act: a speech act merely presenting a social fact, i.e. the predicational content of *Kristian skal gå nu*, as a description. This description does not involve even the slightest element of speaker attitude or modulation. It is possible to check, in the real world, if it really is deontically-socially necessary for Kristian to leave now. It is not the speaker who is responsible for the deontic necessity described. The one responsible is the one who is actually capable of restraining Kristian deontically-socially, for instance Kristian's mother. Thus, the meanings of necessity and possibility do not inherently involve an element of speaker attitude or modulation.

Finally, the meaning domain of modal intensities is not inherently bound up with modification. On the one hand, obviously, a whole number of linguistic items have a modifying function without expressing necessity or possibility. On the other hand, the meanings of necessity and possibility are not necessarily modifying. They are not necessarily modifying in the sense that they are not necessarily dependent on a primary autonomous semantic core and do not necessarily just add a secondary meaning nuance to such a semantic core. In modal logic, of course, necessity and possibility are described as operator meanings operating on – and thus adding a secondary meaning nuance to – a primary predicational content. However, it is not always correct to describe linguistic modal intensities along this line. In (4) and (5), the meaning of *skulle* is not dependent on and does not add a secondary meaning nuance to a predicational content nor to a predicate content or a predicator content (i.e. a relation). In (5), for instance, it does not add a secondary meaning nuance to the predicational content of *Kristian gå (nu)* nor to the content of the predicate *gå*. Rather, as a genuine full verb it expresses a primary autonomous semantic core in its own right. It expresses a relation, a deontic-social relation, the referent of which we may find in the real world, a relation representing a social pressure on Kristian. In (6), it is not even clear that there should be a predication or a predicate for deontic *skulle* to modify.

(6)   *Kristian skal   op   nu.*
        Kristian must   up   now.
        Kristian has to get up now.

As many other full verbs, *skulle* takes a subject, *Kristian*, and a directional complement, *op*. It still, however, expresses necessity: according to (6), it is necessary for Kristian to get up. That is, modal intensities may be expressed by linguistic items that function as modifiers, but often they are not expressed in this way.

The conflation of two, or more, separate areas of linguistic phenomena under the term modality has had severe consequences. Above all, the term itself has become extremely vague. As Brandt has put it, '[t]he term modality is not used with a generally accepted consistent meaning: for instance some authors apply it to almost any kind of logical modification of a predication, others use it more restrictedly [...]' (Brandt, 1999: 19).

One result of this is that the term has lost its value as a tool for linguistic research. Whenever you want to use it, you have to define it anew. In some cases, the extreme vagueness of the term has been directly misleading. In severe cases, the meaning domain of modal intensities has been analysed with explicit reference to one or more of the concepts of mood, modification, speaker modulation, speaker attitude and subjectivity. In less severe cases, the idea that the meaning domain of modal intensities is related to these concepts seems more implicitly to underlie the analysis of the field. As a first example of this, scholars such as Lyons (1977: 452 and 847–8), Palmer (1986: 2), Pelyvás (1996: 69 and 191) and Nuyts (2001: 25 and 193) all characterise or define modality, more or less explicitly, with reference to the concept of speaker attitude, nevertheless treating under this concept not only epistemic but also non-epistemic (dynamic and deontic) necessity and possibility. The result has been characterisations and definitions that are either erroneous or hollow. According to Nuyts, for instance, '[d]ynamic modality involves an ascription of a capacity or a need to the subject-participant in the state of affairs [...]' (Nuyts, 2001: 25). Here, the term 'ascription', in opposition to a term such as 'description', indicates that the language user has a special role when he claims a dynamic necessity ('need') or possibility ('capacity'). However, this role is clearly nothing else than the language user's general role as a selector of the linguistic item that suits him best.

As a second example, a few scholars have used the term mood as a synonym of grammaticalised modality (cf. the critique of this practice in Palmer, 1986: 21–3 and Brandt, 1999: 20). Davidsen-Nielsen (1990: 46), for instance, links the meaning domain of modal intensities to mood in spite of the fact mentioned above that the two are clearly distinct phenomena.

As a third example, analyses of Germanic modal verbs have often focused on the modifying function of these verbs to such an extent that the modal-intensity meanings of these verbs have been underemphasised. Perkins (1983: 10 and 29ff), for instance, describes the function of the English modal verbs as 'relativizers'. According to Perkins, the English modal verbs relate a circumstance (C) to (the occurrence or truth of) a predicational content (X) in accordance with a law (K) deriving from a set of dynamic-physical, deontic-social or epistemic laws. Similarly, Papafragou (2000: 40–1), with reference to Groefsema (1995) describes the function of English modal verbs as relating a restrictor (D – cor-

responding to Perkins' C) to a predicational content (p – corresponding to
Perkins' X). Perkins' and Papafragou's analyses presuppose that English modal
verbs are auxiliaries, i.e. grammaticalised verbs and thus do not express a
primary full-verbal relation, but have a secondary modifying function, adding a
meaning nuance to a semantic core (cf. above). Granted that this presupposition
is correct, these analyses, of course, capture an important aspect of the meaning
of English modal verbs. In a wider perspective, however, neither of the two
approaches seems convincing. Basically, what they do is to analyse a number
of linguistic items to which the meaning domain of modal intensities seems to
be central, with essential reference to the concept of modification with which
this meaning domain is not inherently bound up. The Danish modal verbs,
although they are closely related to the English ones, could not be analysed
even approximately along the line suggested by Perkins and Papafragou because
they are full verbs (at least in many of their occurrences) and thus do not have a
modifying function. An adequate analysis of modal linguistic items should, as
its point of departure, consider the modal-intensity meanings of these items and
only then the question whether the items express these meanings as modifying
meanings. To be sure, both Perkins' and Papafragou's analyses capture essential
aspects of the modal-intensity meanings of English modal verbs. For instance,
Perkins' C and Papafragou's D capture the fact that modal intensities imply
the idea of a 'source' (cf. Section 3.1). Focusing on the modifying function
of these verbs, however, Perkins' and Papafragou's analyses capture such
essential aspects in an ad hoc way. This makes the analyses incoherent and
thus inadequate.

In other cases, the vagueness of the term modality has blurred the understanding of related areas of interest, notably the area of evidentiality. In the
literature on evidentiality one actually finds consensus as regards the definition
of the area and the area is often quite precisely defined (compare e.g. Bybee,
1985: 184; Anderson, 1986: 274; Willett, 1988: 51 and 56; Aikhenvald, 2003:
1). Unfortunately for the study of evidentiality, however, evidentiality seems to
be closely related to epistemic necessity and possibility (cf. e.g. Pelyvás, 1996:
149 for an explicit acknowledgement of the relationship). When the concept of
modality enters the stage of evidentiality research, the consensus and precision
evaporate. The area of evidentiality is sometimes seen as a superordinate area
subsuming the area of modality (cf. e.g. Chafe, 1986: 262; Papafragou, 2000:
121; Ifantidou, 2001: 7–8; Mushin, 2001: 30–3), sometimes as a subordinate
area subsumed by the area of modality (cf. e.g. Bybee, 1985; Palmer, 1986: 51;
Willett, 1988: 52; Crystal, 1991: 127). The result is vagueness also in the term
evidentiality, a vagueness that has licensed a quite abstract use of the term. For
instance, Papafragou uses it as a cover term for 'markers that introduce interpre-

tively used propositions' (Papafragou, 2000: 121), while Chafe states, that '[…] I am using the term 'evidentiality' in its broadest sense, not restricting it to the expression of 'evidence' per se. I will be discussing a range of epistemological considerations that are linguistically coded [...]' (Chafe, 1986: 262).

To sum up, the search for a coherent area of linguistic phenomena that may be covered by the etymological sense of the term modality and which includes the meaning domain of modal intensities seems fruitless. At best, the presupposition of the existence of such a range of phenomena seems misleading. If we want the term modality to be an adequate tool for linguistic description, we have to define it narrowly, precisely and, above all, in a linguistically relevant way. We have to ground the concept of modality in linguistic phenomena. One way to do this is to ignore the concepts related to the etymological meaning of the term and reserve the term for linguistic phenomena that are related to the meaning domain of modal intensities. This meaning domain is, of course, only marginally modal in the etymological sense of the word, but at least it is there. In the following, I shall refer to the meaning domain of modal intensities simply as the meaning domain of modality.

3   The meaning domain of modality

Anchoring the term modality in the meaning domain of modality at first sight seems problematic. This domain is basically a philosophical-logical heritage (cf. e.g. the conception of modality in Hughes and Cresswell, 1974) and the anchoring might be accused of building upon what has been called the 'philosophical fallacy' (Brandt, 1999: 28), i.e. of presupposing that philosophical-logical distinctions are relevant for the description of linguistic facts.

Such an accusation, however, can be countered when we observe actual language. Without claiming a one to one relationship between linguistic and philosophical-logical modality (and, of course, without claiming that linguistic modal meaning should necessarily be described with the descriptive apparatus of philosophical logic), we may definitely observe a linguistic correlate to the latter. First, we find a range of linguistic items that share two characteristics central to philosophical-logical modality:

i)   The meanings of these items may be paraphrased by terms such as necessity and possibility.

ii) The meanings of these items often exist in a number of variants that correspond to the epistemic and non-epistemic (deontic and dynamic) meaning variants in modal logic (the so-called 'alethic' modal meaning variants of modal logic, seem to be analysable, within linguistics, as special cases of epistemic modality) as pointed out by, e.g., Palmer (1986: 11) and Nuyts (2001: 28).

Second, we find that these linguistic items are often grouped together in morphosyntactically delimited paradigms. Such paradigms, then, actually code the above-mentioned meanings as a semantic field.

As examples of such modal linguistic items, we may obviously mention the Germanic modal verbs. The Danish ones are morphosyntactically delimited and grouped together mainly by their capability of being constructed with a bare infinitive (Skyum-Nielsen, 1971: 2–16; Brandt, 1999: 21–6). The meanings of these verbs may all be paraphrased by terms such as necessity, possibility and – indicating an intensity between these two – 'disposition'. And many of the verbs occur in both epistemic and non-epistemic variants (Boye, 2001a: 51–4). Thus, in (7), the modal verb *kunne* may be described as expressing one of three variants of possibility: dynamic, deontic or epistemic possibility, as suggested by the paraphrased translations in (7a) to (c), respectively.

(7)   *Kristian kan være   hjemme.*
       Kristian can be   at-home.
   (a) It is physically possible for Kristian to stay at home.
   (b) It is socially possible (i.e. permitted) for Kristian to stay at home.
   (c) It is epistemically possible that it is true that Kristian stays at home.

Linguistic items that are modal in the narrow sense outlined above are not only found in the Germanic languages. Rather, they seem to be widespread among the languages of the world (cf. Bybee, Perkins and Pagliuca, 1994; van der Auwera and Plungian, 1998). As we have already seen, for instance, Turkish has a suffix system expressing necessity and possibility. This system is capable of expressing not only epistemic necessity and possibility, as in (1) and (2), but also non-epistemic necessity and possibility, as in (8) and (9) (adapted from Kornfilt, 1997: 373–7).

(8)   *Oku   –malı –y   –ız.*
       read   NEC   COPULA I[ST]PLUR
       We have to/must read.

(9)   *Oku   –yabil –ir   –im.*
       read   POSS   AOR   I[ST]SING
       I can/am able to/am permitted to read.

The modal systems are not always as clear-cut as in Danish and Turkish. In Korean, for instance, it is not clear whether the two members of the modal suffix system (-(u)l(i) and –keyss) express different degrees of intensity (i.e. for instance necessity vs. possibility) (cf. Sohn, 1999: 360–2). However, at least –keyss, the meaning of which in my view may be paraphrased by necessity, is capable of occurring with both non-epistemic and epistemic meaning, as in (10) and (11), respectively (adapted from Sohn, 1999: 361).

(10)   *Ce nun an   ka –keyss –e.yo.*
       I TOPIC not   go NEC POLITE
       I don't intend to go.

(11)   *Nwun i   w   –ass   –keyss –ta.*
       snow NOM come PAST/PERF   NEC   DECLARATIVE
       I presume it (has) snowed.

The existence of such less transparent systems of modality in no way speaks against my point that natural languages do code a meaning domain which in central respects correlates with the domain of modality described in modal logic.

We may define this meaning domain extensionally with reference to the two characteristics mentioned above. Thus, it consists of the modal meanings paraphrasable as necessity, disposition and possibility, all of which may occur in epistemic as well as non-epistemic variants. Reserving the term modality for this meaning domain leaves the area of modality no less intriguing than before. Indeed, it seems almost impossible to grasp the common core of it. What is it that unifies the modal intensities? What is the basic function of this meaning domain susceptible to both epistemic and non-epistemic interpretations?

Several scholars have refrained from trying to answer these questions. Apart from sporadic references to the vague concept of speaker attitude, scholars such as Palmer (1979: 2–5), Coates (1983: 18–21) and Davidsen-Nielsen (1990: 43–6) stick to extensional-ostensive definitions, listing all those linguistic items which they find to be modal. However, the only way of coming closer to an understanding of the meaning domain is to try defining it conceptually, i.e. to try anchoring the complexity of the field in a cognitively salient and precisely defined concept that may function as a common conceptual denominator of the meanings encompassed by the field (cf. Bache's requirements for the definitions of 'category concept' in Bache, 1997; 2002). A good defining concept, thus, should, at least:

i)   be capable of functioning as a common conceptual meanings denominator of the content units of necessity and possibility;
ii) make possible an account of the meaning difference between epistemic and non-epistemic modality; and, at best
iii) make possible an account of the vast number of semantic observations related to modal meaning.

The concepts of mood, modification and speaker modulation, etymologically related to the term modality, are all bad candidates for such a defining concept. Two much better candidates are the concepts of 'force dynamics' and 'potential'.

3.1   Modality and the concept of force dynamics

A couple of studies of English and Danish modal verbs try to capture, in a general way, the meanings of these verbs by means of a concept borrowed from the natural sciences, the concept of force dynamics (Talmy, 1988; Sweetser, 1990; Boye, 2001a). Used as a defining concept for the meaning domain of modality as such, the concept has a number of advantages. First and foremost, it seems to provide a good common conceptual denominator of the modal intensities. These are described as stronger or weaker 'forces', so that, for instance, the intensity normally paraphrased as necessity, is identified with a strong force.

Furthermore, it seems to capture in a precise way the actual meaning of the modal intensities (cf. Boye, 2001a: 27–34). Thus, it captures three well-known aspects of modal meaning:

i)   first, the aspect that the modal intensities imply the idea of a 'source'; cf. e.g. Lyons, 1977: 843; Bech's (1951: 7) idea of a *Modalfaktor*, Brandt's (1999: 30) idea of a 'modal source' and Perkins' (1983) 'C' and Papafragou's (2000) 'D' discussed in Section 2. Understood as a force, the modal intensity calls for a source of force;

ii)   second, the aspect that modal meaning implies the idea of something – an 'agonist' – that is affected by the modal intensity; cf. e.g. Brandt's (1999: 31) idea of a 'modal target' and van der Auwera and Plungian's (1998: 80–2) idea of a 'participant'. A force necessarily affects something;

iii)   third, the aspect that modal intensities imply the ideas of a 'result' and 'goal'; cf. Klinge's (1993) idea of a 'resolution' and the idea of 'modal orientation' in Bech (1949) and Brandt (1999: 35–6). A force always has a goal, against which it is directed, and a resultant.

Finally, the concept provides a good abstraction of the different modality types. These are described as different types of force dynamics (cf. Boye, 2001a: 35–40). While dynamic modality is seen as a physical force dynamics, much as a physicist would see it, deontic and epistemic modality are seen as a, respectively, social and mental or rational force dynamics. With a 'force-dynamic' definition of the meaning domain of modality, the dynamic, deontic and epistemic readings of (12) may be paraphrased as in (12a) to (c) respectively.

(12)   *Kristian må   (nødvendigvis) være   i Rom.*
          Kristian must   (necessarily)   be   in Rome.
  (a)   A maximum physical force drives Kristian towards the predicational content
        of *Kristian be in Rome.*
  (b)   A maximum social force drives Kristian towards the predicational content of
        Kristian be in Rome.
  (c)   A maximum rational force drives the predicational content of *Kristian be in
        Rome* towards truth (i.e. verification).

In addition to the advantages mentioned above, the concept of force dynamics is likely to have a cognitive correlate. With this concept, Talmy (1988) is capable of describing not only modal meaning but also the meaning of a range of linguistic items that have no relation to the meaning domain of modality. In this descriptive force resides, however, also the weakness of the concept of force dynamics as a defining concept for the meaning domain of modality. As pointed out by Davidsen-Nielsen (p.c.) and Nuyts (2001: 26), the concept is not capable of delimiting the domain in a satisfying way.

3.2   Modality and the concept of potential

As a defining concept for the meaning domain of modality, also the concept of potential, potentiality or potency (Klinge, 1993; 1996; Langacker, 1990: 25) seems to be equipped with a number of advantages. Building on Bouma (1973) and Marino (1973) Klinge uses this concept as a generalisation of the meanings of a number of English modal verbs:

> [...] I will adopt the terms POTENTIAL and POTENTIALITY to stand for the semantic field shared by the five modals [...]. The cognitive elements of POTENTIALITY are taken to be the following: the object of potentiality is an assumption about a WORLD SITUATION; the WORLD SITUATION is not verified to be the case; one resolution of the POTENTIAL is that the WORLD SITUATION turns out to be the case; and one resolution of the POTENTIAL is that the WORLD SITUATION turns out not to be the case (Klinge, 1993: 323–4, cf. Klinge, 1996: 35–6).

In a broader use, the concept of potential may count as a defining concept for the meaning domain of modality as such. First, understood in roughly the same way as an electrician would use it, the concept functions as a common conceptual denominator of the modal intensities. At one end of the modal intensity scale, possibility may be described as the mere existence of a potential (corresponding to the mere connection between two electric poles). At the other end, necessity may be described as a strong potential (corresponding to the registration of a strong voltage on a voltmeter). Second, the concept makes possible an abstraction from the different types of modality. These may be described as different types of potential.

However, Klinge's use of the concept is not ideal. To begin with, Klinge's use of the concept seems to bind it up with the concepts of modification and speaker attitude. First, Klinge, perhaps rightly, ascribes the English modal verbs operator function (Klinge, 1993: 323) and sees them as semantic modifiers operating on predications. However, in focusing on this modifying operator function, Klinge's analysis, like Perkins' and Papafragou's analyses (cf. Section 2), to some extent underemphasises the modal (intensity) meanings of the verbs. Second, Klinge identifies the object of the concept of potential as 'verification' (cf. the quotation above), thus seemingly binding up the concept of potential with the concept of speaker modulation or speaker attitude. However, only epistemic meaning and thus epistemic modality can be linked to verification. In the dynamic and deontic interpretations of (7) *Kristian kan være hjemme*, the possibility for Kristian to be at home does not concern the verification of the predicational content of *Kristian være hjemme*, but the actualisation of this predicational content. In other words, only epistemic modality is concerned with propositions or third-order entities (i.e. predicational contents with a 'truth-value'); non-epistemic modality is concerned with states of affairs or second-order entities (i.e. predicational contents without a truth-value) (cf. e.g. Palmer, 1979: 35; Lyons, 1977: 842–3).

Moreover, Klinge's definitions of the individual modal intensities seem inappropriate. Klinge describes the individual modal intensities with reference to two possible 'resolutions' of a potential involving a predication: verification and non-verification. For instance, he defines the meaning of *can* as the conjunction of the two possible resolutions: 'the situation representation [i.e. the predicational content] turns out to be a true description of a world situation and the situation representation turns out not to be a true description of a world situation' (Klinge, 1993: 332). And he defines the meaning of *must* as the negation of the non-verification of a predicational content: '[t]he situation representation does not turn out not to be a true description of a world situation' (Klinge, 1993: 351). These meaning definitions are problematic in two respects. From a cognitivist point of view, it is strange that modal meanings, which are often expressed by simplex and often lexical morphemes, should involve logical operators such as conjunction and negation and thus appear as rather complex and modifying meanings. More basically, it seems odd that these meanings should have the structure of predications as is the case in Klinge's paraphrases.

As I have tried to show, neither the concept of force dynamics nor that of potential is completely unproblematic as a defining concept for the meaning domain of modality. Nevertheless, they both have a number of advantages and, I think, a strong intuitive appeal. In the following section, I shall base my attempt of defining the meaning domain of modality conceptually on these two concepts.

4   The concept of force-dynamic potential

The meaning domain of modality, I suggest, should be defined conceptually with reference to the concept of force-dynamic potential. This concept combines the concept of potential with the concept of force dynamics. The combined concept may be conceived of as borrowed from natural science. In physics, the concept of potential designates a situation that causally precedes the realisation of something. For instance, the concept of electrodynamic potential, voltage, designates the situation which causally precedes the actual flow of electrons. On the other hand, the concept of force dynamics may be seen as designating a complex physical situation that may be split up into three causally related subsituations. This complex situation is represented in Figure 1.

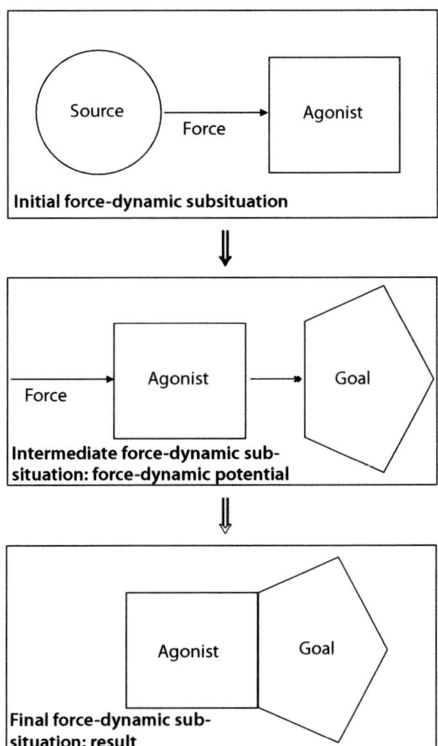

Figure 1: The force-dynamic situation

In the initial subsituation, a force-dynamic source, for instance a car owner, produces a force that affects an agonist, for instance a car. In the intermediate subsituation, the force drives the agonist towards a goal, for instance a garage. In the final subsituation, the agonist has reached the goal towards which it was being driven. Thus, this final subsituation is identical with the result of the force affection: the car is in the garage.

Now, in combination with the concept of force dynamics, the concept of potential points out the causally intermediate subsituation. Thus, in a concrete use, the combined concept of force-dynamic potential may be understood with reference to a physical situation in which a force drives an agonist towards a goal that has not yet been reached. In this respect, as already hinted, it may be understood furthermore as an intermediate step linking together the two subsituations of causation. Thus, the concept of causation might be taken to designate a complex situation involving only the initial and the final subsituations of Figure 1.

In a more abstract use, the concept of force-dynamic potential provides an adequate basis for a conceptual definition of the meaning domain of modality. A definition of this field with reference to the abstract concept of force-dynamic potential has several advantages. Below, I will run through six such advantages.

4.1   Force-dynamic potential and Germanic modal verb meaning

The first advantage is that the concept of force-dynamic potential captures the essence of Germanic modal verb meaning in a precise and coherent way. Although Figure 1 is basically meant as an illustration, for the sake of clarity we may take it to function as an image schematic representation of the deontic meaning of the modal clause in (13).

(13)   Bob must eat because I say so.

The obligatory constituents of this clause together express (i.e. 'designate' or 'profile', in the sense of Langacker) an intermediate force-dynamic subsituation, a force-dynamic potential. The finite modal verb *must* designates a force working within the field of a force-dynamic potential. The primary modal argument *Bob* represents the agonist who is affected by the modal force. And the secondary modal argument *eat* represents the goal – in this case a relational goal – towards which the agonist is being driven by the modal force, but which has not yet been reached. Moreover, just as the intermediate force-dynamic subsituation *presupposes* the initial subsituation, in the same way the meaning of the clause in (1) presupposes (or 'evokes' the idea of) a force-dynamic source. This source is expressed by the non-obligatory clausal constituent *because I say so.* Finally, just as the intermediate force-dynamic subsituation *implies* (or 'evokes' the idea of) a possible final subsituation, in the same way the meaning of the clause in (1) implies a possible force-dynamic result, the possible actualisation of the predicational content *Bob eat*.

It should be noted that the above description focuses on the lexical meaning of modal verbs. For the sake of the argument, the meaning of the English modal verb *must* has been assumed – and will be assumed henceforth – to be a lexical, full-verbal meaning, like the meaning of Danish modal verbs representing a relation between arguments. Thus, the meaning of *must* has been taken to designate a force driving an agonist towards a goal. When it comes to modal meaning expressed by linguistic items with modifying function – for instance, grammaticalised items or adverbs – the meaning might be more abstract. One could speculate, for instance, that the modal meaning of the Turkish suffix in (1) and (8) represents not a strong force, but a strong force-dynamic potential as such, a strong force-dynamic potential for the verification or actualisation of a predicational content, i.e. the total intermediate subsituation of the complex force-dynamic situation. Likewise, to capture the supposedly grammaticalised nature of English modal verbs and thus the fact that their lexical relation meanings have evolved into grammatical modifying meanings, one might suggest that English modal verbs actually do not express a force working within the field of a force-dynamic potential, but a force-dynamic potential as such.

4.2   Force-dynamic potential and the implications of modal meaning

The second advantage is that the concept of force-dynamic potential captures, in a precise and coherent way, a number of more or less well-known semantic implications of modal meaning (especially, of course, of modal verb meaning which is, by far, the most frequently studied type of modal meaning). It captures and relates to modal meaning the ideas, mentioned earlier, of a modal source, a result and something that is affected by the modal intensity. In the representation in Figure 1, the force-dynamic source, the final subsituation and the agonist, respectively, represent these semantic implications.

4.3   Force-dynamic potential and modal intensity

The third advantage is that the concept of force-dynamic potential seems to be a precise common conceptual denominator of the modal intensities. These intensities may be described either, in the case of lexically verbal modal meaning, as weaker or stronger forces working within a field of force-dynamic potential, or, in the case of modifying modal meaning, as weaker or stronger force-dynamic potentials as such (cf. Section 4.1). Thus, we may distinguish between the lexical meanings of the Danish modal verbs *skulle* (shall, must), *burde* (ought to, should) and *kunne* (can, may) in the way represented in Table 1.

(14)   *Bob skal vaske op.*
        Bob must do the dishes.

(15)   *Bob bør vaske op.*
        Bob ought to do the dishes.

(16)   *Bob kan vaske op.*
        Bob can do the dishes.

Force	Maximum	*skulle*
	Non-maximum	*burde*
Mere potential		*kunne*

Table 1: The core meanings of *skulle, burde* and *kunne*

We may describe the necessity meaning of *skulle* as a maximum force, in a non-epistemic interpretation of (14) driving Bob towards the relation *do the dishes*. We may describe the disposition meaning of *burde* as a non-maximum force, also, in a non-epistemic interpretation of (15), driving Bob towards the relation *do the dishes* – but not with the same strength as *skulle*. Finally, we may describe the possibility meaning of *kunne* negatively as an absent barrier, in a non-epistemic interpretation of (16) not preventing Bob from participating in the relation *do the dishes* – or perhaps, as pointed out to me by Klinge (personal communication), positively as the mere existence of a force-dynamic potential, in a non-epistemic interpretation of (16), letting Bob participate in this relation.

4.4   Force-dynamic potential and modality type

The fourth advantage is that the concept of force-dynamic potential constitutes an abstraction of and captures the differences between the epistemic, deontic and dynamic modal meaning variants. The modality types may be regarded as different concrete manifestations of the abstract concept of force-dynamic potential. Manifestations in which the abstract variables result, agonist, goal, force and force-dynamic source semantically, or maybe pragmatically, are ascribed different concrete values.

We may represent the non-epistemic meaning of the modal clause in (17) as the intermediate subsituation in Figure 2.

(17)   Bob must eat.

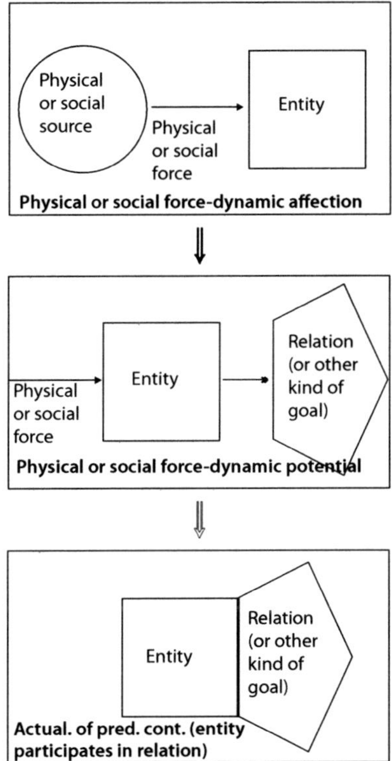

Figure 2: The non-epistemic force-dynamic situation

Still assuming, for the sake of the argument, that English *must* is a lexical full verb (cf. Section 4.1), we may describe the lexical meaning of the non-epistemic variant of this verb in (17) as a non-epistemic maximum force. We may describe the agonist *Bob* that is affected by this non-epistemic force as an entity. We may describe the goal *eat* towards which the entity-agonist is being driven by the non-epistemic force as a physical relation. And we may describe the possible result of this non-epistemic force-dynamic potential as the actualisation of the predicational content *Bob eat*. Moreover, we may distinguish between a dynamic and a deontic meaning of the non-epistemic modal verb. We may, for instance, describe the dynamic meaning as a physical force produced by a physical source and the deontic meaning as a social force produced by a social source.

On the other hand, we may represent the epistemic meaning of the modal clauses in (18) and (19) as the intermediate subsituation in Figure 3.

(18)   It must be the case that Bob is eating.

(19)   Bob must be eating.

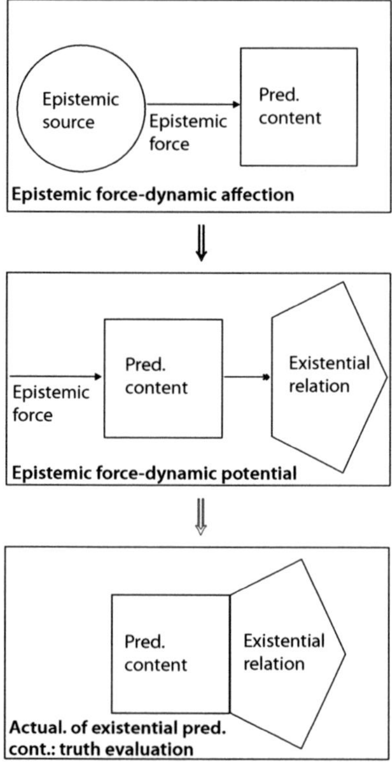

Figure 3: The epistemic force-dynamic situation

The agonist being no longer an entity, this representation captures the sense in which epistemic modal meaning is more abstract than the 'agent-oriented' (Bybee, 1985) or 'participant-oriented' (van der Auwera and Plungian, 1998) non-epistemic modal meaning. We may describe the lexical epistemic meaning of the modal verb *must* in (18) and (19) as an epistemic, mental or rational force. We may identify the agonist affected by this epistemic force with the predicational content of *Bob be eating* or *Bob is eating* rather than with an entity. We may describe the goal towards which the predicational agonist is being driven by the epistemic force as a special existential relation – in (18) expressed by *be the case*, but in (19) latent. Furthermore, we may describe the force-dynamic source of the epistemic force as a special epistemic, knowledge-related source, for instance the knowledge expressed in an adverbial subordinate clause such as *because I know that Bob eats all day long*. Finally, equating verification with the actualisation of a special existential predicational content, we may describe the possible result of this epistemic force-dynamic potential as the actualisation of the special existential predicational content that the predicational content of Bob is eating is the case, i.e. as the epistemic evaluation that this predicational content is 'true'.

Again, the description may be adapted to capture the possibly more abstract modal meaning of modifying linguistic items (cf. Section 4.1). One could speculate, for instance, that the modal meaning variants of the Turkish suffix in (1) and (8) represent not an epistemic and a non-epistemic (dynamic or deontic) type of force, respectively, but an epistemic and a non-epistemic type of force-dynamic potential as such, i.e. a force-dynamic potential for the verification of a predicational content and a force-dynamic potential for the actualisation of a predicational content, respectively.

4.5   Force-dynamic potential and observational adequacy

The fifth advantage is that a description of the meaning domain of modality with reference to the concept of force-dynamic potential seems to be observationally adequate. Some of the linguistic phenomena and observations tied to modal meaning have already been discussed above. For instance, it has been argued that the concept of force-dynamic potential captures some well-known semantic implications of modal meaning. Below, I shall discuss two additional observations, linked to modal meaning, which I think are captured by the concept of force-dynamic potential.

The first observation is that a certain group of Germanic modal verbs are incompatible with deontic meaning. In Danish, for instance, the modal verbs *ville* (will, want), *gide* (bother) and *turde* (dare) never occur with deontic meaning. This fact is related to the observation of a semantic distinction between what the late Danish linguist Gunnar Bech (1951) has called 'intra- and extrasubjective modal factor' and what van der Auwera and Plungian (1998) call 'participant-internal modality' and 'participant-external modality'[2]. Thus, in Bech's terminology, *ville*, *gide* and *turde* can be characterised as being intrasubjective. In a force-dynamic potential description the distinction between intra- and extrasubjective modal factor is captured by a distinction between agonist-internal and agonist-external force-dynamic potential (cf. Boye, 2001a: 32–3). Described with reference to the concept of force-dynamic potential, *ville*, *gide* and *turde* designate modal forces (or mere potentials) which affect the agonist from within and they are produced by sources that originate from the agonist that they affect. In other words, in (20) non-epistemic *ville* designates a force that not only affects but also originates from Bob.

(20)   *Bob vil spise.*
        Bob will eat
        Bob wants to eat.

The distribution of deontic meaning, then, is motivated by the fact that social-deontic forces and absent barriers may only affect an agonist from the outside. The corresponding forces that affect you from within are psychological. Thus, as represented in Table 2, in Danish we may distinguish between on the one hand the agonist-internal modal verbs *ville*, *gide* and *turde* and on the other hand the agonist-external modal verbs *skulle*, *burde*, *kunne* and *måtte*-n (corresponding to *must*) and *måtte*-g (corresponding to *may*) (cf. Boye, 2001a for a discussion of the difference between the two *måtte*-lexemes and the difference between, on the one hand, these two lexemes and, on the other hand, the verbs *skulle*, *burde* and *kunne*)[3].

		Agonist-internal (-deontic)	Agonist-external (+deontic)	
Force	Maximum	*ville*	*skulle*	*måtte*-n
Non-maximum		*gide*	*burde*	
Mere potential		*turde*	*kunne*	*måtte*-g

Table 2: The force-dynamic core meanings of Danish modal verbs

The second observation regards the distribution of directional adverbial complements with Danish modal verbs. As it appears from (21) and (22) only the modal verbs that are classified as 'force modals' in Table 2 are capable of taking a directional complement.

(21)   *Bob vil/gider (godt)/skal/bør/ må(-n) i skole.*
        Bob will/bothers (well)/shall/ought/must to school
        Bob wants to/bothers to/must/ought to/must go to school.

(22)   **Bob tør (godt)/kan/må(-g) i skole.*
        Bob dares (well)/can/may to school
        Bob dares/can/may go to school.

The distribution is motivated by the fact that only the force modals imply a direction. A force necessarily implies a direction towards a goal whereas an absent barrier or the mere existence of a potential only implies the lack of something preventing something else – the agonist – from reaching this goal[4].

4.6   Force-dynamic potential and descriptive and explanatory adequacy

As a sixth advantage, the description of the meaning domain of modality with reference to the concept of force-dynamic potential is, I think, descriptively and explanatorily adequate. It is descriptively adequate in the sense that it has the same descriptive force as the concept of force dynamics (indeed, many of the above mentioned advantages are inherited from this more general concept), but does not share the delimitational weakness, mentioned earlier, of this concept. Unlike the concept of force dynamics, the concept of force-dynamic potential is capable of delimiting modal linguistic phenomena from other phenomena related to force dynamics. The concept of force-dynamic potential relates modal meaning strictly to the intermediate force-dynamic subsituation and in this way it delimits modal phenomena from phenomena that may be described with reference to the initial or the final force-dynamic subsituation.

For instance, the non-epistemic modal meaning of *must* in (17) is distinguished from the causal meanings of *make* in (23), *because* in (24) and *therefore* in (25).

(23)   Bob's mother makes Bob eat.

(24)   Bob eats because his mother has told him to.

(25)   Bob's mother has told Bob to eat. Therefore Bob eats.

When you make somebody do something, you impose a force on him that actually results in something. Thus, as opposed to modal meaning, the meaning of the verb *make* may be described with reference to both the initial and the final force-dynamic subsituations, but not with reference to the intermediate one. On the other hand, the meaning of *because* may be described with reference to the initial force-dynamic subsituation while that of *therefore* may be described with reference to the final one: in (24), *because* introduces a subordinate clause designating a force-dynamic source and thus marks the superordinate clause as designating a force-dynamic result, while, in (25), *therefore* introduces a superordinate clause designating a force-dynamic result and thus marks the preceding superordinate clause as designating a force-dynamic source.

Interestingly, linguistic items such as *make*, *because* and *therefore* seem to occur not only as causal meanings comparable with non-epistemic modal meaning variants but also as inferential meanings comparable with epistemic modal meaning variants (cf. Sweetser, 1990). In the same way as non-epistemic modal meaning is distinguished from causal meaning, the epistemic modal meaning of, for instance, *must* in (18) and (19) is distinguished from the inferential meanings of *make* in (26), *because* in (27) and *therefore* in (28).

(26)   Bob's fingerprints make him the murderer.

(27)   Bob is definitely the murderer because we found his fingerprints.

(28)   We found Bob's fingerprints. Therefore, Bob is the murderer.

In (26), *make* represents an epistemic force produced by an epistemic force-dynamic source, i.e. knowledge, represented by the first argument *Bob's fingerprints* and resulting in the truth of the predicational content of the predicational second arguments *him the murderer*. In (27), *because* introduces an epistemic source producing an epistemic force. And in (28), *therefore* introduces an epistemic result, i.e. the verified 'truth' of the predicational content *Bob is the murderer*. Thus, while modal meaning may be described with reference to the intermediate force-dynamic subsituation, the meanings of *make*, *because* and *therefore* may be described with reference to either the initial subsituation or the final subsituation or both of these subsituations. In other words, *make*, *because* and *therefore* may be described with reference to the less detailed complex situation designated by the concept of causation, while the description of modal meaning necessarily involves the more detailed complex situation of force dynamics represented in Figure 1.

The concept of force-dynamic potential is explanatorily adequate in the sense that it seems to be both functionally and cognitively adequate. First, it seems intuitively reasonable that language should reflect the physical, social and epistemic force-dynamic interactions and potentials of human life. In other words, it seems intuitively reasonable that language should reflect not only the initial and final states of physical, deontic and epistemic force dynamics, but also the intermediate state. Thus, the concept of force-dynamics seems to be functionally adequate. Second, designating the intermediate force-dynamic subsituation, the concept of force-dynamic potential is subsumed by the more general concept of force dynamics. As already mentioned, this concept has been shown by Talmy (1988) to be capable of capturing a number of semantic phenomena and relations. This speaks for the cognitive adequacy of the concept of force dynamics and thus of the concept of force-dynamic potential.

5   Force-dynamic potential and the distinction between modality and evidentiality

With a precise, coherent and adequate conceptual definition of the meaning domain of modality, we are in a position to capture the relations between this domain and the domain of evidentiality. In Section 5.1, I run through the relations. In Section 5.2, on the basis of the definition of the meaning domain of modality with reference to the concept of force-dynamic potential, I sketch an attempt to capture these relations.

5.1   The relations between modal meaning and evidential meaning

On the one hand, two facts suggest that the meaning domain of evidentiality and the meaning domain of modality are distinct:

i)   Evidential linguistic items as expressions of (type of) source of information are often easily distinguishable from modal linguistic items. The evidential meaning of the adverb *allegedly* in (29), for instance, has nothing to do with necessity, disposition and possibility, nor, of course, with deontic and dynamic meaning.

    (29)   Bob is allegedly in Berlin.

ii) In many languages, evidential and (epistemic) modal meaning are encoded in different categories or paradigms (cf. Aikhenvald, 2003). In Danish, for instance, the two types of meaning seem to be expressed by two different verbal groups: the group of modal verbs and the group of perception, attitude, utterance and appearance verbs, respectively (Boye, 2001b; Boye, 2002).

On the other hand, five facts suggest that the meaning domain of evidentiality and the epistemic variant of the meaning domain of modality are closely related.

i)   Epistemic modal linguistic items and evidential linguistic items are semantically both concerned with the truth of a predicational content. In (30), for instance, all the adverbs are concerned with the truth of the content of the predication *Bob is not married*.

    (30)   Bob is probably/possibly/allegedly/apparently not married.

ii) Epistemic modal meaning and evidential meaning both involve the idea of an epistemic source. The knowledge licensing and producing, in the case of epistemic modality, an epistemic, evaluating force or force-dynamic potential, in other words, may be seen as similar to the knowledge functioning, in the case of evidentiality, as evidence for the truth of a predicational content.

iii) In some languages, epistemic modal linguistic items and evidential linguistic items belong to the same category or paradigm. This is the case, for instance, in Hixkaryana (Derbyshire, 1979: 143–5), in Slave (Rice, 1989: 403ff) and in West Greenlandic (Fortescue, 2003: 292–4). It is also the case in Germanic languages. As it appears from (30), the epistemic modal adverbs *probably* and *possibly* and the evidential adverbs *allegedly* and *apparently* all compete for the same position in the clause, mutually excluding each other[5].

iv) Modal meaning and evidential meaning are both organised on an intensity scale. In the same way as we find stronger and weaker modal intensities or forces, we find stronger and weaker kinds of evidence (cf. e.g. Givón, 1982: 25 and 43–4). Direct, visual evidence, for instance, is generally accepted to be stronger, in the sense of more reliable, than indirect, reported or inferential evidence.

v) In certain contexts, epistemic variants of modal linguistic items encoding the meaning of strong modal intensity may have weak, i.e. indirect (reported or inferential), evidential meaning (cf. e.g. Bech, 1949: 17; Palmer, 1986: 72; van der Auwera and Plungian, 1998: 85 on German *sollen*; Traugott, 1989: 41–2 on Old English *sceolde(n)*; Davidsen-Nielsen, 1990: 93 on Danish *skulle*; Anderson, 1986: 274; Sweetser, 1990: 61; van der Auwera and Plungian, 1998: 86 on English *must*; Bech, 1949: 27–8 on German *müssen*). In Danish, for instance, the epistemic variants of the modal verbs *skulle* and *måtte*-n may signal report and inference, respectively, as in (31).

> (31)   *Bob skal/må(-n) være i Berlin.*
> Bob shall/must be in Berlin
> Bob is reported/inferred to be in Berlin.

5.2   Capturing the relations: modality, evidentiality and epistemicity

In order to capture these seven facts, to begin with, I propose to contrast evidential meaning with epistemic modal meaning in the following way:

- Evidential meaning relates a predicational content to an epistemic source (i.e. a knowledge source) that serves as evidence for the truth of this content. It specifies which type of epistemic source is at hand. Because some types of epistemic sources (e.g. directly attested knowledge) are stronger than others (e.g. indirectly attested knowledge), it also implies a specific degree of certainty about the truth of a predicational content.

- In contrast, epistemic modal meaning, as argued above, relates a predicational content to a force-dynamic potential (or a specific force working within this field of potential), the result of which would be (the verification of) the truth of the predicational content. It specifies the strength of the epistemic force-dynamic potential and thus the degree of certainty about the truth of the predicational content. As part of this meaning, it implies an epistemic source that serves as evidence for the truth of this content.

With this contrast, it is tempting to see the difference between epistemic modal meaning and evidential meaning as the difference between reference to the intermediate epistemic force-dynamic subsituation and reference to the initial one, respectively. This way of viewing the difference implies that the relation, represented by evidential meaning, between an epistemic source and a predicational content should actually be interpreted as a force driving the predicational content towards verification. Now, the connection between causation and inference and thus at least 'inferring [or inferential] evidence' (Willett, 1988) is not to be doubted. We have already seen that the causal interpretations of *make*, *because* and *therefore* coexist with epistemic-inferential interpretations. And it is well known that conditional constructions are prone to both causal and epistemic-inferential interpretations, sometimes at the same time, as the two implications (a) and (b) of (32) suggest (cf. Sweetser, 1990).

(32)   If the police are there, there is trouble.
   (a) The presence of the police causes trouble (causal).
   (b) The presence of the police warrants the conclusion that there is trouble
        (epistemic).

However, it is not yet clear to me if it is possible (and useful) to postulate a more general relation between evidential meaning and causation.

In either case, I propose to capture the relations between the meaning domain of evidentiality and the epistemic variant of the meaning domain of modality in the following way. I propose that we view them as constituting separate parts of an epistemic scale (cf. Givón, 1982). By an epistemic scale I mean a continuum consisting of meanings which specify the degree of certainty about the truth (or falsity) of a predicational content. My proposal is in accordance with the conceptual contrast between evidential meaning and epistemic modal meaning proposed above. The epistemic variant of the meaning domain of modality may be conceived of as being inherently part of an epistemic scale: the different degrees of epistemic force-dynamic strength or intensity encoded by epistemic modal linguistic items directly reflect different degrees of certainty about the truth of a predicational content. The meaning domain of evidentiality, on the other hand, may be conceived of as being part of an epistemic scale as well, although not inherently: the different types of epistemic sources encoded by evidential linguistic items only imply different degrees of certainty about the truth of a predicational content.

Figure 4 represents an epistemic scale. It ranges from factive meaning, indicating absolute certainty about the truth of a predicational content, to non-factive (or hypothetical) meaning, indicating absolute uncertainty about the truth of a predicational content.

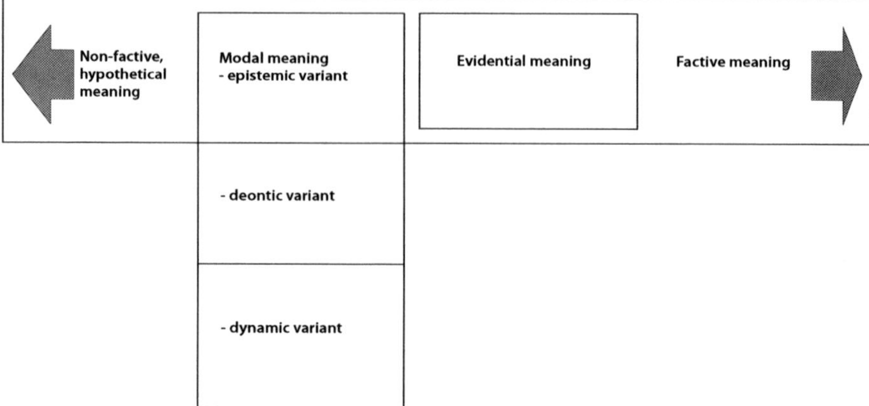

Figure 4: The epistemic scale

As a first observation, Figure 4 captures the fact that the non-epistemic variants of the meaning domain of modality have nothing to do with either evidential meaning or the verification of predicational contents as such. Non-epistemic modal meanings are irrelevant to the scale and therefore placed outside it. The scale itself captures, I think, the relations between epistemic modal meaning and evidential meaning discussed in Section 5.1. On the one hand, it captures the facts:

i)   that linguistic items expressing the two types of meaning are often easily distinguishable; and

ii) that the two types of meaning are often encoded separately from each other.

It does so by representing the meaning domain of evidentiality and the epistemic variant of the meaning domain of modality as constituting separate coherent parts of the overall scale.

On the other hand, the scale captures the five facts that suggest a close relationship between evidential meaning and epistemic modal meaning. To begin with, it captures the further facts:

iii) that epistemic modal linguistic items and evidential linguistic items are semantically both concerned with the truth of a predicational content;

iv) that epistemic modal meaning and evidential meaning both involve the idea of an epistemic source; and

v)   that, in some languages, epistemic modal meaning and evidential meaning are encoded in the same category or paradigm.

It does so by representing both epistemic modal meaning and evidential meaning as constituents of the epistemic scale, thus encompassing the two types of meaning as subtypes of epistemic meaning. In accordance with e.g. Aijmer (1980: 11) and Doherty (1987: 6), epistemic meaning may be defined as meaning concerned with degree of certainty about the truth of a predicational content (cf. e.g.). It may be conceived of as always involving, inherently or by implication, the idea of an epistemic source. In other words, any epistemic evaluation of the truth of a predicational content may be taken to be based on such a source. The factivity presupposed (Lyons, 1977: 808–9; Lyons, 1981: 190) or designated (as coded meaning; cf. Caton, 1969: 28–2; Palmer, 1986: 51; Pelyvás, 1996: 183–4) by the declarative sentence type in (33), for instance, implies that the utterer of this sentence bases his utterance on an epistemic source which is so strong that it does not have to be adduced explicitly. On the other hand, the hypothetical meaning designated by *if* in (34) basically implies that no epistemic source supports the truth of the predicational content of *Bob is in London*. The hypothetical meaning of (34) may be equated with the meaning of absolute uncertainty about the truth of this predicational content.

(33)   Bob is in London.

(34)   ...if Bob is in London.

Moreover, epistemic meaning may be conceived of as constituting a coherent and delimited meaning domain of epistemicity in its own right – a field having the structure of an epistemic scale and encompassing the field of evidentiality and the epistemic variant of the field of modality as subordinate meaning domains (cf. Givón's 1982 notion of 'epistemic space'). When evidential and epistemic modal meaning are found to be encoded in the same category or paradigm, this category or paradigm may be conceived of as encoding (parts of) the meaning domain of epistemicity as such.

Finally, the epistemic scale captures the following facts:

vi) that modal meaning and evidential meaning are both organised on an intensity scale; and

vii) that, in certain contexts, epistemic variants of modal linguistic items encoding the meaning of strong modal intensity may have weak, i.e. indirect, evidential meaning.

On the epistemic scale, the meaning domain of evidentiality is represented as being located closer towards the factivity end than the epistemic variant of the meaning domain of modality. This representation is inspired by Givón (1982). Evidential meaning may be conceived of as involving an epistemic source that is strong enough to serve directly as evidence for the truth of a predicational content. In contrast, epistemic modal meaning may be conceived of as involving an epistemic source that is not strong enough to serve directly as evidence for the truth of a predicational content, but only strong enough to serve as the basis of an evaluation, i.e. only strong enough to produce an epistemic force and thus establish an evaluating epistemic force-dynamic potential. That is, everything else being equal, evidential meaning involves a stronger epistemic source than epistemic modal meaning. In this sense it is epistemically stronger. Evidential meaning, involving a relatively stronger epistemic source than epistemic modal meaning, implies a higher degree of certainty about the truth of a predicational content. The basic advantage of representing evidential meaning as epistemically stronger than epistemic modal meaning, however, has to do with the empirical fact that strong epistemic modal meaning is closely related to weak evidential meaning. Within the epistemic variant of the field of modality, the meaning of maximum epistemic force, or force-dynamic potential, is located at the factivity end of the epistemic scale, whereas the meaning of mere epistemic potential is located at the non-factivity end. Within the field of evidentiality, direct, visual evidential meaning is located at the factivity end of the epistemic scale, whereas indirect, inferential or reported, evidential meaning is located at the non-factivity end. This means that strong epistemic modal meaning is located immediately next to weak evidential meaning. Thus, the epistemic meanings encoded by Germanic modal verbs such as e.g. Danish *skulle* and *måtte*-n are contiguous with indirect evidential meanings. This contiguity, I think, motivates the fact that epistemic *skulle* and *måtte*-n in certain contexts may occur with evidential meaning as in (31): whereas the encoded functional potentials of strong epistemic modal meaning and weak evidential meaning are separate, the actual pragmatic functions of these meanings may overlap.

6 Conclusion

I have argued:

> i) that in order to make the term modality useful as a tool for linguistic description we should use it much more restrictedly than we do today and anchor it in actual linguistic observations.

Restricting the use of the term for the meaning domain of modal intensities, I have argued:

> ii) that this field should be defined and delimited with reference not to any of the concepts etymologically related to the term modality, but to the concept of force-dynamic potential.

On the basis of the definition and delimitation of the meaning domain of modality, I have outlined:

> iii) an attempt to clarify the relations between modal and evidential meaning.

Let me finally add a brief comment to the first and the last of these three undertakings. Restricting the use of the term modality for the meaning domain of modal intensities in a sense makes the term nothing else than an empty shell. There is nothing etymologically modal to this domain. However, the philosophical-logical counterpart of this field has for decades lived with the name modality. Linking the linguistic term modality to the philosophical use, then, provides it with a good deal of interdisciplinary terminological consistency. It should be noted, though, that also within philosophy modality seems occasionally to be used quite vaguely (cf. e.g. Rescher, 1968).

With respect to the attempt to capture the relations between evidential and epistemic modal meaning, I should mention that I am aware that it is no more than a sketch. However, I do think that an understanding of the concept of epistemicity or epistemic meaning is crucial for an understanding of these relations. The growing interest in epistemic meaning, then, will hopefully throw light on the area of modality.

Notes

1   The chapter is based on a more thorough, but unpublished thesis: Boye (2002) I am grateful to the Danish Research Council for the Humanities for granting me a scholarship that has made the final work on the chapter possible. And I am grateful to Annerieke Boland and Peter Harder for valuable criticism and comments on the first draft of this chapter.

2   For van der Auwera and Plungian (1998), the distinction between participant-internal and participant-external modality seems to be something like a modality-type distinction. They regard the distinction as irrelevant when it comes to epistemic modality and they capture the incompatibility of deontic modal meaning and participant- or agonist-internal modal meaning by taking deontic modality to be a special case of participant-external modality. In contrast, I take the distinction between agonist-internal and agonist-external modal meaning to cut across modality types. In Boye (2001a) I have argued that the distinction is relevant also when it comes to epistemic modal meaning and in Section 4.5, I capture the incompatibility of deontic modal meaning and participant- or agonist-internal modal meaning by taking the latter meaning to exclude the former meaning for inherent and natural reasons.

3   The dynamic variant of the Danish modal verb *kunne* like the dynamic variant of the English cognate *can* is normally paraphrased by the word 'ability'. Thus, it may seem counter-intuitive to classify *kunne* as an agonist-external modal verb.

Accordingly, van der Auwera and Plungian (1998) take English *can* to have both 'participant-internal' and 'participant-external' meaning. However, adapting classifications to linguistic facts is clearly preferable to adapting linguistic facts to classifications and while the present classification of *kunne*, as argued, captures the fact that this verb like other agonist-external modal verbs has a deontic variant, van der Auwera and Plungian's classification of *can* seems not to capture any linguistic fact. In accordance with linguistic facts, dynamic or physical ability may be conceived of as an agonist-external property in the sense that, as a physical property, it is external to a psychological core (cf. Boye, 2001a).

4   This motivation, it should be noted, does not apply in the case of at least German and Dutch modal verbs. In German, for instance, all modal verbs seem capable of taking a directional adverbial complement.

5   The co-occurrence of two epistemic adverbs within a single clause, as in *Allegedly, Bob is probably not married*, requires a special reading that involves what Lyons (1977) calls a 'subjective'-'objective' distinction. One adverb (in the example above, *probably*) must be read within the scope of the other (in the example above, *allegedly*). Only the wide-scope ('subjective') adverb can be read as expressing the speaker's epistemic evaluation here and now. The narrow-scope ('objective') adverb must be read as belonging semantically to the predicational content evaluated by the wide-scope adverb.

References

Aijmer, K. (1980) *Evidence and the Declarative Sentence*. Stockholm: Almquist and Wiksell.

Aikhenvald, A. Y. (2003) Evidentiality in typological perspective. In A. Y. Aikhenvald and R. M. W. Dixon (eds) *Studies in Evidentiality* 1–31. Amsterdam: John Benjamins.

Anderson, L. B. (1986) Evidentials, paths of change and mental maps: typologically regular asymmetries. In W. Chafe and J. Nichols (eds) *Evidentiality: the linguistic coding of Epistemology* 273–312. Norwood: Ablex Publishing Corporation.

Van der Auwera, J. and Plungian, V. A. (1998) Modality's semantic map. *Linguistic Typology* 2: 79–124.

Bache, C. (1997) *The Study of Aspect, Tense and Action: towards a theory of the semantics of grammatical categories*. Frankfurt am Main: Peter Lang.

Bache, C. (2002) On categories in linguistics. *Acta Linguistica Hafniensia* 34: 71–105.

Bech, G. (1949) Das Semantische System der Deutschen Modalverba. *Travaux du Cercle Linguistique de Copenhague* IV: 3–46.

Bech, G. (1951) *Grundzüge der semantischen Entwicklungsgeschichte der hochdeutschen Modalverba*. Historisk-Filosofiske Meddelelser 32: 6. Copenhagen: Det Kongelige Danske Videnskabernes Selskab.

Bouma, L. (1973) *The Semantics of the Modal Auxiliaries in Contemporary German*. Haag: Mouton.

Boye, K. (2001a) The force-dynamic core meaning of Danish modal verbs. *Acta Linguistica Hafniensia* 33: 19–66.

Boye, K. (2001b) Evidence for evidentiality in Danish. In H. H. Müller (ed.) *Reflections on Modality*. Copenhagen studies in language 26: 81–127.

Boye, K. (2002) *Modalitet, evidentialitet og epistemicitet: en teori om de tre sproglige kategorier og en analyse af deres verbale manifestationer i dansk*. Unpublished thesis.

Brandt, S. (1999) Modal verbs in Danish. *Travaux du Cercle Linguistique de Copenhague* XXX.

Bybee, J. L. (1985) *Morphology*. Amsterdam: John Benjamins Publishing Company.

Bybee, J., Perkins, R. and Pagliuca, W. (1994) *The Evolution of Grammar: tense, aspect and modality in the languages of the world*. Chicago: University of Chicago Press.

Caton, C. E. (1969) Epistemic qualifiers and English grammar. *Studies in Philosophical Linguistics* 1: 17–54.

Chafe, W. (1986) Evidentiality in English conversation and academic writing. In W. Chafe and J. Nichols (eds) *Evidentiality: the linguistic coding of epistemology* 261–72. Norwood: Ablex Publishing Corporation.

Coates, J. (1983) *The Semantics of the Modal Auxiliaries*. London: Croom Helm.

Crystal, D. (1991) *A Dictionary of Linguistics and Phonetics*. Oxford: Blackwell.

Davidsen-Nielsen, N. (1990) *Tense and Mood in English. A Comparison with Danish*. Berlin: Mouton de Gruyter.

Debyshire, D. C. (1979) *Hixkaryana*. Amsterdam: North-Holland Publishing Company.

Doherty, M. (1987) *Epistemic Meaning*. Berlin: Springer-Verlag.

Fortescue, M. (2003) Evidentiality in West Greenlandic: a case of scattered coding. In A. Y. Aikhenvald and R. M. W. Dixon (eds) *Studies in Evidentiality* 291–306. Amsterdam: John Benjamins.

Givón, T. (1982) Evidentiality and epistemic space. *Studies in Language* 6.1: 23–49.

Groefsema, M. (1995) Can, may, must and should: a relevance theoretic account. *Journal of Linguistics* 31: 53–79.

Herslund, M. (1989) Modality. A presentation. In M. Herslund (ed.) *On Modality. Papers from Meetings and Discussions in the Linguistic Circle of Copenhagen 7–15. Travaux du Cercle Linguistique de Copenhague* XXXIII.

Hughes, G. E. and Cresswell, M. J. (1974) *An Introduction to Modal Logic*. London: Methuen and Co Ltd.

Ifantidou, E. (2001) *Evidentials and Relevance*. Amsterdam: John Benjamins.

Jensen, B. L. (1997) On the use of mood and modal verbs in Italian and Danish. In C. Bache and A. Klinge (eds) *Sounds, Structures and Senses. Essays Presented to Niels Davidsen-Nielsen on the Occasion of his Sixtieth Birthday* 109–25. Odense: Odense University Press.

Klinge, A. (1993) The English modal auxiliaries: from lexical semantics to utterance interpretation. *Journal of Linguistics* 29: 315–57.

Klinge, A. (1996) The impact of context on modal meaning in English and Danish. *Nordic Journal of Linguistics* 19: 35–54.

Kornfilt, J. (1997) *Turkish*. London: Routledge.

Langacker, R. W. (1990) Subjectification. *Cognitive Linguistics* 1(1): 5–38.

Lyons, J. (1977) *Semantics*. Cambridge: Cambridge University Press.

Lyons, J. (1981) *Language, Meaning and Context*. Suffolk: Fontana.

Marino, M. (1973) A feature analysis of the English modals. *Lingua* 32: 309–23.

Mushin, I. (2001) *Evidentiality and Epistemological Stance: narrative retelling*. Amsterdam: John Benjamins.

Nuyts, J. (2001) *Epistemic Modality, Language and Conceptualization: a cognitive-pragmatic perspective*. Amsterdam: John Benjamins Publishing Company.

Palmer, F. R. (1979) *Modality and the English Modals*. London: Longman.

Palmer, F. R. (1986) *Mood and Modality*. Cambridge: Cambridge University Press.

Papafragou, A. (2000) *Modality: issues in the semantics-pragmatics interface*. Oxford: Elsevier.

Pelyvás, P. (1996) *Subjectivity in English. Generative Grammar versus the Cognitive Theory of Epistemic Grounding*. Frankfurt am Main: Peter Lang.

Perkins, M. R. (1983) *Modal Expressions in English*. London: Frances Pinter.

Rescher, N. (1968) *Topics in Philosophical Logic*. Dordrecht: Reidel.

Rice, K. (1989) *A Grammar of Slave*. Berlin: Mouton de Gruyter.

Skyum-Nielsen, P. (1971) *Modalverberne i Nudansk*. Unpublished prize essay.

Sohn, H.-M. (1999) *The Korean Language*. Cambridge: Cambridge University Press.

Sweetser, E. E. (1990) *From Etymology to Pragmatics. Metaphorical and Cultural Aspects of Semantic Structure*. Cambridge: Cambridge University Press.

Talmy, L. (1988) Force dynamics in language and cognition. *Cognitive Science* 2: 49–100.

Traugott, E. C. (1989) On the rise of epistemic meaning in English: an example of subjectification in semantic change. *Language* 65(1): 31–55.

Willett, T. (1988) A cross-linguistic survey of the grammaticization of evidentiality. *Studies in Language* 12(1): 51–97.

4   Modality and subjectivity

Lars Heltoft

1   Introduction

In the present article, I shall offer an analysis of linguistic modality in terms of two basic semantic parameters. One is well-known from both linguistics and modal logic, namely the relatively narrow notion of necessity vs. possibility; the other one is a version of the opposition between subjectivity and objectivity, deviant from most alternatives in the sense that this opposition is not taken to refer to epistemic or doxastic meaning, but – in a sense to be developed below – to the position of the so-called modal factor.

Modality is often taken in a wider sense: a cross-linguistic notional category that grammaticalises in linguistic systems such as mood, modal verbs, particles and clitics, cf. Palmer's article on modality in the *Encyclopedia of Linguistics* (1995). According to Palmer, the areas of semantic substance that grammaticalise in these systems are: attitudes and opinions of the speaker, speech acts, subjectivity, non-factivity, non-assertion, possibility and necessity. Palmer admits the difficulty: 'the semantics is often vague and diffuse and there is no single semantic feature with which modality can be correlated in the way that tense can be regarded as the grammatical expression or "grammaticalisation" of time'.

The main problem, it would seem, is the relation between modality in the narrow sense: necessity and possibility – as found typically in Germanic modal verb systems – and the area of subjectivity or speaker-relatedness, very often grammaticalised in traditional moods (Meillet, 1937: Benveniste, 1958 and Lyons, 1977; 1982) or semi-grammaticalised in constructions or sentence adverbial categories that express attitudes and opinions of the speaker.

In this article, I shall present a possible way of working out the relationship between these two dimensions of modality: necessity and possibility on one hand and subjectivity and objectivity on the other. The emphasis will be on the concept of a modal factor. Where necessity vs. possibility is concerned, I shall assume that this is an inverse system in the sense of G. Leech (1974). Deontic and epistemic senses will not occur as primitive concepts in this system (cf.

Leech, 1969), but I shall assume that these senses will derive in context from combinations of abstract necessity vs. possibility and modal factor position.

Only select examples from the international literature on the subject will be referred to. Most of the examples and material considered will be taken from the Scandinavian languages, especially from modern Danish. These languages are of particular interest for the study of modality because of their extensive sets of semi-grammaticalised modal particles and sentence adverbs. Such particles and adverbs are in many descriptions and treatments considered to be parts of the modal systems of languages since they code degrees of doxastic content, namely certainty, probability and possibility. This is so in Danish, too, but furthermore, they would seem to code evidentiality and even functions of back-channelling and polyphonic viewpoint marking (Nølke, 1994). This brings us closer to mood in the sense of a system coding content functions either directly relevant to the illocutionary system, such as the indicative which is the traditional mood to code constative illocutionary value or its precondition, namely factuality, or indirectly relevant as a system indicating positions of point of view and illocutionary responsibility. An example of the latter coding would be the modern German present subjunctive (see Section 2.1).

2   The concept of a modal factor

In a classic article from the era of Danish structuralism (1951), Gunnar Bech employs the notion of a *Modalfaktor* 'modal factor' in an analysis of the development of the modal verbs in High German. Given that modality will comprise the opposition of necessity versus possibility, Bech defines a modal factor as: '*den faktor… der den inhalt des modalfeldes notwendig… macht bzw. ermöglicht*'[1]. In Bech's descriptive practice, the modal factor can be a semantic argument of the modal verb or some external factor. A simple example of a modal factor would be the subject argument of German *wollen* 'will'.

(1)   *Er   will   das ganze Gebäude   abreissen   lassen.*
        he   wants   the whole building   demolish   let
        he wants to have the whole building demolished.

The opposition to *wollen* is held by the modal verbs *sollen* 'must' and *dürfen* 'may'.

(2)   *Er soll/darf das ganze Gebäude abreissen lassen.*

This is characterised by Bech as the opposition between an intrasubjective modal factor and an extrasubjective modal factor. This terminology refers to the grammatical subject of a modal clause and I shall avoid it from Section 3 onwards to avoid confusion with other notions of subjectivity. Notice that at an abstract level, this relation resembles the notion of subject demotion crucial to the category of voice, cf. Comrie (1977). We can speak of Bech's relation as modal factor demotion: the modal verbs *sollen* and *dürfen,* so to speak bracket the modal factor from realisation as a semantic argument. Where *dürfen* is concerned, the modal factor can emerge as a valency-bound free adverbial, here *meinetwegen/seinetwegen/ihretwegen* 'as for me/him/her', again in a way similar to the demoted subject argument.

(3)   *Er darf meinetwegen/ihretwegen das ganze Gebäude abreissen lassen.*

The second opposition concerning modal factor position is the semantic distinction between causality and autonomy. With the modal verbs *müssen* and *können* the necessity or possibility of the 'modal field' (the modalised predication) is determined by some external law; with the modal verbs *dürfen, sollen, wollen* and *mögen* the necessity or possibility of the modalised predication is autonomous, that is, determined by no external law. The grammatical correlate of this law is, according to Bech, a nexual modal factor (*nexueller modalfaktor,* nexus to be taken in the sense of Jespersen (1924) as a grammatical category with a predicational value): the modal factor is some fact or knowledge about the world that determines the necessity or possibility of the predication. For details, see Bech (1949).

(4)   *Ende April*   *muss man die Rosen schneiden, um ein optimales*
        By the end of April must one   the roses prune,   for an optimal
        Resultat zu kriegen.
        result   to achieve
        By the end of April, one must prune the roses, in order to achieve an optimal
          result.

Thus, Bech's analysis comprises two sets of oppositions of modal factor position, namely:

1	intrasubjektiver	vs.	extrasubjektiver modalfaktor
	intrasubjective		extrasubjective modal factor
	wollen		
2	nexueller	vs.	nicht-nexueller modalfaktor
	nexual		non-nexual modal factor
	müssen		*sollen, dürfen*
	können		*wollen, mögen*

Table 1: Two sets of oppositions

These oppositions are obviously conceived of as a classical case of markedness. The left column holds the marked terms, the right one the unmarked terms. For a recent and convincing functional theory of markedness, see Andersen (2001). The inclusive nature of such oppositions is particularly clear from the opposition nexual vs. non-nexual, where the unmarked modal factor need not be an agent, but could also be some norm or rule, that is, it could take on nexual shape as well.

Notice that German modals are neutral with respect to a distinction that lexicalises in English as *can* vs. *may/might*, that is, to a distinction between the objective world and the speaker's subjective world. German has *können* for both senses. Example (5) (Bech, 1949: 33) is what Palmer (1986) and Davidsen-Nielsen (1990) after him, call dynamic possibility (Bech: Kosmonomische Möglichkeit); (6) (Bech, 1949: 34) is epistemic possibility.

(5)   *Wenn man hier ist, kann man nicht drin sein.*
        If one is here, one cannot be involved.

(6)   *und dieser   da   konnte   wohl   Heinrich Holck sein.*
        and that person   there   can-PAST   presumably Heinrich Holck be
        and that person over there could be H. H.

3   Content form

A point to notice about Bech's position is his focus on 'emic' content distinctions, a focus distinct from that of many recent analyses. The semantic description of the German modal verbs found in Heine (1995) offers itself as an illuminative background for comparison. In Heine's view, the sign relation maps cognitive content onto syntactic frames and lexical material and the question which content distinctions are relevant for a given stage of a language, does not emerge in his approach, since what changes is the target of the mapping, namely the expression.

Heine distinguishes agent-oriented uses of German modal verbs from epistemic uses by means of a set of conceptual properties. Agent-oriented uses are associated with the presence of 'some force (F) that is characterized by 'element of will' (…), i.e. that has an interest in an event either occurring or not occurring'. There is a controlling agent (C) and the situation is dynamic, the event has not yet taken place and there is no certainty that it will occur, only a certain degree of probability.

Epistemic uses involve neither force nor agent, but only the ascription of a certain degree of probability to the event.

The point to notice is the way the two approaches differ with respect to their focus of interest. Bech emphasises the fact that (5) and (6) do not present an 'emic' difference where the modal verbs are concerned. Heine, by contrast, defines a conceptual distinction between epistemic and agent-oriented uses that has certainly proved of use in other descriptions of modal verbs, especially those of English. But his point is that these uses do in fact map onto the German modals, not that they should come out as structurally different content distinctions.

We cannot assume that conceptual structure will glue directly to grammatical forms as their content. We do need hypotheses about the limits and organisation of the notional category of modality, but we cannot assume that linguistic signs have universal cognitive content. Content will be coined differently across languages. In the vein of Danish functional grammar as presented for instance in the preface of Engberg-Pedersen et al. (1996) and in Harder (1996), I shall emphasise the need for empirical studies of the 'emic' content distinctions grammaticalised in particular languages, in Hjelmslevian terms: distinctions of content form. As an ironic comment on Palmer's contention that tense grammaticalises time, I shall call attention to the fact that Danish tense does *not* grammaticalise time, but proximity of the textually constructed worlds; i.e. it is indifferent with respect to distance in time and distance in reality. The tense category of older Scandinavian has in fact in later Danish been absorbed by a more abstract category neutral to traditional tense and mood.

In what follows, I shall follow up on Bech's position, both where the focus on 'emic' distinctions are concerned and with respect to the concept of a modal factor. I shall suggest that this concept can be generalised to comprise other distinctions than those found in German modal verbs.

4   Subjectivity and modal factors

I shall suggest an abstract hypothetical category of modality, including Bech's notion of a modal factor. At this point, we are not addressing the question of 'emic' oppositions found in particular languages, but rather the question of universally relevant cognitive distinctions of semantic substance.

The first dimension, modal factor realised by subject argument or demoted, is peripheral with respect to this discussion, since it is mainly relevant in the analysis of modal verbs and their grammaticalisation processes. The second dimension, causality versus autonomy, is highly relevant, since for one thing, it distinguishes causal from deontic readings of modals. Bech does not, however, draw a distinction between epistemic and non-epistemic modals, for precisely the reason that such a distinction does not lexicalise in German, or in Danish, for that matter. To handle modal phenomena where such a distinction is relevant, we shall need a third dimension, namely that of subjectivity. We shall say that modal factor location can be either in the speaker or outside the speaker and in this sense, we shall speak of subjectivity vs. objectivity, cf. speaker-orientation in Bybee et al. (1994). 'Orientation' is the notion closest to 'modal factor position'.

A caveat with respect to terminology may be in place here. Subjectivity is derived from 'subject' in the sense of *le sujet parlant* 'the speaking subject' of French tradition (Benveniste, 1958; Lyons, 1977; 1982) and has no epistemic content. Thus, objective and objectivity refers to modal factor positions different from the speaker, not to epistemic qualifications. In the description of Danish, it is highly relevant in the description of the content of the modalised passives systems. The so-called *s*-passive in Danish functions as a mood in relation to the system of periphrastic passives, see Heltoft and Falster Jakobsen (1996). We find here a modal factor distinction roughly similar to the difference between subjective and objective modals:

(7) (a) *retten   krydres   med safran.*
          the dish   season-PASS.S-MOOD   with saffron
          the dish is to be seasoned with saffron.

     (b) *retten   bliver   krydret   med safran.*
          the dish   become   season-PERF.PTC.   with saffron
          the dish is (being) seasoned with saffron.

The s-passive functions as an objective mood in the sense that it introduces a point of view or perspective that is different from that of the speaker[2]. In (7a), the modal factor is the set of rules or norms in a cookery book. The periphrastic passive of (7b), by contrast, points to the speaker as the sole viewpoint and is therefore very often used as the straightforward, descriptive mood.

This distinction is drawn at the propositional level in the sense of speech act theory (Austin, 1962; Searle, 1969 and later).

A similar distinction is found at the level of locution and illocution, relevant for the description of sentence adverbials and modal particles. At this level, the distinction refers to differences between points of view articulated in the unfolding of the dialogue. Such views can be the speaker's view or somebody else's, cf. the distinction between different 'locutionary positions' or 'voices' in the linguistic theory of polyphony (Nølke, 1994). Thus, modality will comprise two semantic domains:

   i)   Necessity versus possibility.
   ii) Location of modal factor.

The question of the modal factor's location is bound up with some notion of a predicational hierarchy. For the present purpose, I shall refer to a simplified version of the clause as a layered system, cf. Dik (1989), Dik and Hengeveld (1997) and for the simplification, Christensen (2001).

At the bottom level of the semantic hierarchy, we find Bech's oppositions, see 2. The level of analysis is limited to one single predication and the modal factor is borne by either the subject argument or the demoted subject argument.

The second level, also found in Bech, involves more than one predication and the relevant modal category (mood, modal verb, sentence adverb, etc.) is either neutral, or it insists on having an extrapredicational modal factor position, that is: the modal factor must be located in some predication different from the modal predication.

At the third and fourth levels, the domain of the modal factor is the opposition between the speaker and some non-speaker location. The third level, illustrated by the case of the Danish passives, is the propositional level and the modal factor is either subjective in the sense of speaker-bound, or it is objective in the sense of located in the world described by the speaker. At the fourth level, again, the modal factor can be subjective in the sense of speaker-bound, but at this level, objective modal factor position will mean location in a potential or actual dialogue partner different from the speaker.

> Propositional position:
> subjective (speaker-borne point-of-view) vs. objective
> (view held by some other agent described in the proposition).
>
> Dialogic position:
> subjective (view held by speaker) vs. objective
> (view held by some other locutionary agent).

The modal factor system forms a set of universal oppositions that may grammaticalise differently across languages. It is obvious that at some points in this hierarchy, one dimension may be irrelevant. We have already seen that subjectivity can be irrelevant where the emic structure of modal verbs is concerned. Where mood is concerned, modal factor position can be irrelevant for some languages and third, in the case of sentence adverbial semantics, the opposition necessity vs. possibility can be irrelevant. In what follows, we shall see how far these dimensions will take us in the description of Danish.

5   Modal verbs

Necessity and possibility are probably the semantic building material of all Germanic systems of modal verbs, but not all of these languages lexicalise the distinction between subjective and objective modal factor position where their modal verbs are concerned. English does to some extent, but Danish and German do not.

Bech did not explicitly include the speaker among the set of possible modal factors. This is no defect of his analysis, but a reflection of the major differences in the systems of English and German modal verbs. As in Danish, the lexical modal verb system in German is neutral with respect to speaker-orientedness. Danish and German have not undergone the changes that to some extent introduced lexical specification in English modal verbs in terms of subjectivity. There is no *may/can* distinction in German and Danish similar to the well-known one in English between epistemic *may* and dynamic *can*.

Thus, the semantic changes leading from the middle Danish limited system of modal verbs to the present system need not be characterised in terms of 'subjectification', as cognitive linguists have it. They can simply be characterised in terms of the changes in modal factor suggested by Bech.

In Old Danish (Scanic dialect) the modal verbs *skal* 'must' and *ma* (mā) 'can, may' do not lexicalise the distinction between causality and autonomy (Bjerrum, 1966). Deontic and causal meanings, for instance, cannot be distinguished with these modal verbs. But the opposition to *wil* 'will' is readily described in terms of subject demotion, *skal* and *ma* taking demoted modal factors, *wil* placing the modal factor with the subject argument. The subsystem formed by *skal* and *ma* has been described by Bjerrum (1966) as follows:

(8)   Necessity/obligation: *skal* 'must'
         Possibility/permission/right: *ma* 'can, may'

(8')   Necessity/obligation: *skal taka* 'must take'
         Possibility/permission/right: *ma taka* 'can, may take'

(8")   Semantic merger: *taki* (PRES. SUBJ.)

For ease of exposition I have added the function of the present subjunctive, a semantic merger between *skal* and *ma*. We shall return to the mood system below, but notice that the subjunctive is in fact neutral with respect to both of Bech's dimensions, deontic necessity vs. deontic possibility and modal factor position.

The abstraction process undergone by these modals in the formation of the modern system is not a process of subjectification, but a loss of modal factor opposition. We shall include *kan* (from **kann* 'know intellectually', infinitive **kunnan*), since this furnishes us with enough distinctions to give a brief exposition of the modern core system.

Change of expression	Change of content		
1	**specific modal factor (the subject argument)**	**>**	**non-specific**
kan > kan	intellectual capability	>	possibility
ma > må	ability, permission	>	permission
2	**specific modal factor (the subject argument)**	**>**	**different, but specific (nexual modal factor)**
ma > må	ability	>	necessity
3	**non-spec. modal factor**	**>**	**specific modal factor (1. p. in spec. senses)**
skal > skal	obligation, necessity	>	obligation, necessity, wish, will and promise

Table 2: Change of expression and content

These changes lead to a core system that lexicalises the distinction between causality and autonomy, at the expense, though, of partly blurring the necessity vs. possibility-distinction:

(9)		**causality**	**autonomy**
	possibility	*kan* 'can, may'	*må* 'may, allowed to'
	necessity	*må* 'must, need'	*skal* 'must'

The horizontal dimension is that of causality vs. autonomy, the vertical one that of possibility vs. necessity. Still, we only need a two-dimensional system, since subjectivity does not grammaticalise in the system of the modal verbs in Danish.

This is at variance with the basic assumptions in Hengeveld's treatment of mood and modality in *Dutch Functional Grammar* (1987, after him Dik, 1989; Dik and Hengeveld, 1997). In the Dutch theory, modal verbs fall in three classes, mirroring their position in the layered system. They are either inherent to the predication, that is, they function as predicates and govern their subjects, or they function as predicational operators, or, again, as propositional operators. These three classes are accordingly named inherent, objective and subjective modal verbs.

Using a slightly modified and less technical version of the layered system
(cf. Christensen, 2001), we can illustrate the relations of the modal classes to
the layered system as in Table 3.

Subjective modal verbs	6th layer:	*illocution* (extended proposition) = utterance
	5th layer:	*subjectivity* (proposition) = extended proposition
Objective modal verbs	4th layer:	*reality* (event) = proposition
	3rd layer:	*time* (extended predication) = event
Inherent modal verbs	2nd layer:	*telicity* (predication) = extended predication
	1st layer:	*argument + predicate* = predication

Table 3: Modals and the layered system

According to Hengeveld, the task is to classify modal operators – for a given
language – with respect to their position in the layered system. A universal
set of distinctions is then mapped onto the expression level and through these
mappings – different for particular languages – language specific differences
arise, whether as different lexicalisations or as more grammaticalised systems,
e.g. inflexional systems.

In Danish, the lack of a lexicalised distinction between subjective and
objective modal verbs is compensated for through combinations with other
grammatical systems and, thus, less polysemic readings crystallise. The Danish
s-passive mentioned in (7a) above functions as a mood in relation to the system
of periphrastic passives. We find here a modal factor distinction roughly similar
to the difference between subjective and objective modals.

Notice that the semantic function of the passive mood system with modal
verbs in Danish is to introduce at the constructional level differences of subjectivity that are not found within the lexical system of the modal verbs.

(10) (a) *formuleringen kan misforstås.*   (non-subjective: causal)
         can misunderstand-INF.PASS.S-MOOD
    this wording can be misunderstood.

   (b) *formuleringen kan blive misforstået.*   (subjective: doxastic)
    can become   misunderstand-PERF.PTC.
    this wording may be misunderstood.

(11) (a) *disse roser   må   snart beskæres.*   (non-subjective: causal)
        must soon   prune-INF.PASS.S-MOOD
    these roses must/are to be pruned soon.

  (b) *disse roser må   snart blive   beskåret.*   (subjective: doxastic)
        must soon   become prune-PERF.PTC.
    these roses must be pruned soon.

(12) (a) *den lille sorte høne   må   ikke   spises.*   (non-subjective: deontic)
        must   not eat-INF.PASS.S-MOOD
    the little black hen must not be eaten.

  (b) *den lille sorte høne må   ikke   blive   spist.*   (subjective: wish)
        may   not   become eat-PERF.PTC.
    may the little black hen not be eaten.

(13) (a) *dette problem   skal   løses   snarest.*   (non-subjective: deontic)
        must   solve-INF.PASS.S-MOOD
    this problem must be solved as soon as possible.

  (b) *dette problem   skal   blive   løst snarest.*   (subjective: promise)
        shall   become solve-PERF.PTC.
    this problem shall be solved as soon as possible.

Notice that the product here is asymmetrical and does not directly mirror the layered system. Examples (12b) and (13b) are subjective in the sense of having illocutionary operators with the illocutionary agent as their modal factor; they belong to level 6. Examples (10b) and (11b) are subjective in the sense of hosting propositional operators. Examples (12a) and (13a) have either predicational operators or illocutionary operators; these belong to levels 2 and 6, respectively and finally, examples (10a) and (11a) are non-subjective in the sense of causal. Their modals belong to level 2 only.

The point here is that the combination of modal verb and subjective periphrastic mood results in marked complex signs that must be subjective. The combination of modal verb and *s*-mood, by contrast, results in structures that are unmarked. These unmarked structures can be either objective or subjective, depending on the semantics of the modal. Deontic modal verbs can be either performative (level 6) or predicational (level 2) and thus, there is no direct fit between layers and operators.

The distribution and semantics of Danish modal verbs are at variance with the layout provided by the layered system in that they:

  i)   are neutral with respect to the important distinction subjective vs. objective; and

ii)   in that deontic and causal modal verbs do not behave symmetrically
with respect to the layered system. As expected, the marked term is
confined to one single layer in the system, but the unmarked term is
not and need not be.

6   Types of inflexional mood

Inflexional mood can grammaticalise modal factor distinctions as well, but
need not. At this level, modal factor position can neither be intrapredicational
(Bech's *intrasubjektiver Modalfaktor*) nor extrapredicational (Bech's *nexueller Modalfaktor*), but it must concern the location of locutionary agents.
Indicative moods will normally point to the speaker as the locutionary agent
and thus place illocutionary responsibility with the speaker as well; a normal
function of the subjunctive in such a system is to make reservations with
respect to the speaker's commitment, but this in itself does not call for a
modal factor distinction.

In some languages, however, the subjunctive has the function of indicating
that the text marked by this mood is not to be taken as the locution of the
speaker, but as someone else's locution. The Modern German so-called present
subjunctive is a well known, but instructive example.

(14)   In fast allen Grammatiken steht, dass das adjektivische Attribut mit dem
Kernsubstantiv bezüglich Genus, Numerus und Kasus kongruiert. In **Sie
mag guten Wein** etwa kongruiere **guten** mit **Wein**, es sei Mask. Sg, Akk
weil **Wein** eben diesen Kategorien zugeordnet sei. (Eisenberg, 1989: 55)

The present subjunctives *kongruiere* and *sei* (twice) indicate that the function of
their clauses is to specify the content found in almost all grammars with respect
to adjectival concord. These clauses are therefore marked as citational: they
specify the common content of sets of utterances by locutionary agents different
from the speaker, to the effect that the speaker cannot be held responsible. And
in this opposition, the term possibility is not the relevant term. The present
subjunctive may of course be interpreted in context as an indication of the mere
possibility of the truth of the description. But from (14) it is quite clear that the
structural boundary behind is something different, since the pragmatic function
of (14) is to indicate that this is certainly not what the author holds. The function
of the German subjunctive is to indicate the presence of a non-subjective modal
factor that functions as a locutionary agent and thus as a source of evidence
that the speaker may or may not rely on.

If properly analysed, a classical Indo-European mood system like that of
Old Scandinavian may turn out to include modal factor distinctions as well. In
Old Danish (Scanic) we find a subjunctive that merges both doxastic and deon-

tic (hortative/permissive) meaning. The indicative mood insists on a subjective modal factor, whereas the subjunctive does not. The senses of the subjunctive are doxastic possibility and two deontic senses: permission and obligation. The system is the following for a strong verb like *fara* ('go', 'travel'):

	indicative	subjunctive
present	*far*	*fare, fari*
past	*for*	*fore*

(15) *Summi mæn sigia at   thingmæn mugu æy døma   af   thuifui   øra*
some men say that thingmen must not sentence off thief   ear
some men say that the thingmen are not entitled to sentence an ear off a thief

*vtan   kunungs   vmbutzman   **late***   *thæt døma af.*
unless   the king's representative   let-PRES.SUBJ.   it   sentence off
unless the king's representative should allow it to be sentenced off.

In example (15), we find two possible interpretations, either that the subjunctive marks the text as being part of the text quoted, or that it expresses a reservation on the speaker's behalf with respect to the probability of the representative allowing the thief's ear to be cut off. Example (16) is the hortative sense (deontic necessity) and (17) means 'deontic possibility':

(16) ***læggi***   *thing mæn   femt*
set- PRES.SUBJ. thingmen   a five days' limit
fore hin..   *at   han   **wæri***   *hema.....*
for the other part   that   he   BE-PRES.SUBJ.   at home
the members of the thing must/are entitled to set a five days' limit within
      which he must be home…

(17) ***graui***   *vp   ræf....   Oc   **nyti***   *wæl*
dig-PRES.SUBJ. up   fox..   and   use- PRES.SUBJ. well
he has the right to dig up the fox and use it well

Upon scrutiny, the relation between the indicative and the subjunctive stands out as one including also a coded modal factor position. The indicative is the marked term, which must mark the textual universe as a reality vouched for by the speaker, but the subjunctive – with its hypothetical, citational and deontic senses – need not have the speaker as the modal factor. The subjunctive can refer to other people's view and to norms not necessarily vouched for by the speaker.

(18)   indicative   vs.   subjunctive
certainty   non-certainty / permission,obligation
1.p. modal factor   neutral (non-1.p.)

The modal factor position follows from Bjerrum's analysis (1966), see also above. Like the deontic modal verbs *ma* and *skal*, the deontic uses of the subjunctive need not be speaker-bound with respect to the modal factor, but can be used to refer to some norm. So the indicative marks a sentence as a potential utterance that will describe a textual world as factual. The subjunctive is negatively defined. Its function is restricted to contexts where such pretensions cannot be carried out, that is, in directive (deontic) contexts instead of descriptive ones and in the doxastic area as doxastic possibility.

The main question at this point is whether this is not a covert introduction of yet another notion under the guise of a modal factor. This is of course a pitfall to be aware of, but I think it is in fact possible to relate the subjective notion of a modal factor to Bech's notion and furthermore, once this has been done, we can extend the subjectivity vs. objectivity-distinction to the analysis of modal particles and sentence adverbials.

The similarity between the speaker-bound, subjective modal factor and Bech's notion lies in the fact that the locus of will and intention is already included in his notion at the predicational level, cf. the description of *wollen* 'will'. The analysis to follow rests on the identification of this relation. At the predicational level, the modal factor locates will and cause; at the propositional level, the modal factor no longer rests with an argument bearing the will or intention of the action or activity described, but the bearer of the intention ascribing possibility vs. necessity to the proposition. And at the uppermost level we find the speaker as the locutionary agent, now the agent intending to convey the frame for a certain illocutionary value: constative or directive, as found in for instance the modern Danish distinction between indicative and imperative.

7   Sentence adverbials and modal factors

Once the status of the speaker has been established as one possible realisation of the modal factor, a way seems to be paved for an explicit inclusion of sentence adverbials in the categories of modality.

7.1   Propositional sentence adverbials

Among propositional sentence adverbials I include those marking the propositional attitudes of the speaker: one category consists of doxastic sentence adverbials: those marking degrees (on the scale) of possibility, probability and certainty. Examples are: *formodentlig* 'presumably', *formentlig* 'presumably', *sandsynligvis* 'probably', *egentlig* 'in reality, honestly', *faktisk* 'in fact', *givetvis* 'certainly'. The other one is adverbials of evaluation such as: *desværre* 'unfortunately', *beklageligvis* 'regrettably', *heldigvis* 'fortunately' and *lykkeligvis* 'luckily', which we shall not go into. Adverbials of evaluation mark the speaker's comments on an otherwise constative utterance. They mark a contention on behalf of the speaker that the receiver will share the evaluation given.

The doxastic sentence adverbials are obviously an articulation of the necessity vs. possibility paradigm. But these adverbials are also integrated in another paradigm, a special case of speaker-boundness. A small group of adverbials like *angivelig* 'reportedly', *efter sigende* 'they say', *ifølge nogen/ham...* 'according to sbdy./him...' are citational, in the sense that they mark lexically the clause as a citation and thus as a statement for which the speaker bears no responsibility.

With constative sentence adverbials, then, there is a clear distinction between those that insist on the speaker being the modal factor and those that allow for a non-speaker modal factor.

7.2   Interlocutionary particles

Interlocutionary particles – often counted among the sentence adverbials – are a striking characteristic of the Scandinavian languages. They differ from the sentence adverbials of Section 6.1 by being blocked from occurring in P1-position, Dik's initial position, the fundamental field of Diderichsen's topological model (Diderichsen, 1946; 1966). Within the limits of the main clause, they are distributionally restricted to the main field for sentence adverbials, always in post subject-position. I shall restrict myself to mentioning a handful of them. The semigrammaticalised status of the category is clear from the length of the paradigm: there are at least a score of them.

(19) (a)   *han er   {jo/vist/nok/da/nu/vel/altså/sgu/sikkert}   dumpet   til   eksamen*
       he   is   particles   failed   to   the exam
       he has particles failed his exam

  (b)   *{*jo/ *vist/ *nok/ *da/ *nu/ *vel/ *altså/ *sgu/ *sikkert} er han dumpet til eksamen*

These particles have nothing to do with constative or illocutionary semantics. What they do is to organise what I have called the interlocutionary structure of a dialogue. Their basic structure is a modal factor structure similar to the one claimed for the German present subjunctive, that is, a distinction between locutionary agents, actual or potential. Some of them mark the relevance of a view or stance held by some person different form the speaker, others that only the speaker is involved.

Of particular interest is the subgroup coding a point of view or stance with which the speaker disagrees.

(20)   *pengene   er brugt   på alt mulig halløj//*
        the money   has been spent   on all kinds of fuss

        ja   det skal jeg   da   ikke svare på
        yes,   that have I   particle   not to answer to
        well, I am not the one to answer that question, am I (and you know I am not).

        hvorfor er de det Susan.
        why is that so, Susan.

The interlocutionary particle *da* has an argumentative function in the sense that it marks the assumption by the speaker that somebody else is holding a view at variance with the one proposed by the speaker. This external point of view need not be one taken by (one of) the speaker's interlocutors, but in context, the receiver will of course very often be the relevant person assumed to disagree. No English parallel is found, but I have preferred a version of a tag-question to render the meaning of the example in question.

The adverbs represented in (19) can be described as follows:

(21) (a)   *han er jo dumpet til eksamen.*
            he has – I don't expect to be contradicted – failed his exam'.

     (b)   *han er da dumpet til eksamen.*
            he has – someone/you should have refrained from holding the opposite
                view– failed his exam.

     (c)   *han er nu dumpet til eksamen.*
            he has – in spite of what someone/you think – failed his exam.

     (d)   *han er vist dumpet til eksamen.*
            he has – and I have this piece of information from somebody else – failed his
                exam.

     (e)   *han er vel dumpet til eksamen.*
            he has – wouldn't you agree – failed his exam.

     (f)   *han er nok dumpet til eksamen.*
            he has – all I know points to that – failed his exam.

     (g)   *han er altså dumpet til eksamen.*
            he has – and this may come as a negative surprise to you – failed his exam.

(h) *han er sgu dumpet til eksamen*
     he has – emphatic oath (etym. 'by God') – failed his exam

(i) *han er sikkert dumpet til eksamen.*
     he has – I would expect – failed his exam.

Out of these a majority of 6 against 3 mark the existence of an objective (non-speaker) modal factor that holds some view or is supposed not to hold a particular view:

Subjective	Objective
nok	jo
sgu	da
sikkert	nu
	vel
	vist
	altså

Table 4: Subjective vs. objective particles

Where *da, nu* and *altså* are concerned, these have also productive descriptive uses: *da* 'then', *nu* 'now' and *altså* 'therefore'[3], but the point in this context is the bipartition of the category of interlocutionary particles such that one subcategory is purely subjective in that the speaker is the sole modal factor, whereas the other category has an external modal factor, in the sense that these adverbs include as part of their coded content a reference to a point of view or opinion that is not held by the speaker.

A relatively simple example is the function of the adverbs *vist* and *vistnok* which function as evidential adverbs referring to information from a source different from the speaker himself. This function is similar to the one found in the German subjunctive.

Interlocutionary particles are at a different level with respect to the clausal semantic hierarchy than the constative sentence adverbials. They do concern the semantic domain of probability ranging from necessity/certainty to impossibility, but they code assumptions about locutionary positions or points of view held by others in the context. They either mark the speaker as being the sole locutionary agent relevant, or they mark, by contrast, another locutionary position – potential or actual – as relevant. My point is that this opposition is parallel to the function of modal factors at the lower clause levels considered in the previous sections of this article.

8   Modal factors and the clause as a layered system

In the Dikian tradition of functional grammar, much disagreement has concerned the position of the modal verbs with regard to the layered system (Dik, 1989; Dik with Hengeveld, 1997). Whereas there seems to be general agreement that the epistemic modal verbs (provided that these are relevant for a given language) must be viewed as propositional, disagreement has prevailed with respect to deontic modals. My conclusion is that this controversy seems to rest on the presupposition that the layered model should provide a direct input to the content side of the analysis. It does not. In relation to the Danish functional tradition, the layered system is not a model of the hierarchical potential for content structure (content form), but rather of semantic substance, to be further or even differently structured by the content of empirical languages. Thus, the layered system can serve as a frame of reference for content analysis, but content analysis cannot consist in putting categories on the shelves already provided by the layered system.

The abstract system behind can be summarised as in Table 5.

	Modal factor position	Modal system
Locutionary level and	speaker-bound vs.	necessity vs.
propositional level	non-speaker bound	possibility
Predicational level	argument-bound	necessity vs.
		possibility

Table 5: Basic dimensions of modality

Inherent modalities are bound by an argument at the predicational level. Deontic modalities can be either speaker-bound at the locutionary level or argument-bound, at the predicational level. Epistemic (doxastic) modalities must select their modal factor position from the system speaker-bound vs. non-speaker-bound. They can be either bound at the propositional level (e.g. adverbials of propositional attitudes) or at the locutionary level (dialogic particles).

As far as the final conclusion about modality is concerned, we have not been able to reduce it to one single area of semantic substance. But I have suggested a line of argument and investigation that may lead us to a view that modality can combine from two systems, namely necessity and possibility and modal factor position.

Notes

1   In some of his works, Bech uses no capitals to mark nouns. I respect this practice when quoting him.

2   Among the modern Scandinavian languages, this function is peculiar to Danish and to Dano-Norwegian as well, due to historical influence from Danish. Nothing similar is found with the Swedish s-passive.

3   Jensen (2000a; 2000b) has convincingly shown that many of these particles are the result of extensive processes of 'subjectification' of what were earlier descriptive or cohesive adverbs and that such processes are still going strong.

References

Andersen, H. (2001) Markedness and the theory of linguistic change. In H. Andersen (ed.) *Actualisation. Linguistic Change in Progress* 21–57. Amsterdam/ Philadelphia: John Benjamins.

Austin, J. L. (1962) *How to Do Things with Words*. London: Oxford University Press.

Bech, G. (1949) Das semantische System der deutschen Modalverba. *Travaux du Cercle Linguistique de Copenhague* 4. Copenhague: Einar Munksgaard.

Bech, G. (1951) Semantische Entwicklungsgeschichte der hochdeutschen Modalverba. *Det Kongelige Danske Videnskabernes Selskab. Historisk- Filologiske Meddelelser, bind 32, nr. 6*. København: Ejnar Munksgaard.

Benveniste, É. (1966) *Problèmes de Linguistique Générale I-II*. Paris: Gallimard.

Benveniste, É. (1958) De la subjectivité dans le langage. In Benveniste (1966).

Benveniste, É. (1960) 'Être' et 'avoir' dans leurs fonctions linguistiques. In É. Benveniste (1966) 187–207.

Bjerrum, A. (1966) *Grammatik over Skånske Lov* [*Grammar of the Scanian Law*]. Copenhagen: Københavns Universitets fond til tilvejebringelse af læremidler.

Bybee, J. and Fleischmann, S. (eds) (1995) *Modality in Grammar and Discourse*. Amsterdam/ Philadelphia: John Benjamins.

Bybee, J., Perkins, R. and Pagliuca, W. (1994) *The Evolution of Grammar. Tense, Aspect and Modality in the Languages of the World*. Chicago and London: The University of Chicago Press.

Christensen, T. (2001) Neustik, Tropik og Frastik. Ytringens kommunikative aspekter. In P. Widell and M. Kunøe (eds) *8. Møde om Udforskningen af Dansk Sprog* 62–72. Århus: Institut for Nordisk Sprog og Litteratur. Aarhus Universitet.

Comrie, B. (1977) In defence of spontaneous demotion: the impersonal passive. In P. Cole and J. M. Sadock (eds) *Grammatical Relations. Syntax and Semantics* 8, 47–58. New York: Academic Press.

Davidsen-Nielsen, N. (1990) *Tense and Mood in English: a comparison with Danish*. Berlin: Mouton de Gruyter.

Diderichsen, P. (1946) *Elementær dansk Grammatik*. Copenhagen: Gyldendal.

Diderichsen, P. (1943) Logische und topische Gliederung des germanischen
Satzes. Reprinted in A. Bjerrum et al. (eds) *Helhed og Struktur. Udvalgte
Sprogvidenskabelige Afhandlinger* 52–63. Copenhagen: Gad.

Dik, S. C. (1989) *The Theory of Functional Grammar. Part 1. The Structure of
the Clause*. Dordrecht: Foris.

Dik, S. C. (1997) *The Theory of Functional Grammar.* 1–2. Edited by K.
Hengeveld. Berlin: Mouton de Gruyter.

Eisenberg, P. (1989) *Grundriss der deutschen Grammatik*. Stuttgart: Metzler.

Engberg-Pedersen, E. et al. (eds) (1996) *Content, Expression and Structure.
Studies in Danish Functional Grammar*. Amsterdam: John Benjamins.

Harder, P. (1996a) *Functional Semantics. A Theory of Meaning, Structure and
Tense in English*. Mouton de Gruyter.

Harder, P. (1996b) On content and expression in syntax. In L. Heltoft and
H. Haberland (eds) *Proceedings of the 13th Scandinavian Conference
of Linguistics* 83–92. Department of Languages and Culture, Roskilde
University.

Heine, B. (1995) Agent-oriented vs. epistemic modality. In J. Bybee and S.
Fleischmann (eds) *Modality in Grammar and Discourse* 17–53. Amsterdam/
Philadelphia: John Benjamins

Heltoft, L. and Falster Jakobsen, L. (1996) Danish passives and subject posi-
tions as a mood system. In E. Engberg-Pedersen et al. (eds) *Content,
Expression and Structure. Studies in Danish Functional Grammar* 199–234.
Amsterdam: John Benjamins.

Hengeveld, K. (1987) Clause structure and modality in functional grammar. In
J. van der Auwera and L. Goossens (eds) *Ins and Outs of the Predication*
53–66. Dordrecht: Foris.

Jensen, E. S. (2000a*) Danske sætningsadverbialer og topologi i diakron belysn-
ing*. PhD thesis. University of Copenhagen. Institut for Nordisk Filologi.

Jensen, E. S. (2000b) Sætningsadverbialer og topologi med udgangspunkt
i de konnektive adverbialer. In J. Nørgård-Sørensen et al. (eds) *Ny
forskning i grammatik. Fællespublikation* 7: 141–54. Odense: Odense
Universitetsforlag.

Jespersen, O. (1968 [1924]) *The Philosophy of Grammar*. London: George
Allen.

Leech, G. N. (1969) *Towards a Semantic Description of English*. London,
Beccles and Colchester: Longman.

Leech, G. N. (1974) *Semantics*. Harmondsworth: Penguin Books.

Lyons, J. (1977) *Semantics* I-II. Cambridge: Cambridge University Press.

Lyons, J. (1982) Deixis and subjectivity. Loquor, ergo sum? In R. Jarvella and
W. Klein (eds) *Speech, Place and Action. Studies in Deixis and Related
Topics*. Chichester: John Wiley.

Meillet, A. (1966 [1937]) *Introduction à l'étude comparative des langues indo-européennes*. Forge Village, Mass.: Alabama University Press.
Nølke, H. (1994) *Linguistique modulaire*: *de la forme au sens*. Paris: Éditions Peeters.
Palmer, F. R. (1986) *Mood and Modality*. Cambridge: Cambridge University Press.
Searle, J. (1969) *Speech Acts*. Cambridge: Cambridge University Press.

5 Discourse perspectives on modalisation: the case of accounts in semi-structured interviews

Lars Fant

1 Modality and modalisation from the perspective of communicative needs

1.1 The 'modus' metaphor

The array of linguistic concepts morphologically and semantically based on the Latin noun modus 'shape' or 'manner' – which, in English, includes 'mode', 'mood', 'modality', 'modaliser/modalisation', 'modifier/modification' to mention the most important – is intriguing. On the one hand, each term is intended to correspond to a precise usage in a well-defined subdomain of linguistics, not to be confounded with other terms based on the same radical. On the other hand, there seems to be an original metaphor, which underlies all the terms shaped (and concepts based) on modus and pervades their usage. This underlying idea is that there is some static component which is being subjected to reshaping or remodelling ('modifying') by means of some dynamic component, viz. the modus.

Taken in its widest sense, the modus metaphor could be seen as referring to the structural dualism that characterises all composite linguistic expressions where one (the non-modus part) is commented upon or qualified by the other (the modus part). Here, we find traditional pairs such as theme/rheme, subject/predicate and – precisely! – head/modifier. If understood in a more restricted sense, it refers to the dualism between one component in linguistic expressions (whole utterances, but also with particular reference to verb phrases) which constitutes a dictum, or some 'neutral' propositional content and another component, the modus, which somehow qualifies (attenuates, reinforces, etc.) the content (cf. Bally, 1944: 35). In certain cases, the dictum and modus components are clearly distinguishable, since the modus content has been codified in graphic words, namely those that are boldfaced in the following examples:

(1) (a) My parents are **actually** at home.
     (b) My parents are **unfortunately** at home.
     (c) You **may** leave now.
     (d) It **must** be hot outside.

In (1a), the representation of *my* parents being at home, apart form being stated – and thereby taken responsibility for – by the speaker, is presented as submitted to a cognitive evaluation by means of the adverbial *actually* in the sense 'contrary to your/my/general expectation'. In (b), the same representation undergoes an affective evaluation by means of the adverbial *unfortunately* in the sense 'which you/I/some people do not like'. In (c), the idea of the hearer leaving is presented by means of the modal *may* as something allowed – supposedly by the speaker him/herself – to turn into reality (or as something desirable, an interpretation supposedly brought about by means of a pragmatic, secondary inference). In (d), finally, the idea of high temperatures outside is presented by means of the modal *must* as having the highest possible degree of probability.

It should be obvious from these few examples that the semantic complexity of the modus components is at least as high as that of the dictum components and that even their degree of semantic specificity does not lie very far behind. Still, cognitively speaking, the semantic weight of the modus component is evidently less than that of the dictum component. So there is clearly some feature missing in what we take to be the distinctive characteristics of what we are to understand as modus. The feature to be added is likely to be that of 'cognitive (back)ground'. The dictum part in the dichotomy is sensed as a cognitive figure (foreground), while the modus part is interpreted as backgrounded. If modus is foregrounded, the result will be another dictum, as would happen if the 'modal markers' of (1a) to (d) were converted into whole phrases:

(2) (a) Contrary to what we expected, my parents are at home.
     (b) I'm sorry to have to tell you that my parents are at home.
     (c) Nobody will raise an objection if you leave now.
     (d) It can no longer be doubted that it is hot outside.

1.2   Modalisation as 'qualification of degree'

Traditional semantics, while dealing with the concept of modality, has been concerned with two types of 'filters' through which a propositional content may pass. One is the filter of 'knowledge-packaging', which addresses the issue of how convinced we are of the reality of the worldviews we present. This is what is generally referred to as 'epistemic modality'. The other filter is that of 'necessity-packaging', which addresses the issue of how allowed or recommendable a given action is to be presented as. This latter type is the one generally referred to as 'deontic modality'. Although other kinds of modality have been postulated and included in various authors' modality taxonomies, these two are the constant, recurrent types that appear in all typologies. They can be seen as related to fundamental communicative needs, supposedly that of presenting worldviews (cf. the referential function of Jakobson: Jakobson, 1960) and that of triggering action (cf. the conative function of Jakobson: Jakobson, 1960). Both types of communicative action are, for evident reasons, in need of a fine-tuning mechanism, which is what epistemic and deontic modality would stand for.

A series of other communicative needs could, however, be thought of that are also in need of fine-tuning. Considering the vast number of linguistic choices which we know exists and which we have access to maybe some of, but have no complete control of, how certain can we be that we are expressing ourselves adequately and accurately, so that our interlocutors will understand us in the way we hope? When categorising people and things, will we not need to express nuances and shades that we cannot rely on our lexicon to provide us readily with, especially not in on-line situations when fast retrieval is required? In face-to-face interaction, how certain can we be about the extent to which our interlocutors share our knowledge? And, on the other hand, how sure should we appear to be about the existence of a common cognitive ground, in order not to offend our hearer, but also in order to ensure that our messages actually get across? And how clearly should we allow the illocutionary meaning (opinions, arguments, criticisms, promises, manifestations of gratefulness etc.) of our utterances to be expressed, considering the difficult rapport with our interlocutors that we are deemed to be managing while interacting with them?

The list could be made quite long and yet we would all the time be speaking of 'fundamental' communicative needs, although we would, at the same time, be referring to a number of distinct planes of communication and linguistic expression. The question that arises is: is there any feature or component included in the modality or modalisation concepts that could be applicable to all these specific domains? Or should application of the terms continue to be restricted to the epistemic and deontic spheres, while refraining from accounting for the obvious parallelism between epistemic and deontic modality as anything other than a metaphoric resemblance?

It seems reasonable to think that there is something that the whole series of communicative needs just referred to has in common, which is also what the pair epistemic/deontic modality has in common. An answer to the question of what that something would be is: the (1) need for communicative fine-tuning, (2) along a given scale, which (3) would have common, universal steps. The proposal made in this chapter is that such a fine-tuning scale is identical to that constituted by the well-known quantity operators in traditional logic semantics (cf. Allwood/Andersson/Dahl, 1977). These operators could be seen as related to degree rather than quantity in a restricted sense and could be rephrased as 'modes'. A tentative description could be as follows:

A. The 'maximum' mode, which indicates an absolute degree, beyond which no more qualification is possible.
B. The 'high degree' mode, which indicates a somehow sufficient degree for the communicative content which the modaliser operates on and qualifies to be understood as fully such.
C. The 'some degree' mode, which indicates that the communicative content that the modaliser operates on and qualifies is there to a lower than default degree, without, however, ceasing to exist.

The scale, in fact, would also suppose the existence of a 'zero degree'. The 'zero degree' could be thought of as corresponding to the 'maximum mode' of an inverted scale, along which there would also be a 'high degree' mode and a 'some degree' mode. Translated to the realm of e.g. epistemic modality, the two-faced scale could be reflected and illustrated through the following series of decontextualised sentences:

(3) (a) It must be hot outside. (maximum degree, positive)
     (b) It is probably hot outside. (high degree, positive)
     (c) It may be hot outside. (some degree, positive)
     (d) It cannot possibly be hot outside. (maximum degree, negative)
     (e) It probably isn't hot outside. (high degree, negative)
     (f) It may not be hot outside. (some degree, negative)

Here the examples (3a) to (c) would reflect the first, 'positive' scale and the following examples (3d) to (f) would mirror the inverted, 'negative' scale. This scalar view with discontinuous steps could, incidentally, be thought of as an alternative account for the mirror image relationship found to exist e.g. between the 'must' vs. 'can' modalities, according to Greimas and Courtès (Greimas/Courtès, 1979), while also including the 'intermediate' *should/probably* modality.'

2   Discourse modalisation

Epistemic and deontic modality are well-established concepts that have constituted an area of linguistic study for several decades, in particular within formal
or logical semantics (see e.g. Lyons, 1977; Allwood, Andersson and Dahl,
1977), as well as in the field of grammar/morphosyntax/language structure.
Through the work of scholars such as M. A. K. Halliday (Halliday, 1985), the
study of modality has been extended to the domain of cognitive linguistics and
psycholinguistics. As far as pragmatics and discourse studies are concerned,
various aspects of modality have been addressed (see e.g. Kerbrat-Orecchioni,
1980), although no global framework or model has been proposed to account
for what 'modality' would actually mean, or what precise phenomena it would
cover. Inspiring attempts have been made to associate linguistic phenomena
related to affect and emotion with the modality concept (Barrenechea, 1979,
Kerbrat-Orecchioni, 1992 and 1998, to mention a few). 'Affective' or 'emotive'
modality would thereby stand out as opposed to 'cognition-oriented' (i.e.
epistemic) and 'action-oriented' (i.e. deontic) modality.

More recently, the proposal put forward by Allwood (Allwood, 2000) on
'dialogue modality' has highlighted a great variety of modalisation devices and
classes that could easily be associated with fairly well-defined communicative
needs. The aim of this chapter, while drawing partly on Allwood's (2000)
proposal, is to contribute to the discussion of how to ground the concepts
of modality and modalisation on such needs. The underlying assumption is
that without such grounding, the concepts will remain – as so many other
fundamental notions in linguistics – scientific pseudo-concepts. In this perspective, three important aspects of communication need be addressed and some
corresponding distinctions be developed. One aspect is related to the dialogical
approach (Linell, 1998), which emphasises a view of interaction as negotiation.
Another aspect is the distinction between cognition-oriented, action-oriented
and affect-oriented ways of expression, referred to above. Last but not least,
there is a need for distinguishing varieties of modality as operating on various
planes of verbal expression, e.g. sentence meaning, illocutionary acts, own-
speech management (Allwood, 1998) or interaction management. From this
point and onwards, the term 'modalisation' and 'discourse modalisation' will
be preferred to 'modality' in order to underscore the dynamic nature of the
phenomena in question and, also, to avoid confusion with a term that has its
essential anchorage in semantics.

2.1   Affect-, action- and cognition-oriented modalisation

The claim that affect should be understood as an area in which modalisation operates, along with the areas of cognition and need for action, deserves to be taken
seriously. Linguistic usage is full of markers indicating various types and degrees
of affect, not to mention non-verbal communication, in which the expression of
affect is the main component (for a typology of affective/emotive communication, see the pioneer work by Arndt/Janney, 1987). Here, an association with
Jakobson's expressive function (Jakobson, 1960) comes easily to mind.

The following series of utterances taken from Danish, a language particularly rich in modal adverbs, shows how modal markers oriented towards affect,
action and cognition are compatible within the limits of a sentence:

(4)   (a)   *De bliver **sgu** hjemme.*
            They damn well /will/ stay home.

      (b)   *De **må hellere** blive hjemme.*
            They should stay home.

      (c)   *De er **faktisk** hjemme.*
            They're actually home.

      (d)   *De **må sgu hellere** blive hjemme.*
            They damn well should stay home.

      (e)   *De er **sgu faktisk** hjemme.*
            They're damn well actually home.

      (f)   *De **må faktisk hellere** blive hjemme.*
            They should actually stay home.

      (g)   *De **må sgu faktisk hellere** blive hjemme.*
            They should actually stay home; damn it.

In these utterances, the sentence adverb *sgu* 'damn well' is an affect-oriented
modaliser, the auxiliary-plus-sentence-adverb construction *må hellere* 'should'
is action-oriented, whereas the sentence adverb *faktisk* 'actually' can be seen as
basically cognition-oriented. The modalising markers seem to combine easily.
It could be objected that combinations of affective and cognitive markers, as
in (4e) and (4g), are hardly likely to appear (although, to my ear, the Danish
original sentence sounds a little more acceptable than its English translation).
Probably, however, this is due to logic-based normative thinking. One is not
expected to express simultaneously the idea of something being contrary to
expectation and yet show no surprise but rather indignation regarding that fact.
Still – and empirical research is needed to prove the point – this type of mixture
would no doubt occur in natural conversation. The interesting thing, however,

which regards Danish in particular, is that, if the markers do co-occur, they must appear in an established syntactic order foreseen.

Things are not this simple, however. In actual usage, context-dependent inferred meanings may well occur to complicate the description and create polysemic patterns for each of the modalisers quoted. Non-verbal factors such as intonation definitely play a part in that process. In particular, cognition- and action-oriented markers such as *faktisk* 'actually' and *må hellere* 'should' may readily be interpreted as affect-laden, should the necessary situational and/or prosodic contextualising factors be present. In a combination such as that of (4f), the interpretation of *faktisk* 'actually' as an affective rather than a cognitive marker is probably the most easily available. Notwithstanding, establishing semantic schemata for the modalising markers, in which a basic value in terms of affect-/ action-/cognition-orientation is attributed to each one, is likely to be feasible.

2.2   Representational vs. rapport-management purposes

Verbal interaction can be seen as divided into two basic kinds of meaning negotiation (Linell, 1998: 74) between the participants: the negotiation of 'world views' and the negotiation of social identity (Fant, 2001a; 2001b; in press; cf. the distinction between 'transactional' and 'interactional' made in e.g. Brown/Yule, 1982). In the first type, representations of situations, categories, states, processes, need for action etc. are negotiated among interactants. In the second type, the collective and individual identities of each interactant, along with the relationship to be established between them, is the object of negotiation. The latter could also be said to deal with what has been referred to as politeness phenomena and what could, in a more general perspective, be labelled 'rapport management' phenomena, according to Spencer-Oatey (2000). Modalisation processes may be viewed as oriented towards one or the other type of communicative negotiation. A very simple illustrative example would be the following pair of utterances (which, of course require imagining a suitable context):

(5)   (a)   The water in this part of the estuary is **maybe a bit** too salty for
              pike fry to survive.
       (b)   Your soup was **maybe a bit** too salty, love.

In (5a), a situation is easily imaginable in which the speaker simply wants to express (1) his/her reserve regarding the idea of the water being too salty (*maybe*), along with (2) his/her estimate that the salt content is just slightly and not considerably too high (*a bit*). In a typical situation in which (5b) would be produced, the corresponding intention is hardly likely to be present.

What the speaker would like to convey, here, would rather be his/her wish not to diminish in a socially unacceptable way the hearer's self-image as an acceptably good cook. Obviously, the 'representational' meaning of *maybe* and *a bit* is still present in (5b), but only as a take-off for the correct inferences to be drawn associated with social rapport. This rapport-management function of modalisers has been frequently addressed in the extensive socio-pragmatic literature devoted to politeness under the headings of 'attenuating' or 'mitigating' expressions (and their contrary: 'aggravating' expressions which increase the degree of imposition on or face-threat against an interlocutor). They have received less attention in work whose main concern is modality as such.

It goes without saying that even with regard to this distinction, no a priori dividing line could be drawn that would enable us to predict when one or the other type is at present. Full contextualisation is always required in order to determine to which degree one or the other type of implicature is likely to appear. From a meaning negotiation perspective, it is clear that sentences such as (5a) and (5b) are basically ambiguous and leave room for the hearer to interpret what s/he prefers to interpret.

2.3   Planes of expression

Discourse modalisation should be regarded as related to various planes of expression. This can be illustrated by the appearance of the modalising sentence adverb 'maybe' in the idea unit expressed in a spoken utterance such as the following:

(6)   And they're – maybe – not fully aware of what they're saying.

One intention of the speaker may be, quite simply, to gain time, since s/he has not yet decided how the sentence is to be formulated. Another intention may be to hedge the way s/he is formulating it: 'maybe this could be better expressed with some other wording'. In both cases, we are dealing with 'own-speech management' phenomena (Allwood, 1998) and in the latter case, there is most likely a 'rapport-management' related intention such as that of preserving the speaker's face of being an acceptably good speaker.

However, there are other planes of expression that may be involved as well. The speaker may want to qualify the generalisation possibly contained in the idea unit: 'this is the way those people are, at least to a certain extent'. S/he may also – at the same time or independently – wish to express that the semantic representation included in the idea unit is not entirely certain or to be trusted. Such intentions could be seen as basically associated with sentence meaning (= representational purpose), although here, too, a component of rapport-management may be present, i.e. preserving the speaker's face as an objective and painstaking individual.

On top of that, the speaker's concern may be that of hedging his/her estimate of the level of intersubjectivity (negotiated common ground) between him/her and the interlocutors: 'they may not share my knowledge, expectations or norms.' Here, the plane of expression concerned is no longer just speech-management or sentence-meaning production but rather management of intersubjectivity. It goes without saying that modalisation on this plane of discourse is highly compatible (though not identical) with rapport-management-oriented modalisation.

Yet another plane that can easily become a domain for discourse modalisation is illocutionary force. The idea unit in (6) is naturally understood as having the pragmatic meaning of expressing an opinion and that opinion may need to be qualified by a marker that says 'not too strong'. Here too, there is a high degree of compatibility with rapport-management purposes: 'I don't want to impose my opinion, since (1) I choose to respect my interlocutor's right to have his/her own opinion and not being forced to show it and (2) I want to stand out as a kind and gentle person.'

3   Empirical data: accounts in semi-structured interviews

The data which the following sections draw on are taken from a corpus of semi-structured interviews with mid-level executives at Danish- or Swedish-owned companies in Mexico and Venezuela (Fant, 2001b). There are two sets of respondents. One is locally contracted staff of Mexican or Venezuelan origin, who were asked to tell what they know and think of Scandinavians (Danes or Swedes). The other set is Danish or Swedish staff who had been sent from their home countries to work for a period of time in Mexico or Venezuela and who were asked to present the same kind of account about Latin Americans. The interviewers' purpose was to trigger cultural other- and self-stereotypes through the respondents' accounts. The activity type in question includes a high number of generalising categorisations. There are also a fair number of sequences in which the topic and the length of the account are negotiated between interviewer and respondent. The frequency of modalisers occurring in the dialogue can, without hesitation, be characterised as fairly high. For natural reasons, the type of modalisation that takes place is predominantly cognition-oriented and there are also a considerable number of affect-oriented modalisers, whereas action-oriented modalisation is practically absent. Due to the semi-structured nature of the interviews, which implies a rather informal and colloquial register, rapport-management activities occur frequently, entailing a high number of modalising expressions with various rapport-management functions.

The four samples from which sequences were drawn each have an extension of 100 idea units, each being taken from a different interview. One is in Danish, with a Danish interviewer and a Danish respondent; another one is in Swedish, with a Swedish interviewer and a Swedish respondent. The remaining two are in Spanish, one in which both parties are Venezuelans and the other with a Swedish interviewer and a Mexican respondent. The amount of speech produced in each of the interviews is roughly the same, as is the duration of each sequence (7–8 minutes). Each sample is referred to by means of the respondent's pseudonym: Catrine (Danish), Ken (Swedish), Érica (Venezuelan) and Lorenzo (Mexican).

The samples were coded with regard to the modalising expression detected. Particular attention was given to expressions in which a modaliser was associated with:

i)   a generalising categorisation (sentence meaning);
ii) the illocutionary force of statements with regard to trustworthiness;
iii) intersubjectivity management;
iv) formulation accuracy (own-speech management).

Overall figures regarding these four planes of expression are presented in the table below. Rapport-management functions have not been taken into account here. It should also be noted that certain expressions in which various modalising functions were overlapping have been counted twice or more, depending on the number of domains of application involved.

It can easily be seen that, although there is considerable individual variation regarding the frequency of the various types of modalising expressions, all four domains are substantially represented in each interview sample.

In the following sections, no more attention will be paid to quantitative or distributional aspects of discourse modalisation. Instead the discussion will focus on qualitative features.

	Catrine Lg Dan I+R Dan	Érica Lg Spa I+R Ven	Ken Lg Swe I+R Swe	Lorenzo Lg Spa I Swe R Mex
Total number of modalisers detected	143	124	162	175
Degree of generalisation (sentence meaning)	34	30	69	52
Illocutionary force of statements	28	24	21	48
Formulation accuracy (own-speech management)	47	22	50	40
Intersubjectivity management	19	35	11	16
Other domains	15	13	11	19

Lg = language   I = interviewer   R = respondent
Dan = Danish   Mex = Mexican   Spa = Spanish   Swe = Swedish   Ven = Venezuelan

Table 1: Modalising expressions: number of occurrences per category.

4   Modalisation of propositional content: signalling degree of generalisation in categorising statements

The obvious reason why generalising attributions need be modalised is for the speaker to be able to answer the underlying question 'to what extent could Property P be said to apply to category C?' Generalising categorisations could be modalised with regard to the property attributed ('totally P?'), as well as to the extensional category, regarding time and frequency ('all the time?'; 'always?'), place ('everywhere?'), or the number of tokens/individuals concerned ('all instances of C?).

The modalisation process itself may be conceived as a manifestation of the two-faced three-position scale discussed in Section 1, i.e.:

- total applicability (totally; all);
- high applicability (quite; many);
- some applicability (a bit; some);
- no applicability (absolutely not; no);
- low applicability (not very; few);
- not a very low applicability (not without; at least a few).

Let us examine a few sequences to see how the modalisation process can manifest itself in the domain of categorising statements.

(7)   Sample: Catrine 1 (R = Respondent, I = Interviewer).

21   R   *høflig **på den måde** at de **altid** tænker på: hvordan jeg har det,*
         Polite in the sense that they always care about how I'm feeling,

22   *om jeg har en stol at sidde på,*
         whether I have a chair to sit on

23   *øh altså så er det selvfølgelig også noet mellem mand mand og kvinne ikk*
         er, so then, of course, it's also something between men and women, isn't it?

24   I   *jo.*
         Sure.

25   R   *Æh:*
         Err,

26   *du skal bære jeg må **aldrig** bære noget **som helst***
         you're supposed to carry… I'm never allowed to carry anything whatsoever

27   *jeg må **aldrig** selv åbne en dør.*
         I'm never allowed to open a door myself,

28   *så der er **meget** sådan **meget**- eller **meget** galant.*
         so there is much sort of very… or very gallant

In line 28, the modalisation is explicit, direct and easy to detect: the adverb meget 'very', which qualifies the categorising adjective galant '*gallant*', indicates a high degree of the attributed property. In lines 23–27, the modalising expression *aldrig* 'never', which indicates the maximum degree, is also explicit. Here, however, the property to which it is supposed to apply is less directly expressed: being traditional in one's gender role behaviour ('never' being understood in the sense 'they *always* behave this way').

In line 21, the modalisation of the property *høflig* 'polite' takes place in a less direct way. By adding the clause initiated by *på den måde at* 'in the sense that', the speaker is restricting the meaning of the property 'polite' to deal with 'thinking about how people are feeling', a property which she cannot find an appropriate adjective to express. Thereby, the modalising meaning 'some degree' is applied to 'polite'. On the other hand, to this newly established property the adverb *altid* 'always' is added, indicating the 'maximum degree' mode.

Along with operations of restriction, as in the case of 'polite in the sense that…' just mentioned, expansions may also occur, especially regarding the category to which a property is attributed. One typical example can be seen in the following lines:

(8)   Sample: Lorenzo 1 (R = Respondent).

66 R   *entonces e: no considero que sean individualistas*
        so, err, I don't consider them to be individualists
67   *e: yo más bien creo que:*
        err, I rather believe that…

68   *que lo que hay de sueco a sueco **como todo ser humano** es que*
           hay diferentes personalidades
        that as for Swedes among themselves as among all human beings
           there are in fact different personalities

Here the category 'Swedes' is expanded to apply to 'all human beings', to which the property 'consisting of different personalities' is attributed. Needless to say that such an expansion has a diluting and thereby indirectly diminishing effect on the property attributed (which, incidentally, in this case is already neutral).

5   Modalisation of illocutionary force: signalling trustworthiness of statements

Apart from the sentence meanings associated with generalised attributions, the illocutionary force 'expressing an opinion' or 'putting forward an argument' may be subjected to modalisation. Strengthening this kind of illocutionary force by putting it in the maximum degree mode has the effect of increasing the claimed trustworthiness or reliability of the statement. Analogously, placing the statement in the some degree mode has the effect of weakening the illocutionary force and thereby reducing trustworthiness.

The affinity that the referred kind of modalisation bears to processes of evidentiality (Chafe, 1986) is intuitively obvious and, at the same time, a quite complex matter to account for. The complexity of the issue is mainly due to fact that scholars do not always agree regarding whether a given type of source attribution has a strengthening or weakening effect (Fitneva, 2001; Bermúdez 2002). Whether a source such as 'general knowledge' or 'situational evidence' should rank higher or lower than e.g. 'own experience' is still an open question. Whatever will be the outcome of the trustworthiness ranking between various attributed sources of knowledge, a few remarks could be made from the perspective of how degrees of modalisation are assigned. The following sequence may serve as a point of departure:

(9)　　　Sample: Lorenzo 2 (R = Respondent, I = Interviewer).

9　　R　*E: : y que tiene **pues** e: muchas ventajas*
　　　　　er and that it carries, consequently, many advantages,

10　　　　*porque e: : m: **pues evidentemente** es mucho más fácil ponerse*
　　　　　　de acuerdo cuando llevas una secuencia lógica de las cosas e: :
　　　　　Because, er, erm, well evidently it's much easier to come to an
　　　　　　agreement when you've got a logical sequence of things, er…

11　　　　*también significa **para mí** que e: :*
　　　　　It also means to me that, er…

12　　　　*muchas de estas cosas son apreciaciones debo decírtelo*
　　　　　Many of these things are estimates, I should tell you

13　　I　　　　　　　　　　　　　　　　　　⌊*jum sí sí sí*
　　　　　Hum, oh yes,

14　　　　*pero se trata de eso no,*
　　　　　but that's what it's all about, isn't it?

15　　　　　　⌊*porque **en realidad** no he tenido mucha experiencia fuera de fuera*
　　　　　de de de ericsson.
　　　　　Because, in fact, I haven't had much experience outside ou- ou-
　　　　　　outside Ericsson.

In line 9, the particle *pues*, which could translate simply as 'well' but which, on top of that, carries the constant meaning of referring to preceding discourse (i.e. 'consequently') gives co-textual support to Lorenzo's claim. Mapped onto the modalisation scale, this would imply a 'high degree' mode. However, in line 10, the same particle *pues* is repeated and followed by the adverb *evidentemente* 'evidently', which indicates situational evidence. Here again, although the source of knowledge indicated is a different one, the interpretation 'high degree of trustworthiness' comes readily to mind.

In line 11, the expression *para mí* 'to (for) me', refers to the speaker's own experience, which could here be heard as a disclaimer and, consequently, a 'some degree' mode with regard to trustworthiness.

In line 15, finally, the contrary-to-expectation-referring expression *en realidad* 'in fact, actually' seems to be able to function as a modaliser, since, through the effect of contrasting expectations with reality, the statement stands out as an undeniable fact. This could be interpreted as the trustworthiness of the statement being put in the 'maximum degree' mode.

6   Modalisation of interaction management: signalling degree of intersubjectivity

In negotiating what I have referred to as 'worldviews', speakers not only trade off their cognitive representations to their interlocutors. In order for a full-fledged and sustained communicative activity to occur, the interactants have to make sure there is sufficient common ground for the exchange to be meaningful and the degree and substance of the shared knowledge somehow has to be ascertained and evaluated. This is what feedback processes and interaction management essentially are about (Allwood, 1998), the outcome of which is commonly referred to as 'intersubjectivity'.

Modalisation seems to play a part in these interaction-management proc-esses. There is need not only for sentence meaning and illocutionary force to be qualified, but also for intersubjectivity. This is to say that interactants will consistently, though at different intervals, feel the necessity of giving a qualified representation of the intersubjectivity they perceive with regard to a relevant content. In this perspective, feedback givers and feedback claimers can be thought of as discourse modalisers, with different markers carrying different modes. In the following sequence, there are various types that come to the surface.

(10)   Sample: Érica (R = Respondent, I = Interviewer).

12   R   *Esa es mi opinión personal **no**.*
        This is my personal opinion, right

13   *Sólo que tú me estás preguntando-*
        It's just that you're asking me now…

14   I   ⌊*claro por supuesto sí sí*
        Yes, of course, sure,

15   *y sin el nombre tuyo **no**.*
         and without your name, right?

16   R   ⌊*o sea yo no estoy hablando en nombre de la empresa ni*

     mucho menos.
     That is, I'm not talking now in the name of the company at all?

17   I   ⌊*para nada.*
         Absolutely not

In lines 12 and 15, the particle *no* 'right' can readily be interpreted as a feedback claimer ('uptaker'). However, the falling intonation on each occurrence indicates that the expression should not (or, at least, only indirectly) be interpreted as a request. Rather, it can be seen as signalling something like 'I here perceive intersubjectivity at some degree'. The feedback- claiming effect would then be based on an implicature ('some degree is not enough – assume the responsibility for that and confirm!'), rather than on the core meaning of the expression.

The expressions in lines 14 and 17, on the other hand, are feedback givers: the consecutive markers (1) *claro* 'sure', (2) *por supuesto* 'of course' and (3) *sí sí* 'oh yes' in line 14 and the corroborative negative *para nada* 'not at all' in line 17. All of these can be said to correspond to the 'maximum degree' mode. The modalised content, in this case, does not belong to the speaker but to the interlocutor. In a discourse modalisation perspective, however, this is an irrelevant circumstance. As in all the earlier mentioned cases, there is still a foregrounded content and a backgrounded modalising component.

7   Modalisation of own-speech management: signalling degree of formulation accuracy

The fourth plane to be highlighted, on which discourse modalisation plays an important part, is that of 'own-speech management'. Own-speech management phenomena concern choice and change in the speaker's production of utterances (Allwood, 1998). Some expressions, such as 'er', are used for 'gaining time', whereas others, such as 'that is' or 'I mean' are used for self-reformulation and self-repair. While in the latter case the inaccuracy of the preceding expression is being acknowledged, many of the time-gaining particles and expressions can be understood as disclaimers with regard to how accurate the planned wording is sensed to be by the speaker.

In a discourse modalisation perspective, what comes to mind are all types of disclaimers that we can take as indicating a 'some degree' mode. What may be less obvious is how the two other modes would surface. There is, however, reason to believe that own-speech management is not always about hedging, but can also be about underscoring accuracy of wording. Let us examine a few lines from the data in order to illustrate this point.

(11)   Sample: Ken (R = Respondent).

96   R   *ja har inte upptäckt- (.5) att nåra har varit påträngande- (.5) äh:*
         I have not discovered... anyone being intrusive... err...

97   *äh dom flesta- (.5) tycker ja- (.5) håller en en väldit bra äh äh nivå på*
          vaskajasäja-
          er, most people, I think, keep a very good, er, er, standard with regard
          to, what shall I say,'

98   *ett bra avstånd,(1.)*
          a good distance,

99   *där man **såattsäja** kan umgås-(.5) på ett trevlit sätt*
          where you can, so to speak, be together... in a pleasant way

In lines 96 and 97, the hesitation markers *äh* 'er', *äh*: 'err' and *äh äh* 'er er' obviously function as means for gaining time. Arguably, it could be claimed that a default interpretation of these markers is to indicate 'some though not a high degree' of accuracy.

The same could even more arguably be said about more explicitly disclaiming expressions such as *så att säga* (spoken variety: *såattsäja*) 'so to speak' in line 99, or *vad ska jag säga* (spoken variety: *vaskajasäja*) 'what shall I say'. It is interesting to observe that in line 97 the wording which 'what shall I say' was supposed to modalise, never appears. Instead, by inference, the expression comes to function as a reformulator, which has probably become a conventionalised secondary meaning of expressions such as 'what shall I say'.

What, then, about the 'high degree' or 'maximum degree' modes applied to formulation accuracy? One example can be found in the following sequence:

(12)   Sample: Catrine 2 (R = Respondent).

25   R   *æh:*
         err...'

26   *jo **jeg vil nok sige** altså høflige os- osse pigerne*
          Well, I would rather say, then, polite, als- also the girls,

27   *sådan hvordan har du det*
          like 'how are you doing?'

28   *æh hvordan familien har det-*
       er, 'how's your family?'

29   *hvornår har du hørt sidst hjemmefra,*
       'when did you last have news from home?'

The hesitation markers *æh* 'er' and *æh* 'err' in lines 25 and 28, true enough, belong to the same kind as that commented on in (11) above. However, the expression *jeg vil nok sige* 'I would rather say' seems to be precisely one that carries the function of underscoring the accuracy of the words to come by indicating a high degree mode. There are expressions that could even be interpreted as reflecting a maximum degree mode, such as 'I mean'.

8   Concluding remarks

The stance taken in this chapter is to place modality and modalisation in a wider perspective than is commonly done, namely as a discourse phenomenon. While modality, especially deontic and epistemic modality, have generally been treated as sentence meaning phenomena, further planes of expression can be distinguished in which modalisation processes are at work. Among such planes, illocutionary force, interaction management and own-speech management have been focused on.

One important prerequisite for an expression to function as a modaliser is that it be backgrounded, i.e. perceived as constituting, in some sense, a cognitive background, whereas the expression it operates on is presented, at least relatively speaking, as cognitive foreground. This is a condition of an entirely cognitive-semantic nature. No formal requisites will apply to modalising expressions, since modalisation is taken to be a phenomenon of meaning and not one of form.

Modalisation is seen as the attribution of degrees to a given domain. There are three modes of degree that have been posited: the 'maximum degree' mode, the 'high degree' mode and the 'some degree' mode. The scale can be seen as doubled by positing the existence of a converse negative scale with the modes 'zero degree', 'low degree' and 'not a low degree'. In this perspective, modalisation can be seen as related to quantification processes in semantics.

On the plane of sentence meaning, although deontic modality (action-oriented concerned with the packaging of necessity) and epistemic modality (cognition-oriented concerned with the packaging of certainty) play a dominant part, other domains of modalisation need to be recognised. Two such domains, which are seen as closely interrelated, have been focused on in this chapter, namely (degree of) attribution and (degree of) generalisation in connection with categorising expressions.

Two further classifications of a more global kind have been hinted at, without being specifically developed in the present context. One is the distinction between cognition-, action- and affect-oriented modalisation, which can be seen as related to separate fundamental communicative functions. The second distinction, related to communication in its capacity of interaction, is that between modalisation for representational purposes and modalisation for rapport-management purposes. The former is associated with the process of 'worldview' negotiation in human interaction, the latter with what could be referred to as the negotiation of social identity.

References

Allwood, J., Andersson, L.-G., Östen, D. (1977) *Logic in Linguistics*. Cambridge Textbooks in Linguistics. Cambridge: Cambridge University Press.

Allwood, J. (1998) The structure of dialog. In M. M. Taylor, F. Ne'el and D. G. Bouwhuis (eds) *Structure of MultiModal Dialog*, Vol. II. Amsterdam: John Benjamins.

Allwood, J. (2000) Dialog modality. Paper presented at the OFTI 18 Conference, Helsinki, 29–30 September. University of Helsinki.

Arndt, H. and Janney, R. W. (1987) InterGrammar. Towards an integrative model of verbal, prosodic and kinesic choices in speech. *Studies in Anthropological Linguistics* 29. Berlin, etc.: Mouton de Gruyter.

Bally, C. (1944) *Linguistique Générale et Linguistique Française*. Bern: Francke.

Barrenechea, A. M. (1979) Operadores pragmáticos de actitud oracional: los adverbios en 'mente' y otros signos. In A. M. Barrenechea et al. (eds) *Estudios Lingüísticos y Dialectológicos* 39–59. Buenos Aires: Hachette.

Bermúdez, F. W. (2002) Elevación de sujeto y gramaticalización de la evidencialidad en castellano. Paper presented at the XV Conference of Scandinavian Romanists. Oslo, 12–17 August. University of Oslo.

Brown, G. and Yule, G. (1983) *Discourse Analysis*. Cambridge: Cambridge University Press.

Chafe, W. (1986) Evidentiality in English conversation and academic writing. In W. Chafe and J. Nichols (eds) *Evidentiality: the linguistic coding of epistemology*. Norwood, NJ: Ablex.

Fant, L. (2001a) Creating awareness of identity work in conversation: a resource for language training. In M. Kelly, I. Elliott and L. Fant (eds) *Third Level Third Space: intercultural communication and language in higher education in Europe* 79–93. Bern: Peter Lang.

Fant, L. (2001b) Managing social distance in semi-structured interviews. In E. Németh (ed.) *Selected Papers from the Seventh International Pragmatics Conference* Vol. 2 190–206. Antwerp: International Pragmatics Association.

Fant, L. (in press) Rapport and identity management: a model and its application to Spanish dialogue. In M. E. Placencia and C. García-Fernández (eds) *Research on Politeness in the Spanish-Speaking World*. Mahwah, N.J.: Lawrence Erlbaum.

Fitneva, S. A. (2001) Epistemic markers and reliability judgments: evidence from Bulgarian. *Journal of Pragmatics* 33: 401–20.

Greimas, A. and Courtès, J. (1979) Sémiotique. Dictionnaire raisonné de la théorie du langage. Paris: Classiques Hachette.

Halliday, M. A. K. (1985) *Introduction to Functional Grammar.* London: E. Arnold.

Jakobson, R. (1960) Closing statement: linguistics and poetics. In Th. A. Sebeok (ed.) *Style in Language* 350–77. Cambridge, Mass.: MIT Press.

Kerbrat-Orecchioni, C. (1980) *L'énonciation. De la subjectivité dans le Langage*. Paris: Armand Colin.

Kerbrat-Orecchioni, C. (1992) *Les Interactions Verbales*. Tome II. Paris: Armand Colin.

Kerbrat-Orecchioni, C. (1998) Quelle place pour les émotions dans la linguistique du XXe siècle? In *Actes du Colloque. Les émotions dans l'interaction* Lyon, Octobre (1997) Université de Lyon.

Linell, P. (1998) *Approaching Dialogue. Talk, Interaction and Contexts in Dialogical Perspectives*. Amsterdam and Philadelphia: John Benjamins.

Lyons, J. (1977) *Semantics*. Cambridge: Cambridge University Press.

Spencer-Oatey, H. (2000) Rapport management. A framework for analysis. In H. Spencer-Oatey (ed.) *Culturally Speaking* 11–46. London and New York: Continuum.

6   Categoricality and temporal projection of Spanish modals

Henrik Høeg Müller

1 Object

The present article takes its point of departure in the general assumption that at a primary level the use of modal verbs reflects the way in which the speaker evaluates the amount and type of information he possesses as being either sufficient or not to claim full correspondence between the linguistic representation of a State of Affairs (SoA) and the equivalent, referential world situation. The modal verbs function as linguistic elements through which the speaker can signal – on the basis of the particular information level he has at a specific point in time – whether he considers the propositional content of a given utterance to be a true representation of a corresponding situation in the world, or whether he conceives the propositional content only as a possible representation of a referential situation in the world. As we shall see later on, the group of verbs traditionally referred to as Spanish modal auxiliaries can activate an interpretation of both correspondence and possible correspondence with a world situation.

Moreover, the article aims at accounting for the interaction that takes place, on the one hand between the two temporal elements of the modalised utterance, i.e. the conjugation of the modal verb itself and the occurrence of the infinitive as either simple or compound and, on the other hand, the temporal projection or anchorage of the construction as a whole and the basic epistemic, deontic or dynamic modal values coded into the utterance through the modal. In more abstract terms, the focus of the article is predominantly on a number of observations concerning the interplay between the two basic, grammatical categories of modality and tense in sentences carrying a modal auxiliary. It is suggested that the above-mentioned interaction patterns can shed further light on the frequently debated theme of realisation vs. non-realisation of the SoA in question, i.e. the categorical status of the utterance and furthermore the semantic neutralisation or mitigation of certain forms of the modal auxiliaries, an aspect which to my knowledge is as yet unexplored. Finally the parameters of informational source and level of verification are introduced to account for the distribution of some of the modal auxiliaries in Spanish. It is claimed that these parameters and distinctions are of central importance to the general conceptualisation of modality in language and hence also to the disambiguation of the Spanish modals.

2   The forms

In the Germanic languages a prominent aspect of modal auxiliaries is their more or less deficient verbal paradigm (see e.g. Nuyts, 2001) together with a high degree of regularity in their syntactic manifestations. It is a fairly well established viewpoint that these shared morpho-syntactic features indicate that the modal auxiliaries work as operators within a common semantic field (see e.g. Klinge, 1993: 323).

In Spanish, however, as in the other Romance languages, the verbs generally pointed out as modals are not delimited in their paradigmatic extension – they can occur in all the forms associated with 'normal' lexical verbs – nor do they show a homogeneous, syntactic behaviour (see e.g. Müller, 2001)[1]. Consequently it is not possible to delimit a group of Spanish modal verbs solely on the basis of an established pattern of defectiveness or syntactic homogeneity and hence claim a direct correspondence or identity between the formal and the semantic levels.

However, it is not the intention here to deal with the traditional, morpho-syntactic criteria of auxiliarity, such as substitution of the infinitive by nominal elements, elliptic and cleft constructions and variation of concord in reflexive passive and then discuss their apparent implications for the delimitation and establishment of a fixed inventory list of modal auxiliaries in Spanish[2].

In this article attention will be concentrated on the Spanish modals *deber* and *tener que*, which are capable of conveying shades of meaning corresponding with the English modals 'must' and then *poder* whose semantics can be paraphrased as 'can/may'. In short, these verbs are considered central members of the category of modal auxiliaries, also by Gómez Torrego (1999), because, in opposition to other infinitival constructions conveying meanings of modality or some sort of speaker subjectivity such as e.g. *lograr/conseguir* 'achieve', *intentar/tratar de* 'intend' and *querer* 'want', they do not apparently impose selection restrictions on the subject[3]. In addition to this they are the only modals with which – among other interpretations – we can make claims about the possibility of the propositional content of the utterance (see also Silva-Corvalán 1995: 67). Possibility is here to be understood in a wider form than usual so that it includes both epistemic and deontic possibilities. Following Sørensen (2000: 48ff; 2001: 23ff) both epistemic and deontic sentences are about the possible realisation of something at a present or future point in time; they are not about facts, but '… about the likelihood of the realisation of an SoA in some situation given a particular information context' (Sørensen ibid.). [4]

3 Categoricality, factivity and potentiality

The notions of categoricality, factivity and potentiality are intimately bound up with each other by the fact that all three of them relate to the distinction between realisation and non-realisation of the proposition under the scope of the modal operator.

Klinge (1993) argues in favour of a monosemantic approach to the interpretation of the English modal auxiliaries according to which their function is to instruct the receiver of the utterance about a potential correspondence between the situation representation and the referential situation in the world, however without signalling anything about a future realisation or not of the correspondence. The situation representation can turn out to be a true or false representation of a world situation. So within this framework the inherent lexical semantic feature that all the English modals have in common is that they indicate potentiality, i.e. potential realisation or non-realisation of the SoA denoted by the infinitival phrase and the subject.

The notion of factivity as introduced by Kiparsky and Kiparsky in their almost legendary article, 'Fact', from 1971, builds on the assumption that through its predicates a language indicates as a basic semantic factor whether a given speaker presupposes the truth of the proposition, irrespective of whether the complement is an embedded sentence, a gerund or an infinitive. When the speaker uses a factive predicate as *odd* or *regret,* he believes the complement to express a true proposition, i.e. to be a true linguistic representation of a corresponding world situation. However, when the speaker employs a non-factive predicate as *likely* or *suppose*, he presupposes that there is a possibility that the proposition denoted by the complement may be true or may be false. Kiparsky and Kiparsky (ibid.: 348f.) put forward as an important feature to the notion of factivity that propositions the speaker asserts, directly or indirectly, to be true or false do not follow the factive paradigm and its syntactic consequences. There is, consequently, a clear opposition between the semantic domains of assertion and presupposition and the predicates conveying (non-)factivity only work within the latter.

Categoricality can, in accordance with the content given to this semantic concept by Sørensen (2000: 47ff; 2001: 28ff), be defined in the following way: If, when producing a given utterance, the speaker estimates that he has sufficient information at his disposal to present an SoA as a reality or a non-reality, he is likely to make a categorical utterance. If, on the other hand, the speaker signals that his level of information is insufficient to present an SoA as a reality or a non-reality, the resulting utterance must be considered uncategorical. Both scenarios, of course, require an ideal or honest relation between informational level and the content of the utterance. In other words, if the speaker states that a certain SoA is realised or not realised in a specific world situation, the utterance is categorical and if he states that an SoA possibly is or will be realised or not realised, the utterance is uncategorical.

Although on the surface categoricality and factivity may seem very similar concepts, they actually differ substantially from each other, which can be illustrated on the basis of the following example with the Spanish verb *querer* 'want', by many scholars counted as a member of the group of modal auxiliaries.

(1)   *Pedro quiere comprar   un   coche.*
        Pedro wants buy   a   car
        Pedro wants to buy a car.

When uttering sentences like the above, typically qualified as expressing shades of dynamic modality, i.e. volition, the speaker presents it as an empirical fact that the syntactic subject referent wants to do what is denoted by the infinitive, no matter whether the action to be undertaken by the same subject is yet unactualised. So in this respect the sentence in (1) is fully analogous to any other 'normal', declarative sentence. In his own belief the speaker has secure and sufficient knowledge to enable him to utter that there is a full correspondence between the referent of the subject and the situation denoted by the verb *querer* and consequently the sentence is categorical. The fact that the verb *querer* when conveying a volitive meaning always selects an intentional animated entity as referent of the subject NP supports the claim about a categorical reading.

On the other hand there is no doubt that 'Pedro's buying action' has future time orientation and is therefore by definition non-factive. The realisation of the situation denoted by the infinitival clause is to be understood as posterior to the speaker's time of utterance, but the point is that in this case we talk about the possible realisation of the infinitival clause situation by the subject referent, not the speaker's evaluation of the correspondence between the subject and the infinitive. These are simply two different phenomena.

When operators expressing epistemic or deontic modality are used, the speaker evaluates the information he has as insufficient to describe the relation between the subject referent and the situation denoted by the infinitival clause as categorical. According to his own knowledge, it is uncertain or unverified whether the subject referent has realised the situation denoted by the infinitival clause. The speaker makes claims about the likelihood of the realisation of an SoA in some situation (Sørensen: ibid.).

In opposition to this, sentences interpreted as expressing shades of dynamic modality imply that the speaker estimates his informational level about a certain SoA as being adequate to establish a direct connection of assertion between the subject and the verb conveying dynamic modality.[5]

The parameter of categoricality actually functions at two different levels when applied to the domains of dynamic and epistemic/deontic modality, as can be appreciated in the following figure:

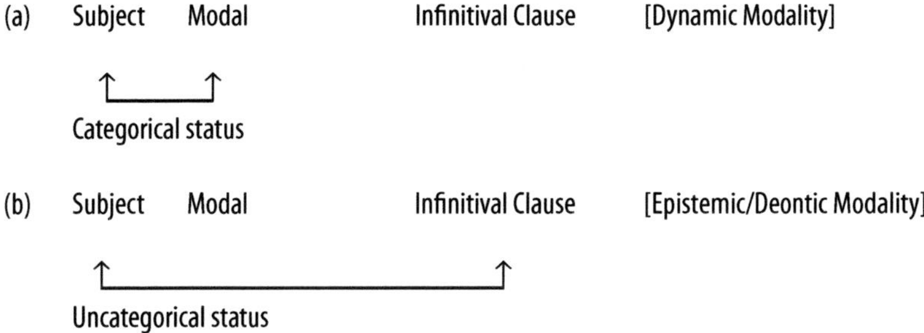

Figure 1: Function of the categoricality parameter

Figure 1 indicates that when a given context favours a dynamic interpretation of an utterance, the relation between the subject and the modal has categorical status, whereas in an utterance of epistemic or deontic interpretational value there is no direct semantic relation between the subject and the modal, but only between the subject and the infinitival clause. This relation is uncategorical because it is explicitly stated by the speaker that the correspondence between the subject and the infinitival clause is only a possibility – we could in fact claim that it is the direct, overt function of the modals conveying epistemic and deontic interpretations to instruct the receiver of the information to decode the utterance as some kind of motivated possibility. These observations are in good keeping with the general idea presented by for example Lyons (1977), Palmer (1979) and Davidsen-Nielsen (1985) that dynamic modality relates to the subject of the sentence and epistemic and deontic to the speaker; the former is subject-oriented and the latter speaker-oriented.

This distinction illustrated in Figure 1 is not captured within the factivity paradigm, according to which both dynamic utterances, at least when expressing volition and epistemic tend deontic utterances presuppose non-factivity, as the factivity notion focuses solely on the relation between subject and complement, in this case the infinitival clause. The parameters of categoricality and factivity cover different semantic areas but on many occasions they overlap with each other. For example, predicates that combine with the infinitive and express likelihood (*poder* 'can/may', *posible* 'possible', *probable* 'probable') are both non-factive and give rise to non-categorical utterances and predicates with infinitive that lexically signal an all-time actualised perspective (*afirmar* 'affirm', *confesar* 'confess', *creer* 'think',) or a past time, iterative or terminative, perspective (*soler* 'be accustomed to', *acabar de* 'to have just done something', *volver a* 'do something again') are factive and produce categorical utterances. However, the parameters come into conflict with each other typically when serving as a theoretical basis for classifying predicates that in combination with their infinitival clause convey a future time, virtual perspective (*querer* 'want', *preferir* 'prefer', *decidir* 'decide', *determinar* 'determine', *elegir* 'choose', *prometer* 'promise', etc.). In this case the predicates are non-factive as the SoA established between the subject referent and the situation denoted by the infinitival clause is unactualised or non-realised seen from the point of utterance of the speaker, but at the same time the utterances convey categorical statements, because the speaker claims the semantic content of the finite verb to be true about the subject referent.

As regards ascribing the monosemantic value of potentiality to the modal operator verbs, which according to Klinge (1993) is a feasible manner to account for the English modals, such a way of conceptualising modality is incompatible with a consistent description of the Spanish paradigm and hence it cannot be successfully transferred to its modals. The reasons why this principle does not allow for a full transfer and direct application to Spanish are several, as we shall appreciate in the following section and just touch upon briefly in this. Firstly, the subject of the verb *poder* 'can/may' used in a dynamic context is submitted to semantic selection restrictions, for which reason *poder* is irreconcilable with taking up the operator status of the modal auxiliary entailed by the potentiality approach, viz. the traditional binary, logical structure 'operator/modal[proposition/descriptive content]'. Secondly, the preterite form of the Spanish temporal system within the dynamic and deontic domains clearly indicates that according to the speaker the situation representation corresponds to a referential situation in the past and therefore the grammatical category of tense in Spanish would, in principle, be capable of invalidating the alleged, inherent lexical content of the modals, i.e. potentiality, which is probably not satisfactory to a monosemantic lexical approach. Thirdly, there are indications at the lexical level that *poder* in some present time dynamic contexts conveys a non-potential reading of the utterance. Finally, the potentiality approach, as I see it, does not explicitly and systematically draw on the informational level of the speaker as a central parameter in the disambiguation of modality and more specifically of the modal operators, although, admittedly, this concept is understood as an underlying premise throughout the article by Klinge (1993).

On the basis of these reflections of a theoretical nature, I believe that the only parameter which can shed some new light on the often, but in my opinion not thoroughly debated group of Spanish modal auxiliaries, is categoricality. In the following we shall see that from an empirical point of view there are good reasons for introducing categoricality as an explanatory point of departure.

4   *Poder* 'can/may'

Basically, the verb *poder* 'can/may' can express three different modal meanings, i.e. epistemic possibility, deontic permission and dynamic ability, exemplified respectively in (2a) (b) and (c):

(2) (a) *¿Usted   cree   que un   tío   que es   capaz   de jugar al   fútbol   un*
      you   think that a   guy whois capable of play of.the football a
      partido   completo   puede estar   enganchado?
      game   whole   may be   hooked
      Do you think a guy who is capable of playing a whole game of football may
         be hooked?

    (b) *La   novela   no   puede estar   nunca en   crisis   en el   país de Quevedo.*
      the novel   no may be   never in   crisis in the land of Quevedo
      The novel may never be in crisis in the country of Quevedo.

    (c) *Sólo   puedo nadar diez vueltas.*
      only   can.I swim ten laps
      I can only swim ten laps.

The status of the sentences in (2a) and (b) is uncategorical as the relation between subject referent and the situation denoted by the infinitive clause in both cases is qualified as a possibility. In accordance with the approach of Sørensen (2001: 25ff.), *poder* is regarded as a lexical item which functions as an operator of possibility between two objects in a transitive structure, i.e. the subject referent and the infinitival clause situation, when *poder* occurs in an epistemic or a deontic context.[6]

Contrary to that, a speaker uttering a sentence expressing ability like the one in (2c) presents it as an asserted, empirical fact that the syntactic subject referent is able to do what is denoted by the infinitive clause, no matter whether the situation denoted by the infinitival clause has been undertaken by the subject referent, is not actualised yet or will ever become a reality. So in the respect of categoricality sentences conveying dynamic modality are fully parallel to all other 'normal' declarative sentences.

4.1   The functionality parameter

For *poder* to convey a dynamic statement there must firstly be a functional agreement between the referent of the subject and the situation denoted by the infinitival clause. This implies that the activity denoted by the main verb must correspond with an inherent functional capacity of the subject referent; i.e. it is a requirement of the subject referent that due to an inherent functional property it is capable of bringing about the situation denoted by the infinitival clause. Therefore *poder* cannot be used in the examples in (3).

(3) (a) *El   sofá no entra aquí.*
      the sofa no enter here
      The sofa doesn't/won't go in here.

    (b) *La   puerta no cierra   herméticamente.*
      the door   no close   hermetically
      The door doesn't/won't close hermetically.

The sofa and the door do not dispose of functional properties that enable them to carry out the activities denoted by the action verbs *entrar* 'enter' and *cerrar* 'lock' and consequently *poder* cannot be used to put forward dynamic statements in these cases. The actions denoted by these verbs require some kind of force or source, an agentive factor, outside the referent of the subject in order to be realised or to come into existence, but the subject referents of sofa and door are not themselves the agentive factors that can, in a given situation, carry out the activities. They act as patients of an outer source, such as the wind, a human being, etc.

(4) (a) *La   puerta no puede   cerrar   herméticamente.*
      the door   no can   close   hermetically
      The door may not close hermetically.

    (b) *Tal vez   la   puerta cierre herméticamente.*
      maybe   the   door   closes hermetically
      Maybe the door will close hermetically.

    (c) **Tal vez la   puerta   pueda cerrar herméticamente*[7].
      maybe   the   door   may   close hermetically
      Maybe the door may close hermetically.

The examples in (4a) (b) (c) support the assumption concerning a necessary functional harmony between the subject referent and the activity denoted by the infinitive, however from another angle. (4a) illustrates that if *poder* is inserted into a context where there is no functionality agreement, the example will be interpreted as epistemic possibility, analogous to the example in (4b). The example in (4c) confirms that *poder* is used epistemically and therefore it cannot occur in the same sentence as the adverb *tal vez* 'maybe', which also expresses an epistemic meaning dimension. They exclude each other in the context in question.

So the conclusion is that in Spanish *poder* can only be used dynamically if there is a functionality agreement between the referent of the subject NP and the situation denoted by the infinitive.

However, the situation is more complicated than that. The examples in (5) and (6) show that even when the requirement of functional agreement is fulfilled, there is still a possibility of choosing between a construction with and without *poder* which results in a difference of meaning.

(5) (a) *No oigo absolutamente nada,   ¿tu   oyes   algo?*
      no hear.I absolutely   nothing   you   hear   something
      I cannot hear anything, can you hear anything?

    (b) *No **puedo** oir   las emisoras   online Visitas.*
      no can.I   hear   the transmitting.stations   online Visitas
      I cannot hear the transmitting stations online Visitas.

    (c) *Cuando la   radiación solar (…) incide sobre una ventana atraviesa*
      when   the radiation solar   fall   on   a   window goes.through.it
      el   vidrio con   facilidad, pero al   incidir   sobre los materiales
      the glass with   ease   but when fall   on   the materials
      del   interior del   ambiente   estos se   calientan, y
      of.the interior of.the environment these themselves warm.up and
      *generan   radiación de onda larga que no **puede** atravesar*
      generate.they radiation of wave long that no can   go.through
      el   vidrio.
      the glass
      When solar radiation falls on a window, it goes through the glass easily, but
        when it hits the materials inside the environment, they warm up and they
        generate long wave radiation which cannot go through the glass.

(6) (a) *Los topos no ven   muy bien, pero poseen   un oído   muy*
      the moles no see.they very well but   possess.they a   hearing very
      sensible.
      sensitive
      Moles cannot see very well but they have a very sensitive hearing.

    (b) *Mientras los ojos de los topos que viven en el   norte   pueden*
      while   the eyes of the moles that live   in   the north   can
      reconocerse   aún   con   claridad, los de los topos del   sur
      recognise.be   even with   clarity   the of   the moles of.the south

> *están recubiertos de una piel protectora, de manera que prácticamente*
> are   covered   of   a   fur protective of   manner   that practically
> *no **pueden** ver nada.*
> no can   see nothing
> While the eyes of the moles that live in the north can be seen quite clearly,
>   the ones of the moles in the south are covered with a protective fur so that
>   practically they cannot see anything.

If *poder* is used in a dynamic context, we are referring to the access of the subject referent to producing the SoA denoted by the infinitive complement. The examples in (5a) have pure descriptive contents in the sense that they constitute a direct, 'objective' reflection made by the speaker of the situations in question. The speaker only asserts that he is unable to engage in the activity denoted by the verb *oir* 'hear'. In the analogous example (5b) *poder* indicates that because of some internal or external factors the speaker is precluded from realising the hearing activity. In other words the use of *poder* codes into the utterances the lack of access of the subject reference to accomplish the activity denoted by the main verb. This means that in (5b) the speaker conveys the information that he believes there is a specific reason why he cannot hear, i.e. the presence of internal or external obstacles such as being hard-of-hearing or not having the necessary equipment, etc. In (5b) the use of *poder* also has the function of signalling a barrier, in this case the window, that prevents the subject referent, the long wave radiation, from producing a certain state of affairs. The pair of examples in (6) point towards the same distinction. (6a) shows that *poder* is not used in generic expressions, because such expressions are *per se* not meant to convey the access to overcome factors that impede or promote the realisation of some situation. They exclusively refer to an inherent, *in casu* functional, feature of the subject referent. In the parallel example (6b) *poder* triggers the interpretation that something is preventing the activity in question, i.e. their fur is preventing the moles in the south from seeing and then the example in Spanish becomes non-generic.

This description of *poder* supports the assumption that the use of *poder* relates the subject and the situation to the existence or not of a particular obstacle or reason and the assumption is further corroborated by the fact that the 'pure' acquired ability in Spanish is expressed by the verb *saber* 'know how to', viz. *Juan sabe nadar* 'Juan can swim'. Moreover it corresponds well with the monosemantic approach of for example Silva-Corvalán (1995) who suggests that *poder* means 'does not preclude', or the force dynamic approach of Sweetser (1990) and Boye (2001 and this volume), who paraphrase *can* and Danish *kan* into 'taking away a potential barrier' or 'absence of a barrier', respectively. The basic idea is that there is nothing that favours the realisation of the situation denoted by the sentence.

On the basis of the observations presented above we may conclude that the dynamic use of *poder* is semantically restricted and above all that there are clear selection criteria in connection with the nature of the subject referent; a fact which also seems to fit quite well with the general assumption that dynamic modality relates to the syntactic subject of the sentence, not to the speaker; it is subject-oriented. This entails furthermore that *poder* used in a dynamic environment cannot be ascribed a status as operator because its function is not to remodel the proposition independently of the propositional content of the sentence. The dynamic *poder* is semantically dependent on the components of the proposition and therefore it would be misleading to represent a dynamic statement as a logical structure of the type m(p), where m is the modal operator and p the descriptive position as an argument of this operator.

4.2   Tense and time aspects of modality

The second type of argumentation that supports the central role of the categoricality distinction concerns the aspects of tense and time and their interplay with modality.

(7)   *Juan puede* PRES./ *podía* IMPER./   *pudiera* IMPER.SUBJ./ *podría* COND. *estar*
        Juan may /   might   /   might   /   might   be
        enfermo.
        ill
        Juan may/might be ill.

4.2.1   Epistemic use

The examples in (7) show that when *poder* is used to express epistemic meaning, some of its forms are subject to semantic neutralisation in the sense that the imperfect, indicative or subjunctive and the simple conditional do not refer to the past, but indicate instead some degrees of factual remoteness or tentativeness in the modal content seen from the present time of the speaker. However, the semantic neutralisation of these forms, sometimes referred to as weakened, polite or mitigated forms, is far from being total, because we communicate more or less confidence in the assertion, which conveys degrees of hypotheticality. Of course, such expressions can occur in direct and indirect speech and then refer to past time, but still the point of utterance and the time of reference are overlapping. This means that epistemic sentences with *poder* in the past, imperfect tense are ambiguous in Spanish, i.e. they can have both past time interpretation, as a result of direct or indirect speech and be weakened forms. It depends on the context whether a past time interpretation is more likely; if past tense is prevalent in the surrounding text, it can probably be conferred on the modal as well.

The general time-overlap between the point of utterance and the time of reference of the proposition constitutes an inherent quality of the epistemic domain and contrary to its dynamic use, *poder* functions as an operator in the epistemic domain because, independently of the semantics of the sentence elements, it conveys an epistemic reading, reshaping the propositional content of the utterance. This observation is also in good keeping with Halliday's (1970) conception of interpersonal modality, i.e. epistemic modality and some shades of deontic modality, as not being subject to or not reacting to tense alternation in the modal verb. The 'time-dependency' between time of utterance and time of reference also explains why *poder* cannot be interpreted to convey an epistemic reading in its non-finite forms, as shown in (8)[8].

(8)   *Juan va   a poder cruzar el   río.* (Silva-Corvalán 1995: 69)
        Juan goes to can   cross the river
        John's going to be able/be allowed to cross the river.
        *It may be the case that John will cross the river.

The only real temporal modification possible, i.e. where we can split the deictic centre of the speaker, the point of utterance, from the time of reference, is the present-perfect alternation of the main verb.

(9)   *Juan puede haber estado enfermo ayer.*
        Juan may   have   been   ill   yesterday
        Juan may have been ill yesterday.

Within the epistemic domain the present-perfect alternation can locate the situation relative to the speaker's deictic centre. The perfect locates the situation in the past relative to the point of utterance, whereas the present locates in an omni-temporal or atemporal time perspective.

4.2.2 Dynamic use

However, when *poder* with the simple infinitive conveys a dynamic meaning, hence bringing about a categorical statement, *poder* is by no means subject to semantic neutralisation. In this case the simple conditional would indicate the apodosis of a conditional construction, the past tense would locate the situation in the past with respect to the deictic position of the speaker and the past subjunctive is simply ungrammatical and consequently ruled out. The dependency between protasis and apodosis in conditionals is a propositional phenomenon independent of the speaker's attitude or commitment which of course belongs to the moment of utterance (see e.g. Verstraete, 2000). These observations are illustrated in (10):

(10) (a) *Sólo podría nadar diez vueltas si hubiera entrenado.* (conditional)
      only could.I swim ten laps   if had.I   trained
      I could only swim ten laps if I had trained.

   (b) *Sólo podía nadar diez vueltas cuando el sol brillaba.* (past imperfect)
      only could.I swim ten laps   when   the sun shone
      I could only swim ten laps when the sun shone.

   (c) **Sólo pudiera nadar diez vueltas.* (past subjunctive)
      only   could.I swim ten laps

In combination with the compound infinitive, as illustrated in (11a) and (b), it is not possible within the dynamic domain to locate the situation in the past relative to the speaker's deictic centre – it simply does not make sense – and for that reason we cannot convey the dynamic reading with the compound infinitive. Such a construction obtains an epistemic reading unless it is taken to refer to a referential world situation in future time, i.e. to be future time oriented, as in (11b), in which case it will inevitably convey a dynamic reading. The compound infinitive, contrary to what is stated by some Spanish grammars, indicates completion in the past or in the future depending on the specific environment, but it does not indicate past time *per se* with respect to the point of utterance.

(11) (a) *Juan puede haber nadado diez vueltas.*
      Juan may   have swum   ten laps
      Juan may have swum ten laps.

   (b) *Juan puede haberlo terminado a las diez.*
      Juan   can   have.it finished   by the ten
      Juan can have finished it by ten.

The explanation for these variations between the dynamic and epistemic domains is that dynamic modality is not modal in the same sense as epistemic and deontic modality, which is in this specific situation corroborated by the fact that the imperfect or the conditional tense morphemes would have past time reference or create the apodosis of a real conditional. *Poder* used dynamically relates, as we have seen, to the subject of the sentence and therefore a dynamic sentence reacts to the time factor in the same way as any other categorical utterance would do, i.e. the situation representation corresponds with a referential situation in the past, an omni-temporal or future situation or a hypothetical situation in relation to the speaker's deictic position.

4.2.3 Deontic use

Epistemic possibility is a possibility in relation to the information available to the speaker at a given point in time in the present or in the past about a situation in the present, the future or the past (signalled by the present-perfect alternation), but to the speaker it will remain a possibility and therefore there is no correspondence with a referential situation.

Whenever *poder* occurs in a deontic environment, as shown in (12), *poder* obtains an interpretation of permission.

(12) *Si lo   desea,   puede   fumar   al   terminar   la   comida,*
      if that wish.you, may.you smoke   when finish   the   meal,
      cuando   sirven   los cafés   y   los licores.
      when   serve.they the coffees and the liquors
      If you wish you may smoke after dinner when they serve coffee and liquor.

The various relevant forms of *poder* do not neutralise in this interpretation, as a past tense morpheme clearly conveys a past time meaning, i.e. the interpretation that at a certain point in the past something was permitted. In fact, this is not really surprising because the permission interpretation requires a human subject which can be affected by a source and which, most importantly, is capable of undertaking the task contained in the permission. In this respect, the subject selection restrictions correspond quite directly to those of dynamic modality.

(13) *Hace cien   años, las mujeres no podían   fumar.*
      do   hundred years, the women   no might.they smoke
      A hundred years ago women were not allowed to smoke.

The only difference is that in connection with the deontic reading we are dealing with a clear future time correspondence relation between the situation representation and the relevant world situation since the hearer cannot fruitfully be permitted or ordered to bring about a situation in past or present time. The situation representation cannot correspond with an already realised world situation. The imperfect of *poder* in a deontic context, as in (13) above, locates the permission itself in the past, which means that *poder* in this case establishes the uncategorical reading that at a given time in the past the subject referent had the possibility to produce the action denoted by the infinitive clause.

To a certain degree in accordance with Palmer (1979), who introduces the term dynamic possibility, we may argue that the underlying subject referent requirements determine the core modality of permission as being equal to that of ability and therefore it is by no means strange that *poder* in this connection is subject to the past tense-past time correlation. It must be possible for the subject referent to undertake what is permitted to him and he must have the ability. So the basic meaning is ability, which is then saturated by semantic and pragmatic factors to convey the interpretation of permission. In this way we obtain an explanation for the fact that morphological tense marking in this case has temporal consequences.

4.2.4 The preterite

The use of the preterite form of *poder* has different effects within the domains of epistemic, dynamic and deontic modality, but the variations corroborate the general picture presented up till now.

(14) (a) *Otros votantes pudieron   estar   enfermos   o viajando   durante el*
        other voters   might   be   ill   or travelling during   the
        periodo de   registro.
        period   of   registration
        Other voters might be ill or travelling during the registration period.

    (b) *También   le   ofrecieron   tabaco   y   Yerba del Medio   pudo   fumar*
        also   him offered.they tobacco and Yerba del Medio   might smoke
        en   las pipas que   sus enemigos   habían   fabricado.
        in   the pipes that   his   enemies   had   made
        They also offered him tobacco and Yerba del Medio was allowed to smoke
          the pipes that his enemies had made.

    (c) [...] *y   pudo   nadar por   el   río   y   cruzarlo en*
        and   could.he   swim through the   river   and cross.it in
        aproximadamente   dos horas, [...]
        approximately   two hours
        [...] and he was able to swim across the river in approximately two hours, [...]

When *poder*, as in (14b), occurs in the preterite and in an environment that favours a deontic reading, a categorical interpretation is established. In this case the situation must be interpreted in the way that in the past *Yerba del Medio*, the subject referent, was given the permission to smoke and at the same time, in fact, he engaged in the activity of smoking, for which reason we are not talking about a possible action, but a description of reality. There is a full correspondence between the situation representation and a referential situation in the past as is the case with the dynamic example of (14c), where the referent of the subject in fact produced the swimming activity.

Finally, the epistemic sentence in (14a) stands apart because in this environment *poder* cannot prompt a reading of correspondence with a world situation. The interpretation difference between epistemic and dynamic readings can be illustrated with the examples of Gómez Torrego (1999: 3361), reproduced as (15).

(15)   *El   portero   pudo   parar ese balón.*
        the goalkeeper   could/ might stop   that ball
        The goalkeeper was able to stop/could have stopped that ball.

This example may mean either that the goalkeeper actually stopped the ball, was capable of doing it, or it may mean that although he had the opportunity, the possibility, he did not succeed in doing it. In this last case the simple and the compound infinitive neutralise and the preterite neutralises with the imperfect in combination with the compound infinitive. So once again we have clear evidence of the fact that the categoricality distinction plays a major role in defining the semantics and pragmatics of modal verbs.

5 *Deber* 'must'

The modal verb *deber* serves as a vehicle for conveying both epistemic and deontic meaning possibilities, viz. (16)[9].

(16) (a) *El   especialista   aseguró que Elián   debe   sufrir de   síndrome de*
          the specialist   assured that Elián   must   suffer from   syndrome of
          estrés postraumático   y   debe tener pesadillas y   miedo al   agua.
          stress posttraumatic   and must have nightmares and fear   of.the water
          The specialist assured that Elián must suffer from posttraumatic stress
              syndrome and must have nightmares and fear of water.

   (b)   *?Debe   estar   Saviola en el   plantel   que va   al   Mundial?*
         should be   Saviola in the team   that goes to.the world.cup
         Should Saviola be in the team that goes to the world cup?

If we compare *deber* with *poder* within the epistemic domain, we may establish that, what on the surface at least looks like a full neutralisation between the forms of *poder*, does not find a counterpart in the forms of *deber* as they do not neutralise. The epistemic use of *deber* is not subject to the neutralisation process. By contrast, within the deontic domain a number of forms of the verb *deber* neutralise when combining with the simple infinitive, as illustrated in (17).

(17)   *La policía debe* PRE/ *debía* IMP./*debería* COND./ *debiera* IMP.SUBj. *meterlo*
        the police must /   should /   should /   should   put.him
        en   la   cárcel.
        in   the   jail
        The police must/should put him in jail.

The situation is reversed, so to speak, in comparison with the epistemic domain which entails that there is no direct correlation between the neutralisation phenomenon and the modal categories of logic. The claim here will be that the reason why all the forms of *deber* neutralise with the simple infinitive is the inherent future time orientation of the deontic domain; there are simply no other possibilities[10]. The simple infinitive, as mentioned before, indicates an omni-temporal and definitely non-past temporal perspective and the deontic environment forces the situation to obtain a future time orientation. The joint effect of these two factors implies that past tense morphology of the modal *deber* cannot under any circumstances convey past time anchorage. Therefore the forms neutralise and express various degrees of speaker commitment or involvement instead.

From the examples in (18) we can observe that there is a contrast between the present and the other forms when they combine with a compound infinitive. When *deber* is in the present, the compound infinitive does not locate the situation in the past relative to the speaker's deictic centre, as was the case for *poder*, but it indicates that actualisation or completion is desired by a certain point in time.

(18) (a) *Debes   haberlo hecho para mañana.*
  must.you have.it done for   tomorrow
  You must have done it by tomorrow.

   (b) *Debías/ deberías/debieras   haberlo hecho ayer.*
  should/ should/ should.you   have.it done yesterday
  You should have done it yesterday.

The other examples with *deber* and the compound infinitive are more or less self-explanatory in the sense that they convey the meaning that the speaker wishes that the subject referent had produced the action, but in fact it did not happen. *Deber* can never indicate completion or accomplishment, not even in the preterite, which usually serves the purpose of just that.

(19) (a) *La policía debió   meterlo en la   cárcel.*
  the police   should   put.him in the jail
  The police should have put him in jail.

   (b) *Elián debió tener pesadillas.*
  Elián should have   nightmares
  Elián must have had nightmares.

(20) (a) *La policía debió/ debía/   debería/ debiera haberlo   metido en la cárcel.*
  the police should/ should/ should/ should   have.him put   in the jail
  The police should have put him in jail.

(b) *Elián debió   haber   tenido   pesadillas.*
     Elián must   have   had   nightmares
     Elián must have had nightmares.

The complex of examples in (19) and (20) firstly reveals that *deber*, neither when expressing epistemic nor deontic meaning, can indicate accomplishment of the SoA in question, i.e. *deber* never signals that the propositional content composed by the subject referent and the situation denoted by the infinitival clause corresponds with a referential world situation. Secondly, not even the preterite form, which usually serves the purpose of indicating realisation of an SoA, triggers a reading of correspondence between linguistic representation and world situation. Instead, when occurring in the preterite, the whole construction obtains past time reference and then it neutralises with the compound infinitive, which is illustrated in (19) and (20). This neutralisation is the only possibility left.

6   Comparison of *poder* and *deber*

One question still remains to be commented on: the difference between *deber* and *poder* with respect to the patterns of neutralisation of their forms. The hypothesis presented here is that the epistemic use of *poder* does not presuppose an informational source. When using *poder*, the speaker does not necessarily infer anything from internal or external circumstances. He does not directly communicate the existence of pieces of evidence that favour or entail the realisation of the content of the proposition.

Uttering a sentence like *Juan puede estar enfermo* 'Juan may be ill', the only intention of the speaker would be to convey the objective possibility of the fact that human beings can be ill, i.e an almost generic utterance about a member of the human race. The speaker does not communicate that the speculations about the possible situation of *Juan* are inferred from any specific internal or external circumstances, although, of course, it is possible overtly to indicate, for example via a causal conjunction, that in a specific case the utterance is provoked by certain informational source, viz. *Juan puede estar enfermo ya que ayer parecía bastante pálido* 'Juan may be ill because yesterday he looked quite pale'. However, the point is that *poder* in itself does not presuppose or signal the presence of a source.

When using *deber* the situation is different, because the speaker overtly indicates that there is a source, some internal or external information that he takes into consideration. According to the speaker some pieces of information favour, require or entail a correspondence between the subject referent and the situation denoted by the infinitive. Some factors related to the subject referent or some circumstances surrounding it, in the widest sense, influence the utterance of the speaker and make him think as he does. In the speaker's mind there is a relation between the subject referent and the situation denoted by the infinitive; there is a motivation. This implies that when *deber* occurs in the present, imperfect or conditional, the speaker communicates, precisely because of this relation between subject referent and the denotation of the infinitival clause, that now in the present or before in the past there are/were some factors related to the subject referent that influence(d) the utterance of the speaker and for that reason the whole situation is understood as pertaining to the present or the past. The motivated relation in the speaker's mind between a source and the clear suggestion of this source of a realisation of the proposition in question entail that the epistemic environment activated by *deber* is subject to temporal variation and for that reason the epistemic use of *deber* admits no semantic neutralisation.

Generally, *deber* differs from *poder* because in all its forms, both within the epistemic and deontic domains, it operates on the relation between subject referent and infinitival clause denotation conveying uncategorical statements. *Deber* is therefore a true operator whose main function it is to prompt an interpretation of uncategoricality, which, as we shall see in the following section, is under the influence of the parameter of level of speaker verification. The preterite influences *deber* and *poder* in its epistemic use in an identical manner in so far as both verbs in this form are unable to render the meaning of accomplishment. They express possibility and the usual effect of the preterite, namely to let the content of the utterance correspond with a realised past time world situation, is suppressed.

7   Comparison of *deber* and *tener que* in a perspective of verification level

The two lexical items *deber* and *tener que*, both capable of conveying epistemic and deontic modal meanings which can be paraphrased by the English *must* or *have to*, seem to a large degree to be semantically identical although most scholars recognise a difference between them, commonly attributed to a distinction between an internal and external perspective, subjective vs. objective. However, in Müller (2001) this explanatory platform is rejected and instead it is suggested that their lack of functional equivalence should be connected to a distinction between strong and weak informational force, instantiated via *tener que* and *deber,* respectively. The same line of approach will be pursued here and some of the arguments put forward in Müller (ibid.) in favour of this force perspective will be repeated in the following. However, 'strong and weak informational force', will here be replaced by the notion of 'high and low level of speaker verification', as this notion is considered to cover the phenomenon and its consequences more adequately.

Distinguishing between *tener que* and *deber* within a perspective of the level of speaker verification, it is assumed that *tener que* signals a high level of verification in the sense that the information available to the speaker provides him with a maximum degree of confidence in the realisation, still only possible, by the subject referent of the situation denoted by the infinitive clause. A semantic paraphrase of *tener que* could be 'necessarily have to' which indicates that the speaker expresses almost blind confidence in the subsequent correspondence between the content of the utterance and the situation, while *deber* is semantically more equivalent to 'probably is', i.e. a lower level of information and consequently less speaker confidence in the validity of the information.

(21) (a)   *Ese tío va   tan lento que no tiene   que sentirse   muy bien.
            that   guy walks so   slowly that no has.he to   feel.himself very well

    (b)   *Ese tío va   tan lento   que tiene   que no sentirse   muy bien.
           that   guy walks so   slowly   that has.he to   no feel.himself very well
          That guy walks so slowly that he can't be feeling very well.

(22) (a)   *Ese tío va tan lento que tiene que no sentirse muy bien.*
           Ese tío va tan lento que debe no   sentirse muy bien.
           Ese tío va tan lento que no debe   sentirse muy bien.
           That guy walks so slowly that he can't feel very well.

    (b)   *Ese tío va   tan rápido que debe/tiene que sentirse   muy bien.*
           that guy walks so   fast   that must.he   feel.himself very well
          That guy walks so fast that he must be feeling very well.

According to Silva-Corvalán (1995: 91), from whom the examples in (21) are taken, neither *tener que* nor the infinitive can be negated and express epistemicity, viz. (21a) and (b). Silva-Corvalán (ibid.) asserts that these restrictions are examples of indications that the use of *tener que* in what she refers to as possibility contexts may be a recent development in Spanish. Originally *tener que* only signalled deontic modality and it is natural to assume that it is probably traces of this original deontic meaning that still show today when we describe *tener que* as conveying the meaning of a high level of verification and thereby a high level of speaker confidence in the possessed information, which is closer to a necessary consequence than something which is just likely. However native speakers of peninsular Spanish accept the negation of the main verb infinitive, a fact I shall take into consideration in the following argumentation.

The data presented in (21), (22) and (23), including especially the variation pattern between *tener que* and *deber* can be accounted for on the basis of the assumptions about a level of verification. When *tener que* is negated as in

(21a), it amounts to uttering: 'that guy walks so slowly that it is not a necessary consequence that he feels well', which is not the intended meaning, of course and therefore the sentence seems semantically and pragmatically odd. However, if we accept, contrary to the claim made by Silva-Corvalán (ibid.), that the main verb infinitive can be negated separately as in the first example of (22a) we can actually present a good explanation of this phenomenon which is consistent with the speaker verification level approach. In the first example of (22a) the negation does not have scope over *tener que*, i.e. it does not have the semantic structure NO(necessary consequence), but it has scope over the infinitival clause, which means that the example translates into the following: 'that guy walks so slowly that it is a necessary consequence that he does not feel well'. In this way *tener que* obtains scope over the negated complement and therefore we express a high level of speaker verification in relation to 'his *not* well-being, NO[well-being], which is fully compatible with the intended meaning of the sentence.

Because of the 'true' operator status of *deber*, the normal scope relations of the negation are annulled in connection with the use of *deber* so that in a sentence with *deber* it is always the propositional content of the complement which is negated, irrespective of the position of the negation, viz. the fact that the second and third examples in (22a) have identical semantic contents. Due to the interpretation of low verification level signalled by *deber*, the negated examples with *deber* can be paraphrased into: 'that guy walks so slowly that he is probably not feeling well or it is not a probable consequence that he feels well', which of course is a pragmatically sound utterance.

The analogous positive examples in (22b) do not evidently pose equivalent scope problems and consequently the two sentences just express different degrees of belief in his well-being, according to the different levels of speaker verification implied by the two lexemes.

The examples in (23) also corroborate the assumption of a distinction between a high and a low level of verification, just from a deontic perspective this time. Within the deontic environment the notion of speaker verification level must be taken one step further so that a level of obligation is directly derived and inferred from the verification level. In short, this means that the verification level which the speaker estimates to possess has consequences for his view on the subject referent in the sense that the referent is seen as being more or less obligated to engage in or refrain from engaging in a situation. In this way the degree of obligation becomes a directly derived effect of the speaker verification level.

(23)   *Siento*   **deber/tener que molestarle a usted.*
         regret.I.to   must/ have to   bother   to you
         I am sorry to have to bother you.

Because of the high level of speaker verification and derived subject referent obligation, triggered by the use of *tener que,* in (23) the speaker conveys the information that: 'I am sorry, but there is no other way out than to bother you', while the use of *deber* indicates the following: 'I am sorry and actually I could have chosen another solution than bothering you', where the two parts of the sentence become pragmatically contradictory. Actually, the implications of (23) have wider and more general consequences because they entail that *deber* cannot ever subordinate another predicate and occur in the infinitive, a syntactic restriction which is also pointed out by Gómez Torrego (1999: 3349). The explanation is that the clear volitional semantic feature conveyed by the first verb will always be in contradiction with the low level of obligation expressed through *deber.* The first verb and *deber* semantically require two different types of subject referent, a requirement which is syntactically incompatible with a construction of the type main verb 1 + infinitive, where the two predicates share the subject. This restriction is not relevant for *tener que* because the first verb and the modal in these cases pull in the same semantic direction, so to speak. The high level of obligation triggered by the modal is fully compatible with the semantic subject selection requirements of the first verb. There is no contradiction between the asserted willingness or volitional force of the subject referent, which is implied by the semantics of the first verb and the high obligation level triggered by the employment of *tener que.* The variation of acceptance in (24) further supports this line of argumentation[11].

(24)   *Me gustaría   tener que/*deber ayudaros.* (Gómez Torrego, 1999: 3349)
me would.like.to have to /   must help.you
I would like to have to help you.

The pair of examples in (25a) and (b) illustrate the same distinction between high and low obligation level, but from an aspectual angle.

(25) (a) *La policía   tuvo   que meterlo en la   cárcel.*
the police   had   to put.him in the jail
The police had to put him in jail.

   (b) *La policía debió   meterlo en la   cárcel.*
the police debió put.him in the jail
The police should have put him in jail.

(26) (a) *La policía   debió/   debía/   debería/ debiera haberlo   metido*
the police   should/ should/ should/ should   have.him   put
en la cárcel.
in the jail
The police should have put him in jail.

(b) *La   policía   tuvo   que haberlo   metido   en la cárcel.*
the police   had   to   have.him   put   in the jail
The police must have put him in jail.

Both examples of (25) occur in the indefinite preterite form. (25a) implies that the action denoted by the infinitive phrase *meterlo en la cárcel* 'put him in jail' actually took place, whereas *debió* in (25b) conveys the meaning that the speaker wishes that the subject referent had produced the action, but in fact did not do it.

The high obligation level signalled by the use of *tener que* results in an interpretation where the SoA actually was realised, while *deber* entails that the level of obligation was not high enough to make the subject referents carry the action into effect. The realisation interpretation becomes a necessary consequence of the use of *tener que* in the preterite, while this is not the case with *deber.*

The interpretation of low obligation level conveyed by *deber* means that *deber* can never indicate accomplishment, not even in the preterite, as mentioned before. Instead, when occurring in the preterite, the whole construction obtains past time reference and then it neutralises with the other forms when combining with the compound infinitive, which is illustrated in (26a).

Tener que does the opposite. In the preterite it triggers the interpretation of accomplishment, so when it combines with the compound infinitive, it cannot express the deontic meaning anymore, which requires non-accomplishment, so in the preterite *tener que* changes to the epistemic domain, as shown in (26b).

(27) (a) *Cuando les   oigo hablar de la   necesidad de   una nueva reforma*
         when   them hear.I talk of   the necessity of a   new   reform
         laboral,[…], *llego a la   conclusión de que la   sonda Mars Pathfinder*
         labour,[…], come.I to the conclusion of that the probe Mars Pathfinder
         les   ha   debido   reenviar desde Marte.
         them have   must   sent   from Mars
         When I hear them talk about a new labour market reform,[…], I come to
           the conclusion that the space probe, Mars Pathfinder, must have sent them
           from Mars.

    (b) *El   presidente de Iberia, Xabier Irola,*[…], *ha tenido   que recordar al*
        The president   of Iberia, Xabier Irola,[…], has had   to   remind to.the
        Gobierno   que   se   avecina   un   verano caótico para el   tráfico
        Government that   itself approach a   summer chaotic for   the   traffic
        aéreo[…]
        air[…]
        The president of Iberia, Xabier Irola,[…], has had to remind the Government
          that the air traffic is facing a chaotic summer,[…]

Finally, when *deber* and *tener que* occur in the perfect as in (27) the verification/obligation level variation is evident again, this time, however, with the consequence of a shift in the modal category. The low level of *deber* favours an epistemic reading, whereas the high level of *tener que* conveys the deontic reading.

8   Conclusion

Organising the semantic field of modalities around speaker information as the fundamental parameter enables us to describe the central Spanish modals *poder,* *deber* and *tener que* on the basis of three, strongly interrelated, dimensions: categorical status of the utterance, status of the informational source as either direct or presupposed and the speaker verification level.

The notion of categoricality, which is the most important of the three dimensions, provides a powerful tool for perspectivising the auxiliaries' capability to express variants of modal meanings. The categorical status of an utterance, including the related subject selection restrictions, has direct influence on temporal deixis, i.e. the temporal anchorage or projection of the utterance, activated by the morphological tense marking of the modals and the dependent verbs and subsequently in the derived phenomenon of semantic neutralisation.

However, the semantic neutralisation patterns are not just determined by the categorical status of the utterance, but are also clearly connected to the distinction between a cognitively, overtly manifested informational source, which is present whenever *deber* and *tener que* are employed and an informational source that can be presupposed, but does not necessarily have to exist, which is conveyed by the use of *poder.*

Finally, the distribution of *deber* and *tener que* reflects the speaker's own assessment of the level of verification provided by the informational source he possesses. The phenomenon of verification/obligation level cuts across the categories of epistemic and deontic modality, it manifests itself in the temporal and aspectual systems and in general its employment as a descriptive device gives rise to new insights in the field of modality.

Notes

1   As in other languages the Spanish modals do not have an imperative form. A discussion of the relation between the imperative mood and the Spanish modal auxiliaries is found in Müller (2001: 42ff.).

2   The application of a set of morphological and syntactic criteria to the Spanish modals is debated in Müller (2001: 40f.).

3   The phrastic auxiliaries *deber de* 'must' and *haber de* 'must' are not treated in this article for the following reasons: *haber de* is becoming less and less frequent in current language use and today it is considered literary and somewhat archaic. As for *deber de* many language users do not distinguish between *deber de* and *deber*, so their meanings have to a certain extent become neutralised.

4   Sørensen (ibid.) mentions that this conception of possibility goes back to von Wright (1951) and is found in many later works on modality as for example in those of Davidsen-Nielsen (1990) and Boye (2001).

5   Of course, the speaker's use of operators leading to epistemic or deontic interpretations indirectly imply that the subject referent is capable of taking part in the situation denoted by the infinitive. The sentences *el chico puede estar enganchado* and *el chico no puede fumar aquí*, conveying epistemic and deontic meanings respectively, presuppose that the subject referent *el chico* is a semantically sound or logical 'participant' in the situation denoted by the infinitive.

6   According to Sørensen (ibid.) '… any obligation (or permission) is also about the possible realisation of something at some point in time after the obligation (or permission).' Expressed in other terms, this viewpoint is also found in Ridruejo (1999: 3214) who with reference to Kiparsky and Kiparsky (1971), points to the fact that deontic modality implies a certain kind of epistemic modalisation as well, because both modal categories indicate the non-factivity of the proposition in question.

7   This construction is of course possible in its reflexive passive version, i.e. *la puerta no puede cerrarse herméticamente* 'the door cannot be closed hermetically', where an active agent is inferred.

8   That the restriction concerns the epistemic domain as such and not just the verb *poder* is illustrated by the following examples where the verbs *deber/tener que* are used epistemically:

Juan va a	*deber/tener*	*que*	*cruzar*	*el*	*río.*
Juan goes to	must/have	to	cross	the	river.

John's going to have to cross the river.
*It's very likely that John's going to cross the river.

(Silva-Corvalán 1995: 69. The original example does not include *tener que*)

9   For the sake of presenting a coherent picture, it should be mentioned that *deber* may receive an epistemic hear-say interpretation, viz. *este vino debería ser muy bueno, según me han dicho* 'this wine should be very good, I have heard'. However, I shall have nothing specific to say about this construction, as it falls outside the scope of this article.

10   Here we disregard the descriptive function of deontic statements, as is (18b).

11   Data from Silva-Corvalán (1995: 92), in casu the example *Juan quiere deber hacerlo* 'Juan wants to have the obligation to do it', constitutes an argument against the verification level hypothesis, but according to my informants and my own intuitions such a construction is considered semantically odd.

References

Boye, K. (2001) The force-dynamic core meaning of Danish modal verbs. *Acta Linguistica Hafniensia* 33: 38–74.

Davidsen-Nielsen, N. (1985) Contrastive English-Danish linguistics with special reference to modality. *CEBAL* 7: 7–28. Copenhagen: Nyt Nordisk Forlag Arnold Busch.

Gómez Torrego, L. (1999) Los verbos auxiliares. Las perífrasis verbales de infinitivo. In I. Bosque and V. Demonte (eds) *Gramática Descriptiva de la Lengua Española, Tomo II* 3323–89. Madrid: Espasa Calpe.

Halliday, M. A. K. (1970) Functional diversity in language as seen from a consideration of modality and mood in English. *Foundations of Language* 6: 322–61.

Kiparsky, P. and Kiparsky, C. (1971) Fact. In D. Steinbeck and L. A. Jokobovits (eds) *Semantics. An Interdisciplinary Reader in Philosophy, Linguistics and Psychology* 345–69. Cambridge: Cambridge University Press.

Klinge, A. (1993) The English modal auxiliaries: from lexical semantics to utterance interpretation. *Journal of Linguistics* 29: 315–57.

Lyons, J. (1977) *Semantics.* Cambridge: Cambridge University Press.

Müller, H. H. (2001) The Spanish Modal Auxiliaries. In *Reflections on Modality.* Copenhagen Studies in Language 26, H. H. Müller, (ed.) 39–66.

Nuyts, J. (2001) *Epistemic Modality, Language and Conceptualization.* Amsterdam/Philadelphia: John Benjamins.

Palmer, F. R. (1979) *Modality and the English Modals.* London: Longman.

Ridruejo, E. (1999) Modo y modalidad. El modo en las subordinadas sustantivas. In I. Bosque and V. Demonte (eds) *Gramática Descriptiva de la Lengua Española, Tomo II* 3209–251. Madrid: Espasa Calpe.

Silva-Corvalán, C. (1995) Contextual conditions for the interpretation of poder and deber in Spanish. In J. Bybee and S. Fleishman (eds) *Modality in Grammar and Discourse* 67–105. Amsterdam: John Benjamins.

Sweetser, E. (1990) *From Etymology to Pragmatics.* Cambridge: Cambridge University Press.

Sørensen, F. (2000) *Om danske modalverber og P-led.* Unpublished manuscript.

Sørensen, F. (2001) Modals and modality. Some issues and some proposals. In H. H. Müller (ed.) *Reflections on Modality.* Copenhagen Studies in Language 26: 11–37.

Verstraete, J.-C. (2000) Subjective vs. objective modality in functional grammar: criteria, types and unmarked options. Handout for the Ninth International Functional Grammar Conference. Madrid, Spain, 20–23 September.

von Wright, G. (1951) *An Essay in Modal Logic.* Amsterdam: North Holland.

7 On the modal values of the Italian Pluperfect – with occasional reference to Danish and English

Iørn Korzen

1 Introduction: simple and compound verb forms

The aim of this chapter is to focus on the use of the Italian Pluperfect, or Past Perfect[1], with special reference to its modal usages and with brief comparisons with Danish and English. The Pluperfect has generally been treated somewhat superficially in Italian linguistics[2] and its modal values especially are often reduced to very brief remarks, if indeed they are mentioned at all. On the following pages I hope to make it clear that any description that tends to ignore or reduce the importance of the modal content of the Italian Pluperfect, will delimit the question of modality to a much too narrow field of investigation.

The Italian verb system boasts two Pluperfect forms, both compound forms composed of the auxiliary verb, *avere* or *essere* ('to have'/'to be'), in a synthetic past tense and the Past Participle of the lexical verb (I here confine myself to the active system). Since Italian has two synthetic past tenses, the imperfective *Imperfetto* and the perfective *Passato Remoto*, we obtain both the so-called *Trapassato Prossimo* and the *Trapassato Remoto*, as exemplified in (1) and (2) with the verb *scrivere* ('to write') in the third person singular:

	Simple forms:	→	Compound forms:
(1)	*Imperfetto* [imperfective] (e.g.: *scriveva*)	→	*Trapassato Prossimo* (e.g.: *aveva scritto*)
(2)	*Passato Remoto* [perfective] (e.g.: *scrisse*)	→	*Trapassato Remoto* (e.g.: *ebbe scritto*)

Such compound forms arose in the neo-Latin languages – together with the Future Perfect, the *Futuro Anteriore*, which has the auxiliary verb in the Future tense, cf. (3) – in the same way as the compound form with the auxiliary verb in the Present form, the *Passato Prossimo*, cf. (4):

Simple forms: → **Compound forms:**

(3)   *Futuro* (e.g.: *scriverà*) → *Futuro Anteriore* (e.g.: *avrà scritto*)

(4)   *Presente* (e.g.: *scrive*) → *Passato Prossimo* (e.g.: *ha scritto*)[3]

This latter form was known already in classical Latin and originally it expressed a lasting state or effect in the present, e.g. *epistolam scriptam habet,* lit.: 'S/he has the letter written'. But gradually, as the subject was seen more and more as responsible for the event or action that had caused the given state or effect, it eventually came to express the event itself (Rohlfs, 1969: 727) and it thus included the event *and* its consequences for the present (one of the possible contents of the Latin *Perfectum* – the other one being the aoristic sense), see also Tekavčić (1972: 290–300).

In this way, the grammatico-semantic content of all compound forms of modern Italian can generally be described as:

(5)   the designation of a terminated event, the consequence or following state
           of which is relevant in the temporal or modal frame expressed by the
           auxiliary verb.

Closest to this description, but omitting the modal part, are Bach/Schmitt Jensen (1990: 442). Most other Italian grammars simply state that the compound forms express events that precede the reference point expressed by the auxiliary verb. I hope that the validity of (5), at least as far as the Pluperfect goes, will become clear as this chapter progresses.

While the aspectual distinction between *Imperfetto* and *Passato Remoto*, cf. (1) and (2), is absolute, this is not so in the case of the compound forms. The *Trapassato Remoto* is always perfective, but the *Trapassato Prossimo* may be used both perfectively and imperfectively, cf. Korzen (2001: 174 and 2002: 203). The *Trapassato Remoto* is quite rare and archaic in modern Italian. It only occurs in subordinate temporal clauses joined to independent clauses that have the verb in the *Passato Remoto,* and with its perfective auxiliary verb it simply denotes an event that is terminated before another terminated event of the past. Thus, like the *Passato Remoto*, the *Trapassato Remoto* does not hold any particular modal values and in the rest of this chapter I shall therefore confine myself to the *Trapassato Prossimo*, i.e. the type in (1), *aveva scritto.*

2 Modal 'remoteness'

Even though Italian – like the other neo-Latin languages – has grammaticalised mood oppositions (the Indicative vs. the Subjunctive and the Conditional), the indicative forms are often used with specific modal values, i.e. adding some subjective or objective modal qualification to a given reality. In some cases, the indicative forms express particular qualifications that are not found in the Subjunctive or the Conditional, in other cases, as e.g. in (15) below, the choice between an indicative and a subjunctive form is simply a question of formality and linguistic register (cf. also Lepschy and Lepschy, 1979: 226–8). The precise interpretation depends on the lexical content of the verb and on the cotext and I am therefore generally a little sceptical about very rigorous mono-semantic descriptions of verb forms.[4] They seem to be correct only at a level of such abstraction that the actual value and usefulness of the description is counter-productively reduced to a minimum, making more specific description and analysis necessary anyhow for a full understanding of the grammatico-semantic possibilities. Generally, verb forms are multidimensional, even if in some of their semantic possibilities we may talk about a 'common denominator', as we shall see below.

The grammatico-semantic values of the Italian *Trapassato Prossimo* originate, at least in part, from those of the auxiliary verb in *Imperfetto*, a tense form that basically expresses the 'removal' of the verbal situation (i.e. event, process or state) from a surrounding context. This removal, or 'dislocation', may be (primarily) temporal or (primarily) modal and this feature of the preterite is well known in many languages. As for Danish, Wiwel (1901: 140–2) was the first to explicitly take the terminological consequences of this fact by suggesting the term *afstandsform* ['distance form'] (op.cit. 141) for the Danish preterite. Diderichsen (1971[3] [1946]: 123) calls this a 'just choice' and it is followed also by Heltoft (1999: 152ff)[5].

The same point of view has been expressed by several other more or less recent scholars, who find that the primary semantic content of past tenses is generally that of *distance from present reality*. Only the co- or context will clarify the temporality and/or modality of the distance. Lyons talks about 'the interdependence of time and distance':

(6)   by virtue of the interdependence of time and distance (in that what is
          further away takes longer to reach), there is a direct correlation between
          temporal and spatial remoteness from the deictic zero-point of the here-
          and-now [...]. [W]hat is commonly regarded as past-tense [...] is perhaps
          better analysed, in certain languages at least, in terms of the more general
          notion of *modal remoteness*. (Lyons, 1977: 718–9, my italics)

Similarly, features or properties different from [+ past] have been put forward in the descriptions of past tenses made by other scholars. In the same vein as Wiwel, Seiler (1971: 84, 87) and Steele (1975) for instance suggest the feature [dissociative][6], Halliday (1978: 869) the term [distal][7] and Jensen (2001) [+ distance][8].

In the same way, Herslund (1987 and 1988) sees the temporal use of tense forms as a secondary dimension that follows the primary one, which is the modal dimension of 'topicality' or 'actuality' of the denoted verbal situation, meaning whether or not it is 'relevant or belonging to the actual world of the speaker' (Herslund, 1988: 294):

(7)

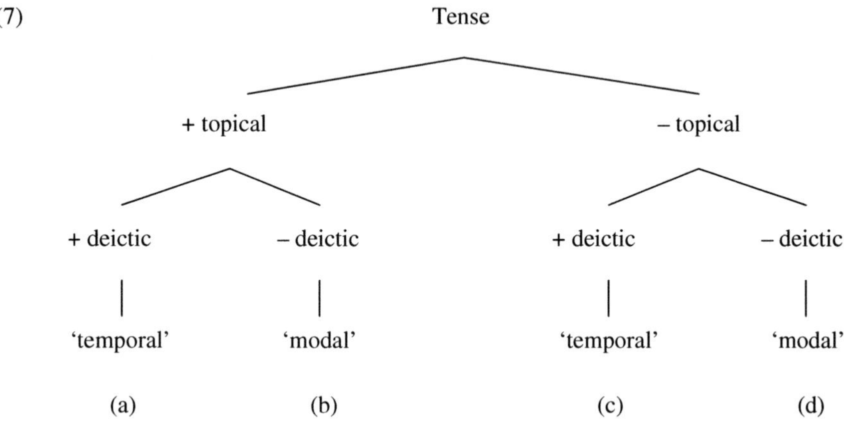

In (a) we find specific verbal situations taking place at the moment of speech, in (b) various generic expressions in the present tense and in (c) and (d) the temporal and modal uses respectively of past and future tense forms. It should be added that very often the dichotomy temporal/modal of the right branch, '− topical', is not a clear and distinct one. Often we must limit ourselves to talking about *primarily* temporal or *primarily* modal uses, as we shall see below.

The notion of 'topicality' is very close to the notion of 'current relevance/ irrelevance' found in Bhat (1999: 173–5) who was inspired by the Tibeto-Burman language Mao-Naga where two different suffixes, *Ti* and *oTi*, distinguish current relevance from irrelevance, e.g.:

(8) (a) *ole apru-Ti-e.*

     pot break-RELEVANT-PRED

     The pot has broken (and is still in the broken state).

(b) *ole apru-oTi-e.*

     pot break-IRRELEVANT-PRED

     The pot had broken (but is no longer in the broken state). (Bhat, 1999: 173)

As in the cited examples, these suffixes may – at least in some of their usages – be translated as Present Perfect and Pluperfect respectively, a phenomenon which is extremely relevant to this chapter.

Both Herslund and Bhat define their notions of 'topicality' and 'current relevance' or 'irrelevance' as modal notions.

3   The Italian *Imperfetto*

The Italian *Imperfetto* – as well as the equivalent tense in the other Romance languages – communicates the content of dissociation or 'removal' *par excellence*. As I said before, the verb form expresses the feature [+ imperfective] and this feature explains on the one hand its function as a dependent verb tense, i.e. its use as an anaphoric or cataphoric connective[9] and, on the other hand, its modal uses. The feature [+ past], also expressed by the *Imperfetto*, removes the situation from the actual world of the speaker and the imperfectiveness means that the denoted verbal situation may be neither temporally specified nor considered as terminated or completed. This points to 'indeterminacy' as the fundamental characteristic of this tense[10].

Some of the most exhaustive descriptions of the modal values of the Italian *Imperfetto* are found in Bazzanella (1990: 440–7; 1994: 98–102). Bazzanella defines the following examples of the *Imperfetto* as modal uses, since as common denominator they all perform a 'kind of translation from the real world into another, created by the speaker' (1990: 440). As is seen in the translations, in many cases the equivalent English verb is a compound form or a phrasal verb:

(9)   (a)   The 'oneiric' meaning:
Ho sognato che avevo fame.
I dreamt I *was* hungry.

(b)   The 'fantasy' meaning:
A: *Peccato che non ci siamo portati via quella bella insegna.*
B: *Già e poi magari passava un vigile e ci conciava per le feste.*
A: What a shame that we didn't steal that nice signboard.
B: Sure and then a policeman *came/would have come by* and *gave/given* us a good thrashing.

(c)   The meaning of 'attempt and/or imminence':
Giovanni cadeva già nel burrone quando gli ho steso la mano: sono arrivato appena in tempo.
Giovanni *fell/was going to fall* into the gorge when I gave him my hand: I was just in time.

(d)   The 'hypothetical' meaning:
   Se potevo, venivo.
   If I **could/had been able to*, I **came/would have come*.

(e)   The 'potential' meaning:
   Vincenzo doveva essere qui; non capisco cosa gli sia successo.
   Vincenzo *should be/have been* here; I can't understand what has happened to him.

(f)   The 'ludic' meaning:
   Io ero l'albero, tu il cavallo.
   I **was/'ll be* the tree, you the horse.

(g)   The 'epistemic-doxastic' meaning, where the speaker hints at previous knowledge or beliefs:
   Che cosa c'era domani al cinema?
   What *was/is* on at the movies tomorrow?
   where one may imply a *verbum dicendi* in a past tense, e.g. What did you say was on...

(h)   The meaning of 'politeness or modesty':
   A: *Desiderava?*
   B: *Volevo un caffè.*
   A: What did you want?
   B: I *wanted/would like* a coffee.

(i)   The meaning of 'planning':
   A: *Non puoi farlo domani?*
   B: *Domani andavo in biblioteca.*
   A: Can't you do it tomorrow?
   B: Tomorrow I **went/was going to go* to the library.
   Like in (h), the *Imperfetto* indicates that there is room for negotiation.

(j)   The meaning of 'fondness' particularly used with children:
   Aveva fame la mia bambina?
   My little girl **was/is* hungry?

The examples (a) to (c) refer to a past time, whereas (e) to (j) do not. Example (d) is temporally ambiguous. Generally, the meaning of (h) occurs with verbs of a particular lexical type and (i) and (j) may be said to be particularly context dependent and so to say less 'standardised' than the rest.[11]

Furthermore, we find – in Italian as well as in other languages – uses such as the following, which may be defined as *Imperfetti* 'of irrelevance':

(10) A: *Lo sai che mi ha lasciato Luca?*

    B: *Chi?*

    A: *Quello che **era** alto due metri e che **aveva** due figli con Anna.*

    A: Did you know that Luca left me?

    B: Who?

    A: The guy who *was* two metres tall and *had* two children with Anna.

(11)   *Ho perso i miei guanti ieri sera. E' un vero peccato. Mi **piacevano** molto,*
        erano *così belli.*

        I lost my gloves yesterday evening. It's a real shame. I *liked* them very
        much, they *were* so nice.

In (10) Luca is probably still two metres tall and still has children with Anna and in (11) my gloves are probably still nice and I still like them even if they are no longer in my possession. Instead, the *Imperfetti* indicate that the denoted states are no longer relevant to the speaker, cf.:

(10 ')A: *Lo sai che ho sposato Luca?*

    B: *Chi?*

    A: *Quello che è alto due metri e che **ha** due figli con Anna.*

    A: Did you know that I married Luca?

    B: Who?

    A: The guy who *is* two metres tall and *has* two children with Anna.

(11 ')   *Sto cercando i miei guanti; mi **piacciono** molto, **sono** così belli.*

        I am looking for my gloves; I *like* them very much, they *are* so nice.[12]

Such removal or dislocation of the content of a proposition to a created or imagined world also means its removal to a *cognitive and psychological background*, since it expresses an alternative mode to the real world foreground, cf. Reinhart (1984: 802):

(12)   Modal propositions (including 'irrealis' statements of alternative modes of
    events) and negative propositions (reporting events which did not take
    place) are background. Such propositions function as clues for the
    understanding of the foreground by comparing its events to alternative
    modes of development.[13]

4 The Italian *Trapassato Prossimo*

As hinted at in the introduction, with rare exceptions the Italian *Trapassato Prossimo* has not been at the centre of linguistic research, and in Italian grammars it is generally reduced to brief remarks stating that it expresses the occurrence of an event prior to some reference point of the past. Such a description does not, however, do justice to the tense form, which is very widely used in Italian and has quite a large semantic and modal range. Furthermore, it serves important co- and contextual purposes such as pragmatic and/or narrative backgrounding, as we shall see.

All semantic, modal and pragmatic content of the *Trapassato Prossimo* derive from the fundamental value of the *Imperfetto* as indicator of *distance* and *non-topicality* and the semantic content of the Past Participle of an event having taken place, cf. also (5). On the one hand, the *Trapassato* occurs with the same modal values that we saw in (9) – with the exception of three cases that are not relevant in the sense of an event having taken place, namely the meaning of 'attempt or imminence' (9c), the 'potential' meaning (9e) and the meaning of 'planning' (9i). On the other hand, precisely because of the Past Participle it can express some modal nuances that are not found in the *Imperfetto*.

The uses and functions of *Trapassato Prossimo* can be divided in two basic domains: a contextual one, where the verb relates directly to the communication situation and a co-textual one, where the verb relates to a surrounding text (and thereby possibly indirectly to the communication situation).

4.1   Contextual use of *Trapassato Prossimo*

If a *Trapassato Prossimo* relates directly to the communication situation, it always expresses a modal content in the sense of 'removing the event in question into a world created by the speaker' or in some other way reducing its importance. With the three exceptions mentioned, we find all the modal values of (9) here: i.e. the 'oneiric' meaning, cf. (9a):

(13)   *Ho sognato che avevo vinto un milione.*
        I dreamt I *had won* a million.

the 'fantasy' meaning, cf. (9b):

(14) A: *Peccato che non ci siamo portati via quella bella insegna.*
     B: *Già e poi magari passava un vigile che **aveva visto** tutto.*

     A: What a shame that we didn't steal that nice signboard.
     B: Sure and then a policeman who *had seen* everything would have come.

the counterfactual meaning, corresponding to the 'hypothetical' meaning of (9d):

(15) (a)   *Se tu **avevi** effettivamente **spedito** la lettera, come promesso, adesso non
           staremmo qui a recriminare.* (cit.: Bertinetto, 1986: 465)
           If you *had* really *sent* the letter like you promised, we wouldn't sit here
           and complain. (The Pluperfect Indicative in the protasis corresponds to a
           Subjunctive *Trapassato Prossimo* in a more formal register)

(b) *Voglio ridarla indietro questa roba qui e tanti saluti [...] Se non era che*
     *per due giorni la villa è stata chiusa, senza segno di vita, lo **avevo** già **fatto***
     ***prima!** (Carlo Lucarelli: Il giorno del lupo. Torino, Einaudi, 1998, p. 34)*
     I want to give this stuff back. If the villa hadn't been closed for two days
     without any sign of life, *I *had* already *done* it (I would already have
     done it). (The Pluperfect Indicative in the apodosis corresponds to a Past
     Conditional in a more formal register)

the 'ludic' meaning, cf. (9f):

(16)   (*Facciamo che*) *io ero la mamma e ti **avevo** appena **preparato** la cena.*
        (Let's play that) I *was/am the mother and that I *had/have just *prepared*
        your dinner.

the 'epistemic-doxastic' meaning, cf. (9g):

(17) A: (*guardando nella sua borsa*): *Costanza, non c'è il portafoglio!*
     B: *Ma non è possibile, guarda bene.*
     A: *No guarda: occhiali, agenda, chiavi, fazzoletti, non c'è. [...] Dobbiamo*
          assolutamente fare la denuncia; tu non sai dov'è la questura?
     B: *No, non lo so.*
     A: *Non **eri** già **stata** a Firenze?* [*Non avevi detto che...?*]
     B: *Sono stata a Firenze ma non sono mai stata in questura, non conosco*
          bene Firenze. (I. Korzen: *Scene Italiane*. Copenhagen Business School,
          1995: 39).

     A: (checking her handbag): Costanza, the purse is missing!
     B: That's impossible. Check again.
     A: No, look: glasses, notebook, keys, handkerchief, it's gone. We must
          absolutely report it. Do you know where the police station is?
     B: No I don't.
     A: *Had*n't you *been* to Florence before? [Didn't you say that...?]
     B: I have been to Florence but I have never been to a police station. I don't
          know Florence well.'

the meaning of 'politeness or modesty', cf. (9h):

(18)   *Suona un campanello. Teresa apre. Entra Elena.*
        TERESA *Buongiorno.*
        ELENA *Buongiorno. **Avevo telefonato** stamattina. Vengo per l'inserzione sul*
        'Messaggero'. Mi chiamo Elena Tesei.
        (N. Ginzburg: *Ti ho sposato per allegria e altre commedie.* Einaudi, 1976:
        79; the beginning of the play *L'inserzione*).

        A doorbell rings. Teresa opens the door. Elena comes in.
        TERESA Hello.

> ELENA Hello. I *had phoned/phoned this morning. I've come about the ad in
> the 'Messaggero'. My name is Elena Tesei.

the meaning of 'fondness', cf. (9j):

(19)   *La mia bambina non **aveva mangiato** abbastanza?*
        My little girl *hadn't/hasn't eaten enough?

In such cases, perhaps with the exception of (19), we also find the Pluperfect in Danish, in the 'ludic' meaning, cf. (16), often with the adverb *jo* [≈ as I would]: *Så var jeg jo moren og havde netop lavet middagsmad til dig* [So I was the mother and *had* just *made* supper for you [as I would].

Where the *Imperfetti* of (9) express the removal of states or imminent or ongoing events from the actual world into a world created by the speaker, the *Trapassati* in (13) to (19) all designate terminated events that are removed (or 'backgrounded', in Reinhart's words, cf. (12)) to a potential or particular speaker's world. In the case of the 'polite or modest' *Trapassato* in (18), the event in question did actually take place, but *its consequences* are removed from the actual world in order to reduce its importance. This too entails a *pragmatic backgrounding*, which in fact turns out to be another common denominator of the *Trapassato*, also in the textual uses of the *Trapassato*, as we shall see in 4.2 below (cf. also Korzen 2001, 2002). The opposite is found in the *Passato Prossimo*, e.g.:

(18')   Ho **telefonato** *stamattina. Vengo per l'inserzione sul 'Messaggero.'*
        I *phoned* this morning. I've come about the ad in the 'Messaggero.'

which will express the *relevance* of the event at the speech time and thereby a relative foregrounding of it. This use of the *Trapassato* is very common in many languages, including English and Danish. Cf. examples such as:

(20) (a) *Veramente **avevo preparato** un discorso sull'articolo partitivo, ma vedo
           adesso che non è pertinente.*
           I *had* really *prepared* a paper on the partitive article, but I see
           now that it is not relevant.
           *Jeg **havde** egentlig **forberedt**...*

     (b) *Avevo pensato di passare stasera, ma forse è una cattiva idea.*
           I *had thought* of dropping by tonight, but it may be a bad idea.
           *Jeg **havde tænkt mig**...*

     (c) *Kommer du i aften? Nej, det **havde** jeg ikke **tænkt** mig.*
           Will you be coming tonight? No, I *hadn't planned* to do so (I *wasn't*
           going to).

where the *Trapassato Prossimo* (or preterite in (c)) indicates that there is room for negotiation, cf. (9i). The equivalent *Passato Prossimo* would occur in contexts such as:

(20')(a) ***Ho preparato*** *un discorso sull'articolo partitivo* ***che intendo tenere fra un'ora.***

    I *have prepared* a paper on the partitive article *which I intend to deliver in an hour.*

    Jeg ***har forberedt****…*

(b) ***Ho pensato*** *di passare stasera;* ***ti va bene verso le 8?***

    I *thought* of dropping by tonight; *would 8 o'clock be OK?*

    Jeg ***har tænkt mig****…*

(c) *Kommer du i aften? Nej, det* ***har*** *jeg ikke* ***tænkt*** *mig*

    Will you be coming tonight? No, I wasn't meaning to.

Similarly, an event may be backgrounded in order to express the speaker's own *uncertainty* as to whether or not it was opportune. In the following exchange I is Interviewer and C is the Interviewee Cristina:

(21) I: *Tu hai detto che torni a lavorare in autunno. Vuol dire che usufruisci di tutte le possibilità di aspettativa che ti dà la legge?*

    C: *In un certo senso sì, perché io sono rimasta… rimango a casa nove mesi dopo l'arrivo della bambina. E per i tre mesi successivi, fino a che la bambina non è in casa nostra per l'arco di un anno, avrei due possibilità: o tornare al lavoro, con orario ridotto, di circa il 25% in meno, ma il mio stesso stipendio, oppure posso chiedere, se ho bisogno, un'aspettativa dal lavoro senza stipendio. Io* ***avevo pensato*** *di tornare al lavoro in ottobre, insomma, in metà settembre…*

    I: *Ciò sarebbe dopo quanti mesi?*

    C: *Dopo i nove mesi regolari.* (I. Korzen: *Gli italiani vivono (anche) così 1.* Copenhagen, Samfundslitteratur, 1989, p. 85)

    I: You said that you'll go back to work in the fall. Does that mean that you use all the possibilities of leave of absence that the law gives you?

    C: In a certain sense it does, because I stay home for nine months after the baby arrives. And for three more months, until the baby has lived with us for a year, I shall have two possibilities: either to go back to work with about a 25% reduction of the working hours but the same salary, or I can ask to continue the leave of absence without salary. I *had thought* of going back to work in October, or rather in mid September …

    I: That would be after how many months?

    C: After the usual nine months.

Another reason why an event or its consequences may be backgrounded is that it took place in a past that is felt to be very remote:

(22)   *Su questo argomento tanti anni fa N. ci **aveva scritto** un libro.*
        On this topic N. *had written/wrote a book many years ago. (cit.: Squartini, 1999: 58).

(23)   *Quel disegno lo **avevo fatto** io il primo giorno che lavoravo all'istituto.*
        I *had done/did that drawing on the first day I worked at the institute. (cit.: loc.cit.).

As the English translation shows, such usage of the Pluperfect is very marginal, if at all possible, in English, unless another reference point of the past is expressed in the co-text. The same is true of Danish.

In other cases, the *Trapassato* will express that the consequences of the event in question are no longer relevant because *in the meantime the situation has changed*. This is the case in the following exchange. P is Police officer and A the interlocutor:

(24) A: *Io non sono italiana, sono svizzera.*
     P: *Ah, lei è svizzera.*
     A: *E avevo con me il passaporto.*
     P: *Ho capito. E quando deve fare rientro in Svizzera?*
     A: *Eh, **avevo deciso** di stare qui in Italia per una settimana.*
     P: *Sì.*
     A: *Ma visto quello che è successo forse partirò prima.* (I. Korzen: *Scene italiane* cit. p. 41 – the scene following that of Example (17)).

     A: I'm not Italian, I'm Swiss.
     P: Oh, you're Swiss.
     A: And I had my passport with me.
     P: I see. And when do you go back to Switzerland?
     A: Ah, I *had decided* to stay in Italy for a week.
     P: Yes.
     A: But in view of what has happened, I may leave earlier.'

(25)   'Domani parto.'
        Sul momento, Livia, pigliata a tradimento, continuò a sorridere.
        'Ah, sì? E dove vai?'
        'Torno a Vigàta'.
        'Ma se **avevi detto** che restavi fino a lunedì' disse, mentre il sorriso le
            si astutava lentamente come un cerino. (A. Camilleri, *Gli arancini di*
            Montalbano, Arnoldo Mondadori, I Miti, 2000, p. 23)

I leave tomorrow.
Livia was taken aback and continued to smile.
'Oh yeah? And where will you go?'
'I go back to Vigata'.
'But *had*n't you *said* (didn't you say) that you would stay until Monday?'
   she said while her smile slowly extinguished like a match.

Squartini (1999) has – very aptly – labelled such cases 'reversed result' and they can be compared with the *Imperfetti* in (10) to (11). Here, we generally find the same occurrence of the Pluperfect in English and Danish: in (24) *Jeg havde besluttet,* in (25) *Havde du ikke sagt.*

The cross-linguistic situation is different in the case of *Ti avevo detto di/che...* [*I had told you that...*]. This may be defined as a fixed expression that states either that a piece of advice or an order issued by the speaker was not followed by the interlocutor, or that some prediction of the speaker's turned out to be correct – unlike a prediction of the interlocutor's:

(26)   '*Ti **avevo detto** di avvertirmi subito se succedeva qualcosa!*'
      '*E io ti **avevo detto** che non è successo niente! E' arrivato un furgoncino,*
        poco fa, e ha portato della roba all'ingegnere...' (C. Lucarelli: *Lupo*
        mannaro. Torino, Einaudi 2001, p. 78).

      'I *told/had told* you to let me know if anything happened!'
      'And I *told/had told* you that nothing has happened. A van arrived a little
        while ago and brought some stuff to the engineer...'

Here English and Danish *may* use the Pluperfect, *I had told you... / Jeg havde (jo) sagt at...,* but the preterite seems just as frequent.

In some parallel cases, the Pluperfect occurs in Italian but not in Danish and English. These are cases in which the consequences of the event are no longer relevant or topical because a *new event of the same kind* is taking place. For instance, in a situation where an Italian speaker (or writer) is composing a new letter to the same recipient, s/he would say:

(27)   *Ti **avevo** già **scritto** un mese fa.*
    I **had* already *written/wrote* to you a month ago.

The following example comes from a TV-film in which the speaker, a police-man, is entering yet another building during an investigation:

(28)   *Quanti palazzi **avevamo** già **controllato**?* (from the TV-film *Law and*
      Order).

    How many buildings **had* we already *checked out/did* we already *check out*?

In all cases in this section, the *Trapassato Prossimo* expresses the 'removal' or dislocation of the event or its consequences from the actual world, thus adding a modal qualification to the content. In (13) to (17) and (19) the speaker removes both the event and its consequences into a world of his or her own; in (18) and (20) to (28) the *Trapassato* expresses the dislocation of the consequences of an event that already took place and thereby it reduces its importance. In both cases the event is removed from the pragmatic foreground. The expression *Ti avevo detto…* cf. (26) normally functions as a personal comment on, or reaction to, an element of the pragmatic foreground.

Exactly the same thing is found in the textual use of *Trapassato Prossimo*.

4.2   Textual use of *Trapassato Prossimo*

In this section we shall see how a *Trapassato Prossimo* can relate to verbs in other tenses in the same text and thereby express a distinction at a text pragmatic level, namely a distinction between textual foreground and background. The fundamental content of the *Trapassato* is still the removal of the denoted event or action or of its consequences from the actual world, but in these cases, 'actual world' means the 'actual text world' or the 'ongoing discourse universe'. The removal may here be either (primarily) temporal or (primarily) modal, cf. the right branch of the tree in (7), but in all cases it will result in a removal from the text pragmatic or narrative foreground. Best described and very frequent are examples such as:

(29)   *Appena Luca **era tornato** dal lavoro, partimmo per il mare.*
        Right after Luca *had returned/returned* from work, we all left for the
            seaside.

with a primarily *temporal removal* of the proposition in question and a text pragmatic reduction to a time setting function. In cases such as:

(30)   *Bianchi ha perso l'aereo per Copenaghen: **era arrivato** tardi in aeroporto*
        Bianchi missed his plane to Copenhagen. He *had arrived/arrived* late at the
            airport

the temporal relation between the two propositions is pragmatically irrelevant and logically ambiguous. If technically the time in which you miss your plane is when the plane takes off and you are not on board, this moment may be before, during or after your arrival at the airport. Instead, the function of the *Trapassato Prossimo* is here to indicate that the proposition expresses a background feature, namely the *cause* of the main event, i.e. that Bianchi missed his plane.

However, whole text sequences may be put in the *Trapassato Prossimo*. Quite common in journalistic and narrative texts is the *Trapassato* used for instance as a prologue or epilogue to a foregrounded text sequence. By choosing to put some events or actions in the *Trapassato*, the speaker or writer reduces them to a background level, which may constitute the opening or the closing frame of the main story. The following is an example of an '*opening Trapassato*':

(31)   *Finiti gli studi universitari, due studenti* **avevano avuto** *due borse di studio per preparare le loro tesi di specializzazione, ed* **erano partiti** *verso una città straniera dove abitava un celebre maestro con cui volevano studiare. Studiare con una persona così importante era una fortuna, dicevano molti. I due* **erano cresciuti** *insieme,* **avevano** *sempre* **studiato** *assieme, e s'erano anche* **abituati** *a pensare le stesse cose, come una coppia di vecchi sposi.* (G. Celati: *Cinema naturale*, Feltrinelli 2001, p. 81; the beginning of the short story *Novella di due studenti*).

Having finished their university studies, two students *had got* two grants in order to prepare their theses and they *had left* for a foreign city where a distinguished teacher that they wanted to study with lived. Many people said that they were very fortunate to study with such an important person. The two *had grown up* together, they *had* always *studied* together and they *had got* used to thinking the same things, like an old married couple.'

Conversely, the final paragraph of the novel *La voce del violino* by Andrea Camilleri (Palermo, Sellerio, 1999) constitutes a sort of *conclusive elaboration* on behalf of the narrator:

(32)   *Tutto* **era stato**, *fin dal principio, uno scangio dopo l'altro. Maurizio* **era stato** *scangiato per un assassino, la scarpa scangiata per un'arma, un violino scangiato con un altro e quest'altro scangiato per un terzo,* [...]. (op.cit. 206)

Right from the start, it *had* all *been* one mistake after another. Maurizio *had been* mistaken for a murderer, the shoe mistaken for a weapon, a violin mistaken for another and this other violin mistaken for a third one.

A similar conclusive frame is found in the TV version of the novel, where the last scene has a voice-over, namely the voice of the main character, the inspector Salvo Montalbano, who comments:

(33)   *Adesso che la storia* **era finita, avevo capito** *che tutto* **era stato** *fin dal principio uno scangio dopo l'altro. Maurizio di Blasi* **era stato scangiato** *per un assassino, la scarpa per una bomba a mano, un violino scangiato per un altro violino. Il piccolo François* **aveva** *addirittura* **scangiato** *famiglia.* (*La voce del violino*, director: Alberto Sironi).

> Now that the story *had finished*, I *had understood* that right from the start
> everything *had been* one mistake after another. Maurizio di Blasi *had been*
> mistaken for a murderer, the shoe for a hand grenade, a violin mistaken for
> another. The little François *had* even *changed* families.[14]

In this way, the writer chooses which actions should be located in the narrative foreground and which should serve as a background frame. The latter are formally moved to a time frame prior to the main action, but as I have shown in Korzen (2001 and 2002), each case may express various semantic nuances other than (just) a different time frame, e.g. cause, result, consequence or other elaboration on the main event, see also (30).

In such cases, the Pluperfect is generally possible also in Danish and English. The following example is an exception, due to the time adverb *oggi* (today) and the absence of a past reference point:

(34)   *Oggi **avevi chiesto** a Fausto cosa pensava… o meglio, scusate, come
         pensava sarebbe stata la società italiana quando Giorgio fosse cresciuto.
         Giorgio è nostro figlio. […]* (Korzen, *Gli Italiani vivono* cit., p. 21).

         Today you **had asked/asked* Fausto what he thought, or rather, sorry, how
         he thought the Italian society would be when Giorgio grew up. Giorgio is
         our son.

This text is the beginning of a videotaped interview with a Milanese woman and it constitutes so to speak the 'introduction' to her following reflections.

Due to the same text pragmatic function, the *Trapassato* may have the illocutionary role of *inviting the hearer to speak*. By withdrawing an event from the textual foreground, it prompts the interlocutor to produce a *new* textual foreground:

(35) A: *Beh, io credo che me ne farò un altro [di aperitivo].*
     B: *Bene. Poi vogliamo anche ordinare?*
     A: *Cameriere!*
     B: *Ah, al telefono mi **aveva accennato** a una grande donazione per l'ospedale
         pediatrico di San Clemente.*
     A: *Sicuro; so quanto le stia al cuore quel posto, come a tutti del resto. […]*
         (from the TV-film *La signora in giallo*).

     A: Well, I think I'll have another [aperitif].
     B: Good. Then perhaps we should order?
     A: Waiter!
     B: Oh, on the phone you **had hinted/hinted* at a big donation to the
         children's hospital in San Clemente.
     A: Sure. I know how important it is to you, as it is to all of us by the way.

With *aveva accennato,* A expresses a background of previous knowledge shared by both A and B. This means that A is not saying anything new and the pragmatic function is to invite the hearer to elaborate on the subject in question. Likewise:

(36)   *Mi avevi telefonato?*
        Had you *phoned*/Did you phone me?

will – much more directly than *Mi hai telefonato? (Passato Prossimo)* – express the request to supply a textual foreground, i.e. to explain *why.* A simple *yes/no* answer would not be sufficient, rather it would be quite rude – unlike in the case of *Mi hai telefonato?*

In cases equivalent to (35) and (36), the Pluperfect will not be possible – or at least it will be quite marginal – in Danish and English. On the whole, the Pluperfect is used much more frequently in Italian than in languages such as Danish and English[15].

5 Conclusion: (modal) remoteness and (con)text pragmatics

The Italian *Trapassato Prossimo* is a 'backgrounding tense'. In all its uses it expresses the removal of a verbal situation (event, process or state) from a con- or co-textual foreground to a background. In all its contextual uses, this backgrounding may be considered a modal qualification. In its co-textual uses, we can talk about a specific text pragmatic function. Remoteness, be it (primarily) modal or (primarily) temporal, cf. Section 2, is strongly inter-related with (con)text pragmatics, more precisely the pragmatic distinction between (con)textual foreground and background. What is removed from the actual or current world, whether it is the concrete contextual situation or the current co-textual universe, will become background. The contextual, modal backgrounding of a verbal situation will signal its removal from the real world foreground or in other ways weaken it in the ongoing communication. Similarly, textual backgrounding will remove the verbal situation from the central 'event-line' and thereby enhance the distinction between different pragmatic or narrative text levels.

Notes

1   In this chapter I shall follow the Italian tradition and distinguish between denominations of physical time, e.g. *future,* with small initials and denominations of verb tense or forms with capital initials, e.g. *Futuro.*

2   Among the fortunate exceptions are Bertinetto (1986) and Squartini (1999). For a presentation of other scholars on the Italian Pluperfect see Korzen (2001; 2002).

3   In fact, to all synthetic verb forms in Italian, finite as well as *Infinito* and *Gerundio*, correspond equivalent compound forms with the Past Participle.

4   Cf. also Bazzanella (2000), who offers a series of examples of the varied content and functions of Italian verb forms.

5   '*Forskellen mellem præsens og præteritum er således en forskel mellem en nærhedsform* (proksimal form) *og en afstandsform* (distal form)' (Heltoft, 1999: 154) [The difference between present and preterite is thus a difference between a form of closeness and a form of distance].

6   'I have argued that *past* and *irrealis* are actually modifications along tense/aspectual and modality parameters respectively of the semantic primitive dissociative. I have argued this specifically for Uto-Aztecan, but given the cross-linguistic relationship between *past* and *irrealis*, I should like to suggest that dissociative is a universal semantic primitive.' (Steele, 1975: 217).

7   '[T]he term distal is meant to suggest distance from G[round], not in a temporal but in an epistemic sense. This morpheme dissociates the predicate in its scope from G and from the speaker in particular – removing the lower predicate from the domain of accepted present reality and implying a longer epistemic path from the speaker to the ultimate objective content.' (loc.cit.).

8   See other references in James (1982), who also presents a number of examples of 'dissociation marking' by past tenses in different languages.

9   Cf. Herslund/H. Korzen (1999: 25–26, 43–45) for the similar phenomenon in French.

10   Cf. also Bertinetto (1986: 158) and Bazzanella (1990: 448).

11   In cases of a high degree of standardisation, the receiver's expectations of the modal content of the *Imperfetto*, i.e. the 'translation' from the real world, is already activated by the co- or context to a relatively high degree, whereas in cases of a low degree of standardisation, the pragmatic impact of the verb form itself may be felt as stronger.

12   See similar French, English and Danish examples in Herslund (1987 and 1988).

13   Bernhardt (2003) reaches a similar conclusion in an analysis based on Fauconnier's mental spaces (Fauconnier, 1994).

14   See other examples of this in Korzen (2001; 2002). For more examples of the 'prologue' use of the Italian *Trapassato Prossimo*, cf. also Miklič (1998).

15   And, in fact, Greek and Swedish. Cf. Squartini (1999) and, for a comparison with Danish, Korzen (2001). In op.cit., I cite a series of examples of how the Italian translator of a Danish novel (Leif Davidsen: *Den russiske sangerinde*) has changed Danish Preterites into Italian *Trapassati Prossimi* in order to render explicit text pragmatic distinctions between foreground and background, which in the original Danish text would only result from the analysis of a larger co-text. For a more thorough elaboration on the textual use of the Italian *Trapassato Prossimo*, cf. Korzen (2001; 2002).

References

Bach, S. and Schmitt Jensen, J. (1990) *Større Italiensk Grammatik.* Copenhagen: Munksgaard.

Bazzanella, C. (1990) 'Modal' uses of the Italian indicativo Imperfetto in a pragmatic perspective. *Journal of Pragmatics* 14: 439–57.

Bazzanella, C. (1994) *Le facce del parlare. Un approccio pragmatico all'italiano parlato.* Milano: La Nuova Italia.

Bazzanella, C. (2000) Tense and meaning. In D. Marconi (ed.) *Knowledge and Meaning – Topics in Analytic Philosophy* 177–94. Vercelli: Mercurio.

Bernhardt, L. (2003) Tekstuelle bistrukturer – definition og funktion. *Hermes* 30: 129–58.

Bertinetto, P. M. (1986) *Tempo, aspetto e azione nel verbo italiano. Il sistema dell'indicativo.* Firenze: Accademia della Crusca.

Bhat, D. N. S. (1999) *The Prominence of Tense, Aspect and Mood.* Amsterdam/ Philadelphia: John Benjamins.

Diderichsen, P. (1971) *Elementær Dansk Grammatik.* First edition 1946. Copenhagen: Gyldendal.

Fauconnier, G. (1994) *Mental Spaces. Aspects of Meaning Construction in Natural Language.* Cambridge University Press.

Halliday, R. W. (1978) The form and meaning of the English auxiliary. *Language* 54(4): 853–82.

Heltoft, L. (1999) Det verbale system. In E. Hansen and L. Heltoft *Grammatik over det Danske Sprog.* Kapitel 4–6. Pre-publication.

Herslund, M. (1987) Catégories grammaticales et linguistique textuelle: la catégorie du temps en français. *Copenhagen Studies in Language, CEBAL* 10: 89–108.

Herslund, M. (1988) Tense, time and modality. In V. Rosén (ed.) *Papers from the Tenth Scandinavian Conference of Linguistics* 289–300. University of Bergen.

Herslund, M. and Korzen, H. (1999) *Det franske sprog. Kapitel VIII, I. Den komplekse prædikation 1.* Pre-publication. Copenhagen Business School.

James, D. (1982) Past tense and the hypothetical. A cross-linguistic study. *Studies in Language* VI(3): 375–403.

Jensen, B. L. (2001) Det italienske verbalsystem. De finitte formers semantik. In C. Bache et al. (eds) *Ny forskning i grammatik. Fællespublikation 8. Gilbjerghovedsymposiet 2000* 149–69. Odense Universitetsforlag.

Korzen, I. (2001) Pluskvamperfektum; modale og retoriske relationer. In C. Bache et al. (eds) *Ny forskning i grammatik 8. Gilbjerghovedsymposiet 2000* 171–89. Odense Universitetsforlag.

Korzen, I. (2002) Il Trapassato Prossimo in un'ottica pragmatico-testuale. In H. Jansen, P. Polito, L. Schøsler and E. Strudsholm (eds) *L'infinito and oltre. Omaggio a Gunver Skytte* 203–26. Odense University Press.

Lepschy, A. L. and Lepschy, G. (1979) *The Italian Language Today*. London: Hutchinson.

Lyons, J. (1977) *Semantics* Vols. 1–2. Cambridge University Press.

Miklič, T. (1998) Uso cataforico del Trapassato Prossimo italiano: un espediente testuale per la messa in rilievo. *Linguistica* XXXVIII(2): 183–95.

Reinhart, T. (1984) Principles of gestalt perception in the temporal organisation of narrative texts. *Linguistics* 22(6): 779–809.

Rohlfs, G. (1969) *Grammatica storica della lingua italiana e dei suoi dialetti. Sintassi e formazione delle parole*. Torino: Einaudi.

Seiler, H. (1971) Abstract structures for moods in Greek. *Language* 47(1): 79–89.

Squartini, M. (1999) On the semantics of the Pluperfect: evidence from Germanic and Romance. *Linguistic Typology* 3: 51–89.

Steele, S. (1975) Past and irrealis: just what does it all mean? *International Journal of American Linguistics* 41(3): 200–17.

Tekavčić, P. (1972) *Grammatica storica dell'italiano. Volume II: Morfosintassi*. Bologna: il Mulino.

Wiwel, H. G. (1901) *Synspunkter for dansk Sproglære*. Copenhagen: Det Nordiske Forlag.

8 Where there is a *will*, there is a modal[1]

Alex Klinge

1 Preliminaries

Linguistic approaches to the topic of modality have been many and varied. An overview of the literature of the past 50 years reveals that there is no general consensus as to the kinds and degrees of modality that are necessary for an adequate theoretical framework that will capture modality and modal expressions in language. Some writers simply employ intuitive paraphrases such as possibility, permission, prediction, doubt, etc. Other writers rely on various subdivisions of a general notion of modality into for instance extrinsic and intrinsic modality, or speaker-, hearer- and subject-oriented modality, or various force-dynamic concepts. Some writers interpret modality narrowly as including only the formal class of modal auxiliaries, other writers include all shades of attitudes to propositions and some even include negation, cf. e.g. Frawley (1992: 384).

The most persistent source of inspiration for the study of linguistic modality has been the work by von Wright in philosophical logic, in particular his seminal publication on modal logic in 1951. Von Wright distinguished several *modi*, some of which have become the stock-in-trade of many linguists:

- Alethic modality, or modes of logical truth;
- epistemic modality, or modes of knowing;
- deontic modality, or modes of obligation.

In a footnote (1951: 28) he also introduced dynamic modality, which he took to be concerned with abilities and dispositions. One particularly fruitful way in which von Wright's *modi* have been employed as a framework for organising linguistic expressions is by treating epistemic, deontic and dynamic as kinds of modalities which are internally organised into degrees of modality, viz. possibility/permission vs. necessity/obligation (see Palmer, 1990: 36). Most linguists have assumed that alethic modality, the modality of logical truth, is not encoded in natural language (for a different view cf. Durst-Andersen, 1992 and 1995 and this volume). Furthermore, it should be noted that some writers choose to conflate deontic and dynamic modalities into non-epistemic, or 'root', modality, which seems to be the linguistically most salient split observable in many languages.

One thing that a majority of writers on modality in language seem to agree on is that modality is somehow fundamentally a notion covering the difference between presenting a proposition in an unqualified manner as verified and true and presenting a proposition in a qualified manner as non-verified and only potentially true. The basic opposition is illustrated by the two prototypical sentences in (1).

(1) (a)   John is in his office. (non-modal)
     (b)   John may be in his office. (modal)

In a standard utterance of (1a) the speaker presents the proposition *John be in his office* as verified relative to the situation she is referring to, encouraging the hearer to process and store the proposition as true of the world the speaker is referring to. In a standard utterance of (1b), on the other hand, the speaker presents the proposition as unverified but with an indication that it is her belief that it is potentially true of the world she is referring to, thereby encouraging the hearer to process and store the proposition as only potentially true relative to the current state of knowledge of the speaker. In other words, the traditional line of reasoning is that by uttering (1b) the speaker signals that she has less than perfect access to the truth of the proposition. This precise feature is generally taken to be the hallmark of modality.

The conception of modality illustrated is usually turned into a definitional delimitation of modality which hinges on the speaker. Palmer (1986: 16) provides the following delimitation:

(2)   Modality in language is, then, concerned with subjective characteristics
           of an utterance and it could even be further argued that subjectivity is
           an essential criterion for modality. Modality could, that is to say, be
           defined as the grammaticalization of speakers' (subjective) attitudes
           and opinions.

In this way subjectivity becomes a central, even criterial, feature of the definition of modality.

Writers who adopt speaker subjectivity as their point of departure will have to decide how to interpret possible utterances of the following sentences containing the modal *will*.

(3) (a) The service to Carlisle will arrive at platform two in ten minutes.
     (b) We will bring the wine.
     (c) They will be home at this time of the day.

Neither (3a) nor (3b) would seem to qualify as seriously subjective in the manner intended by the traditional definition of modality, while, conversely, (3c) would seem to constitute a perfect exemplar of modal semantics. Various solutions to this descriptive problem have been proposed. Some writers rely on morpho-syntactic criteria and operate with *will* as a modal auxiliary on a par with the other modals. Other writers operate with a polysemous *will*, which only sometimes qualifies as modal. Yet other writers exclude *will* completely from treatments of the semantics of the modal auxiliaries, arguing that the semantics of *will* is essentially non-modal with a few modal-like uses. The radical option of exclusion of *will* on the grounds that it is basically semantically different from the other modal auxiliaries is found in for instance Palmer (1986), Davidsen-Nielsen (1988), Groefsema (1992), Bache and Davidsen-Nielsen (1997) and, most recently, Papafragou (2000).

   In the following I intend to address the question whether the division or exclusion of *will* is really warranted. Does the motivation for division or exclusion follow from the inherent semantics of the modal auxiliaries, or does it follow from the *a priori* definition in (2), which may or may not have anything to do with the semantics of the modal auxiliaries?

2   Morpho-syntax, grammaticalisation and tree climbing

The object of my chapter is the English modal auxiliary lexeme *will*, which has the present tense form *will* and the past tense form *would*. The lexeme also has the enclitic forms *'ll* and *'d*. Etymologically, the modern forms derive from Old English present tense base *will*[-] and past tense base *wolde*[-], which in turn had their roots in shared Germanic forms which seem to cluster around the semantic ground of 'want to', 'desire' and 'intend to'. The cognate modern Danish forms are the infinitive *at ville*, the past participle *villet*, present tense *vil* and past tense *ville* and the cognate modern German forms are the infinitive *zu wollen*, the past participle form *gewollt*, the present tense bases *will*[-] and *woll*[-] and the past tense base *wollt*[-].

   However, although they share common ancestry, the current morpho-syntactic status of the three lexemes is very different. The interesting observation is that in fact in all three languages, the lexemes *will, ville* and *wollen* are glued to the morpho-syntactic characteristics of the other central modal auxiliaries. In the case of modern standard English, the central modal auxiliaries *can, may, must, shall* and *will* exhibit some quite distinct morpho-syntactic features:

(4) English modal auxiliaries:

    (a) have no lexical counterparts, i.e.:
       *He will a lot;

    (b) have no non-finite forms, i.e.:
       *You need to will win.
       *She was in the habit of willing win.
       *She had willed win for a long time;

    (c) cannot be stacked, i.e. ;
       *She will could win;

    (d) do not take person/number agreement, i.e. ;
       *She wills win.

Danish and German modal auxiliaries do not display a similar impressive array of peculiar features. Subject to some distributional constraints, the details of which are irrelevant to our concern here, Danish and German modal auxiliaries have non-auxiliary counterparts, they have non-finite forms, they allow stacking and in German they carry agreement features. If we assume that the pronounced deficiencies of English modal auxiliaries reflect a higher degree of grammaticalisation, we would also expect a concomitant greater level of semantic bleaching. In other words, the standard grammaticalisation argument would be that in English the loss of lexical function has been mirrored by a loss of lexical content.

If we accept the traditional observation that the original Germanic *will*-lexemes clustered around the semantic ground of 'want to', 'desire' and 'intend to', the basic effects of grammaticalisation processes would lead us to predict that modern English *will* is likely to be more abstract relative to the original semantic ground than German *wollen*. And indeed, while English *will* is vague enough to be used both in sentences uttered to convey volition/intention and in sentences uttered to convey simple future-time reference without any hint of volition/intention, German *wollen* retains too much of its lexical content to be used in sentences uttered to convey simple future-time reference. In German the auxiliary *werden* is used for non-volitional future-time reference.

(5) She will leave us. (= intends to or non-volitional future)

(6) (a) *Sie will uns verlassen.* (= intends to)
     (b) *Sie wird uns verlassen.* (= non-volitional future)

So it would appear that English *will* is semantically vaguer and thus more versatile than its German counterpart. Not only does this mean that an adequate framework of English *will* does not necessarily simultanously amount to an adequate framework of German *wollen* or, I will assume, of Danish *ville*, but it also suggests that the semantics of English *will*, like the semantics of all the English modal auxiliaries, has climbed higher up the semantic tree, as it were. English modals are inextricably bound up with tense, indicating that their semantic point of insertion is directly attached to the illocutionary level as a sister of the propositional content.

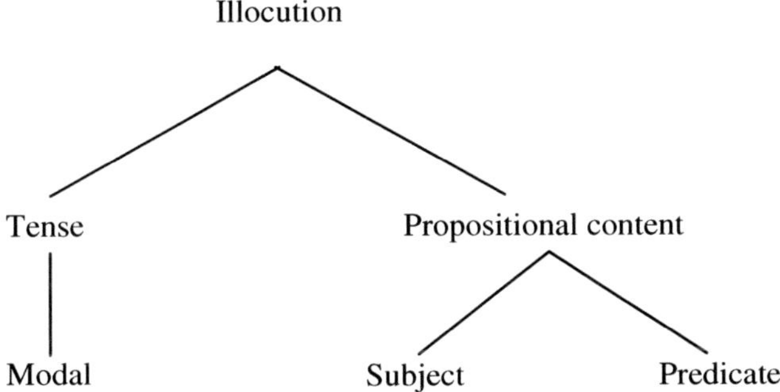

Figure 1: The semantic tree

My point of departure is that English modals plug into a higher operator position and have to be pragmatically interpreted 'down' to affect subject-predicate relations such as volition and ability, a point to which I will return below.

The basic morpho-syntactic fact is that *will* is glued to *can, may* and *must*, sharing all their idiosyncracies as auxiliary verbs. The interesting question is why *will* should have been such a faithful companion in morphology and syntax. Might it not plausibly be the case that *can, may, must* and *will* (and *shall* in the relevant dialects of English) stick together simply because they have a shared semantic *raison d'etre*? Those who treat *will* as semantically detached from the other modal auxiliaries implicitly reject the possibility that it is really semantic coherence which keeps the modal auxiliaries tightly together morphologically and syntactically. In an attempt to reconcile semantic exclusion with morpho-syntactic membership, Harder (1996: 369 and cf. Harder, 1997: 89ff) called *will* 'a squatter in the modal paradigm'. The way I see it the onus of plausible explanation rests *a priori* on the shoulders of the exclusionists. We turn now to the statement of their case.

3   The grounds for exclusion

In traditional literature relying on intuitive paraphrases for the modals the individual modals are inevitably described as polysemic, each conveying at least two or three meanings. So, for instance, writers have argued that *may* conveys meanings such as epistemic possibility, deontic permission, dynamic possibility and benediction (cf. Palmer, 1990 and Coates, 1983). In the context of intuitive polysemic frameworks, *will* takes the prize when it comes to the number of meanings allegedly uncovered. Leech (1997) identifies no less than five discernible meanings, viz. future-time reference, willingness, insistence, intention and predictability, illustrated in (7a) to (e). The number in effect rises to six because characteristic behaviour is given as an independent meaning under predictability, illustrated in (7f). And we might also add another meaning often singled out, viz. order, illustrated in (7g), bringing the total number up to seven.

(7) (a)   Tomorrow's weather will be cold and cloudy. (future time)
    (b)   My chauffeur will help you. (willingness)
    (c)   He ˈwill go swimming in dangerous waters. (insistence)
    (d)   I will write tomorrow. (intention)
    (e)   That will be the milkman. (predictability)
    (f)   He'll go all day without eating. (characteristic behaviour)
    (g)   You will do as I tell you. (order)

While such intuitive renderings are woefully inadequate and quite misleading as representations of the semantics of the lexeme *will*, I will nevertheless assume for now that the sentences illustrate a range of potential utterance meanings to which *will* somehow contributes. It follows that I also assume, for now, that they illustrate a range of potential meanings which any adequate theory of *will* will have to be able to account for at some level of description going from morpheme to utterance processing in context.

As pointed out in the introduction, several of the meanings identified in (7) seem to fall unproblematically under the headings of epistemic, deontic and dynamic modality. The question we need to ask, then, is what it is that motivates some writers to exclude *will* from the other modal auxiliaries. Two related, but independent, arguments are usually appealed to by exclusionist writers (cf. Davidsen-Nielsen, 1988; Palmer, 1990).

(8) (a)   The semantics of *will* basically remains anchored in volition, but has undergone so much semantic bleaching that it may also express volitionless future time;

    (b)   the semantics of *will* basically developed from volition into categorical temporal reference to future time, synchronically yielding a separate non-volitional will with a synchronic prediction sense, which is extended to certain modal uses.

The argument in (8a) puts volition at the centre of *will's* semantics. The three clearly volition-related utterance interpretations are illustrated in (7) (b) *My chauffeur will help you*, (c) *He ¦will go swimming in dangerous waters* and (d) *I will write tomorrow*. A speaker who utters either of the three sentences (b), (c) and (d) would standardly be taken to state the objective facts that the referents of the subjects *my chauffeur*, *he* and *I* are in a given volitional/intentional relation to the situations denoted by the semantics of the predicates *help you, go swimming* and *write*. This means that on the assumption that (7b), (c) and (d) represent core occurrences, *will* fails to meet the criterial speaker subjectivity of modality set out by Palmer in the quotation in (2) above. Thus, on such a conception of modality, *will* is non-modal as a point of departure.

Will shares this fate with *can* to the extent that *can* is taken basically to mean ability, because a speaker who utters a sentence such as *John can speak Italian* (Palmer, 1986: 102) would standardly be taken to state an objective fact that the referent of the subject *John* possesses a given ability relative to the situation denoted by the semantics of the predicate *speak Italian*. In fact, Palmer's (1986: 103) conclusion about *can* meaning ability and *will* meaning volition is that:

(9)   They are subject-oriented in that they are concerned with the ability or
        willingness of the subject, not with the opinion or attitude of the speaker.
        This type can be omitted from the strict typological classification of
        modality, although it is of interest that modal verbs have these meanings.

In effect, Palmer is relegating von Wright's dynamic modality to the realm of the non-modal. So one argument excluding *will*, together with *can*, is that its basic semantics does not meet the speaker subjectivity requirement and, thus, in such a perspective, it is simply not modal.

Another line of argumentation takes its point of departure in the future-time reference in (7a). Some writers argue that future-time reference inherently falls under the heading of epistemic modality (cf. Coates, 1983: 169–83 and Palmer, 1990: 161–3). Lyons (1977: 677) argues that 'futurity is never a purely temporal concept; it necessarily includes an element of prediction or some related modal notion.' However, against this, Davidsen-Nielsen (1988: 6–8 and cf. Bache and Davidsen-Nielsen, 1997: 290–3) argues that statements about the future may indeed have a determinate truth value which may be used to make categorical statements. Thus, an utterance of the sentence *Tomorrow's weather will be cold and cloudy* would be factually binding on the speaker in respect of the weather the day after the utterance is made in precisely the same way that an utterance of *Today's weather is cold and cloudy* would be factually binding on the speaker at the time of utterance. Examples which are clearly epistemically and deontically modal, such as (7e) *That will be the milkman* and (7g) *You will do as I tell you*, are interpreted by Bache and Davidsen-Nielsen (1997: 316–317) as secondary modal uses of the otherwise categorical future tense marker.

Davidsen-Nielsen uses distributional tests to argue that the future tense lexeme *will* is a different lexeme from (dynamic) volitional *will*. First of all, future tense *will* does not occur in conditional subclauses, but volitional *will* does.

(10) (a)   *If he will help me tomorrow, I can finish before Friday. (future tense)
     (b)   If he will help me tomorrow, I can finish before Friday. (volition)

Secondly, according to Davidsen-Nielsen (1988: 11), ambiguity can be shown to be an either-or choice between the two meanings of one form, i.e. formal syncretism.

(11) (a)   He will take care of all the rest. (future tense)
     (b)   He will take care of all the rest. (volition)

Thirdly, according to Davidsen-Nielsen, volitional *will* is highly constrained in (non-negated) passive clauses.

(12) (a)   I will be brought back in disgrace. (future tense)
     (b)   *I will be brought back in disgrace. (volition)

Fourthly, according to Davidsen-Nielsen, future tense *will* is like the other tenses in having secondary modal uses.

(13) (a)   They will be home at this time of day.

While Davidsen-Nielsen (1988: 12–13) concedes that 'from a strictly formal point of view it is impossible to operate with two *will's*, one of which is temporal and the other of which is modal', he argues that one form may turn into two semantically distinct linguistic entities.

I have now introduced and illustrated the two main arguments, i.e. lack of required speaker subjectivity and categorical future-time reference, which are used to stigmatise or exclude *will*. I intend to argue that they are both based on untenable premises and yield unwarranted conclusions.

4   The grounds for inclusion

In order to counter the exclusion arguments I intend to show that the semantics the exclusionists claim for *will* is erroneous and that its semantics is really closely tied to the semantics of the other modals, thus giving weight to the argument that the morpho-syntactic kinship of *will*, *can*, *may* and *must* reflects semantic kinship. This in itself ought to suffice to vindicate the view that *will* is a fully paid-up member of the modal club. Nevertheless, to ensure that my points will not be isolated observations I will also show that subjectivity in the sense in which it is employed by Palmer in (2) above is not a defining feature of the semantics of the modal auxiliaries. And, finally, I will question whether the distributional tests proposed by Davidsen-Nielsen can really be used to show that there are two semantically distinct *will*-forms.

My first purpose is to refute the claim that *will* has a core semantics centering on volition, paraphrasable by for instance *want to*, *willing to* and *intend to*. The preferred utterance interpretations of a couple of minimally opposed sentences containing *will* will cast serious doubt on whether it is reasonable to say that will encodes volition. Consider contexts in which a prize fighter might conceivably utter:

(14) (a)   I will win a stunning victory if I ever fight him again.
    (b)   I will suffer a crushing defeat if I ever fight him again.

In all likelihood we would be happy to interpret the fighter's utterance of (14a) as conveying his intention to knock the stuffing out of his opponent at the next available opportunity. However, I am sure that we would be reluctant to interpret the fighter's utterance of (14b) to convey his intention to be defeated, though of course in a match-rigging context such an interpretation might be fine. Anyone who argues that *will* in (14a) encodes volitional meaning will have to explain why it is most naturally not present in (14b). And anyone, such as myself, who argues that volition is not a synchronic semantic feature of *will* will have to be explicit about where the intentional interpretation of (14a) comes from.

In order to understand why the intentional interpretation applies to (14a) but not to (b), we only need a basic, informal understanding of what intention is. Let us say that we fundamentally see normal human beings as potential agents capable of choosing to bring about new states of affairs in the world, as long as they have the requisite control and are not subject to blocking external constraints. In other words, I postulate that we have, or form, assumptions about our own relation with the world in future time that enable us to plan future activities and actions. And by extension we also make assumptions about other people and their plans for the future. Moreover, in a normal course of events we expect potential agents to choose to bring about new states of affairs that are desirable to them, and only subject to external motivation, e.g. coercion or persuasion, do we expect agents to choose to bring about new states of affairs that are non-desirable, or undesirable, to them. Intention, then, is a planned future activity or action by an agent to bring about a state of affairs that previously had no correlative representation in the assumptions held by the agent about the course of the world. Normal agents only intend to bring about non-desirable states of affairs if they are subject to external motivation.

If we consider the semantics of (14a) and (b), a reasonable rendering would be to say that the speaker encourages the hearer to store a representation of respectively *I win* and *I lose* as representations which do not have verified referential correspondence situations in the world at the time of utterance but which, according to the speaker, will subsequently turn out to have a verified correspondence relation with a referential situation in the world. Assumptions about desirability and internal and external motivation linking the prize fighter to situations where he is a winner or a loser will determine whether we expect him to be an intentional or a non-intentional agent of the situations referred to in (14a) and (b). In other words, the type of context sensitivity involved is a good indication that the intention meaning is a property of utterance interpretation rather than of the semantics of *will*.

I can now expand my critique of the exclusionists' semantic argument. Consider some possible interpretations of utterances of:

(15) (a)   I will help him.
    (b)   You will help him.
    (c)   She will help him.

We would be inclined to infer intention and willingness on the part of the speaker in the case of (a), but in the case of (b), we would not at all be likely to infer that the referent of *you* has any intention or willingness to help. In fact (b) would most likely receive a directive interpretation. In (c) we may either assign intention to the referent of *she* or not, depending clearly on assumptions that are not an encoded part of the sentence uttered. Why should the interpretations in terms of the alleged basic volitional semantics be so unstable? An adequate explanation certainly does not follow in any non-arbitrary way from a theory that postulates a basic volitional meaning for *will*.

Above I argued that semantic bleaching has taken *will* irrevocably out of the subject-predicate relation and into a higher operator position where it is always bound up with tense. The semantic *raison d'être* of the tense category lies in setting up a correspondence relation between the representation derived from a clause and a referential state of affairs. Elsewhere I have suggested that the semantic *raison d'être* of the English modals is to signal that the representation derived from the clause is a representation with non-verified but potential correspondence with a referential state of affairs (see Klinge, 1993). In other words, what *can, may, must, will* and *shall* share semantically is that they signal that there is a potential correspondence relation between the representation derived from a clause and a referential state of affairs in the world. Each modal auxiliary represents a different constellation of potential between representation and referential state of affairs (for details cf. Klinge, 1993). It is only in the instance of utterance that the hearer figures out on the basis of assumptions activated in the context whether the correspondence hinges on:

   i)   Circumstances in the general course of the world;
   ii)   an intentional agent, who may be internally or externally motivated; or,
   iii) whether he is himself the agent being motivated by the very utterance.

So all the modal auxiliaries encode that the correspondence relation is non-verified but potential and the specific place that *will* has carved out for itself is that the correspondence is currently unverified but will turn out to become verified. Only assumptions activated in a given instance of utterance can supply the additional information whether correspondence should be taken to follow as a result of the general course of the world, i.e. prediction and future-type interpretations, or as a result of the activities of an agent, internally or externally motivated, i.e. volition- and directive-type interpretations. If we apply such a semantics to (15a) to (c) in conjunction with the informal definition I gave of intention above we can approximate the preferred interpretations.

In (15a) the speaker presents to the hearer the semantics that the correspondence relation between a representation of the referent of *I* engaged in the activity of helping the referent of *him* is non-verified to the speaker at the time of utterance but turns out to become verified. Seeing that the speaker has inserted a pronoun referring to herself in the subject position and seeing that the subject is interpreted as representing the agent of helping, the hearer can only conclude that the speaker is in conscious control of her own future activities in respect of helping the referent of *him*, so the speaker is taken to be internally motivated. Up to this point an intentional interpretation is clearly warranted. If we further add the specific desirability assumptions activated by the two-place predicate *help* (x, y), we take it that helping is more desirable to the person being helped than to the person helping. Intention to produce an activity in future time which is desirable for someone else without external force amounts to willingness. Note that if we block the assumption of agent control, the intention or willingness interpretations are immediately lost, cf. *I will receive my exam results next week.*

Turning now to (15b), the assumptions activated will turn out to be very different. In (15b) the speaker inserts the hearer as the agent in control of creating the correspondence relation between the representation of the sentence uttered and a referential situation. In effect, the speaker is saying that it turns out to be true that the referent of *you* produces the activity of helping the referent of *him*. The hearer already holds very good assumptions about his own future and his own subsequent planned activities, so if the speaker asks him to store the representation, which to him of course is an *I will help him* representation, he can either store it as information about the general course of the world, which is a bit odd, because in normal circumstances he ought to hold better assumptions about his own future than the speaker, or he can store it as a new assumption where the speaker has inserted him as controlling agent of producing the relevant state of affairs in the world. Such an interpretation amounts to direct motivation through the utterance and has to be backed by some kind of speaker-authority to persuade him to store it as a new assumption about his own future activity. It is interesting and quite revealing, to note that some sets of perception verbs contrast in terms of active perception with inherent agent control as against passive perception with no agent control, such as 'note' vs. 'notice', 'see' vs. 'look at', 'hear' vs. 'listen to', etc. If a speaker combines those verbs that are specified for agent-control with the semantics of *will* and *you* as the subject and thereby the hearer as the underlying agent, she will also automatically interfere with the future activity of the hearer and thus be taken to utter the sentence for directive purposes, which is not the case with the passive perception forms, cf. *You will note the warning on the lid* vs. *You will notice the warning on the lid* and *You will look at me when I am talking to you* vs. *You will see me when I am talking to you*. The assumptions that result in the directive interpretation are triggered by the combination of *you*, *will* and agent-control and a speaker making claims about subsequent correspondence. There is no reason whatsoever to argue that the directive meaning is derived exclusively from the semantics of *will*.

Finally, the interpretation of (15c) sits squarely between a willingness and a simple future-time interpretation, both equally possible. In either case the semantics is the same: there is no verified correspondence between the representation derived from *She will help him* and a referential state of affairs but, according to the speaker, the potential is that correspondence turns out to become verified. However, the hearer has to figure out on the basis of contextual assumptions whether the speaker intends the utterance to be processed and stored as information about the general course of the world, leading to a future-time interpretation, or as information about the referent of *she* as an internally – or possibly externally – motivated agent, leading to a willingness interpretation or, less likely, a directive interpretation.

How is it possible to test my claim that the volitional interpretation does not come from *will* and that the only contribution *will* makes is to convey that the correspondence relation between representation and state of affairs follows subsequently to the utterance? Consider the minimal pairs in (16):

(16) (a)   I want to help him but unfortunately I cannot.
     (b)   I am willing to help him but unfortunately I cannot.
     (c)   *I will help him but unfortunately I cannot.

It is perfectly consistent for the speaker to ask the hearer to process and store a representation of the speaker's intention or willingness to produce a subsequent helping-activity, but that the actual referential helping-activity is unfortunately blocked. It is, however, not consistent to ask the hearer to process and store a representation which the speaker says will subsequently correspond with a referential state of affairs and then to say that that same state of affairs is known by the speaker to be blocked.

On the approach presented, the preferred interpretations rely on assumptions which go far beyond the semantics of *will*. More important to our present purposes, however, are the observations that:

i)   The semantics of *will* is not at all volition, which renders irrelevant exclusion on the grounds that volition is not speaker subjective and thus not a modal concept on Palmer's interpretation;

ii)   the semantics of non-verified but potential correspondence runs through all the modals and *will* fits in snugly; and

iii)   the type of semantics proposed combines smoothly with contextually activated assumptions to produce preferred interpretations. It will even unproblematically account for examples which are more obviously epistemic in a traditional sense, such as (17) below, quoted from Davidsen-Nielsen (1988):

(17)   They will be home this time of day.

Again, the speaker simply presents the representation of *They be home this time of the da*y as not having verified correspondence with the referential state of affairs at the time of utterance but the correspondence is potentially true and the specific potential is that the correspondence turns out to become verified. Assigning only potential correspondence, strong though the potential might be, commits the speaker less than assertion of verified correspondence, so an utterance of *They will be home this time of day* will commit the speaker less than *They are home this time of day*.

Note that the semantics of *will* proposed has absolutely nothing to do with future-time deictic reference, it is only to do with the potential of correspondence between a representation and a referential state of affairs. Whether the state of affairs is located temporally in the past, at the time of utterance or in the future is simply not part of the semantics of *will*. So there is neither anything odd nor any 'secondary usage' in having a referential state of affairs temporally located in past time.

(18)   They will have left yesterday.

Of course it also follows that on the analysis proposed there is no separate *will* which is a grammaticalised deictic marker of future time. Future-time reference follows from the course-of-the-world assumption about verification of correspondence between a representation and a referential state of affairs.

This leaves the question of the distributional evidence presented by Davidsen-Nielsen in favour of two different semantic *wills*. According to Davidsen-Nielsen future *will* does not occur in conditional and temporal subclauses, but 'volitional' *will* does. And 'volitional' *will* is highly constrained in passive clauses. At first blush this seems to be borne out nicely by (10) and (12) above. However, it is doubtful that the acceptability contrasts illustrated may reasonably be used to draw the conclusion that it is two different *wills*, or even two different semantics of *will*, which result in the acceptability involved. Most obviously, if on Davidsen-Nielsen's distributional test in (10) we have to operate with a future-tense *will* contrasting with a non-future-tense *will*, then apparently we find similar acceptability contrasts with other modals.

(19) (a)   *If he {may, must} help me tomorrow, I can finish before Friday.
        (possibility, necessity)
   (b)   If he {may, must} help me tomorrow, I can finish before Friday. (permission, obligation)

It is a well-attested fact that conditional and temporal subclauses do not lend themselves to subjective epistemic interpretation, a fact which also blocks epistemic adverbials, cf. (20).

(20)   *If fortunately he helps me tomorrow, I can finish before Friday.

In other words, the only thing the contrast in (10) shows is that subjective epistemic interpretations of *will* are not available in conditional and temporal subclauses. That it is the epistemic interpretation of *will* which is blocked becomes quite clear in (21).

(21)   *If they will be home this time of the day.

In a similar manner, the distributional test which applies to passive constructions does not really show what Davidsen-Nielsen would like it to show. We have already seen how volitional interpretations depend crucially on assumptions about agents and their relation with subsequent states of affairs. Agents cannot consciously control states of affairs in which they are patients, so it is very difficult to assign the requisite control to the subject of a passive construction that will result in volition-type interpretations. Thus again the most reasonable conclusion is that the volition interpretation is simply not available as an utterance interpretation of *will* in passive constructions.

Obviously, if volition and deictic future-time reference are not meanings encoded in *will* but interpretations derived from utterances of sentences containing *will*, the traditional grounds for exclusion are simply invalid. Nevertheless, the intuition remains that if modality is to do with speaker-subjectivity as suggested by Palmer in (2) above, *will* has a considerable range of contexts in which it does seem to be binding on the speaker in a sense which is more 'objective' and truth-evaluable than *may* and *must*. Of course the intuition only applies in those contexts where *will* is not involved in clearly epistemic and clearly deontic interpretations. This intuition only becomes relevant as a ground for exclusion of *will* from the other modal auxiliaries in so far as we accept speaker-subjectivity as an *a priori* definition of what counts as modality and thus, by extension, what counts as a modal auxiliary. However, we need to bear in mind that the definition we choose for the notion of modality is a matter of consensus (cf. for instance Nuyts, this volume). It does not necessarily reflect the semantics of the modal auxiliaries. And, accordingly, it may be used to exclude *will* from the consensus definition of modality, but it may not necessarily be used to exclude *will* from the other modals.

In actual fact, if speaker-subjectivity in the sense it is traditionally employed is used as a criterion of modality, all the modals may be disqualified in certain contexts. Lyons (1977: 828, cf. Nuyts and Herslund, this volume) introduced the distinction between a deontic utterance which creates a permission or an obligation and a deontic utterance which reports the existence of an obligation. The distinction we have to make is between a deontic performative and a deontic statement. Consider (22):

(22)   You mustn't tell lies.

A speaker may utter (22) in order to impose her will on the hearer by means of the utterance, which would count as a deontic performative, or a speaker may utter (22) in order to say that such are the rules we all have to obey, which would count as a deontic statement. In the deontic performative the obligation is created performatively in making the utterance and so there is no correspondence relation with an already existing situation that may be either true or false. In the deontic statement, however, the speaker reports the existence of an obligation, which gives rise to a correspondence relation which may be either true or false. Deontic statements are simply not modal in the traditional speaker-subjectivity sense. But does *must* mean two different things, one counting as modal, the other counting as non-modal? Of course not. *Must* has exactly the same meaning in both cases. Speaker-subjectivity is simply not encoded in the modal auxiliaries, so it cannot be used as a criterion to exclude *will*, or *can* for that matter, from the other modals.

Moreover, the traditional belief that in central epistemic utterances the speaker is uncommitted to the truth-value of her assertion is strictly speaking also not true. Let us reconsider our point of departure, viz. (1), repeated here for convenience as (23).

(23) (a)   John is in his office.
     (b)   John may be in his office.

In (a) the speaker asserts a verified correspondence relation between the representation the hearer derives from the content of the sentence uttered and the referential state of affairs it is supposed to represent in its instance of utterance. Under normal circumstances the speaker becomes committed to the truth of the unmodified correspondence relation and the hearer, in so far as he has no reason to doubt the quality of the speaker's background information, will process and store the representation as a verified and thus true representation of the referential state of affairs.

In (b) a modal auxiliary has been inserted, which makes the correspondence relation potential – in this case undecided between whether it turns out to be the case that there is a referential state of affairs where the referent of *John* is in his office or not. Under normal circumstances the speaker does not become committed to the truth of the correspondence relation and thus she does not become committed to a referential state of affairs where the referent of *John* is in the location *in his office*, but she does become committed to the potential asserted in respect of the correspondence relation. (23b) may actually either receive an epistemic or a deontic interpretation in different contexts depending on the assumptions activated, but note that in either case the speaker is in fact bound by her assertion of the potential: if the utterance receives an epistemic-type interpretation, the speaker is held to believe that the state of affairs is in fact possible; and if the utterance receives a deontic-type interpretation, the speaker will be bound to accept it both if the referent of *John* actually chooses to occupy *his office* and if he chooses not to. All that has happened between (23a) and (b) is that the locus of assertion has moved from the semantics of tense alone to the semantics of a tensed modal auxiliary. The basic semantic facts are of course precisely the same in sentences containing *will*. The only difference is that the specific potential which the speaker asserts is that the correspondence relation actually turns out to become verified, such as in (24a) and (b).

(24) (a)   John will be in his office tomorrow.
    (b)   John will have been in his office yesterday.

The difference between (a) and (b) lies primarily in the best quality of information that is available about the world at past time relative to the time of utterance and about the world at future time relative to the time of utterance. The world at past time is in principle accessible, so a speaker may have verified information, which may in the best of situations be conveyed by unmodalised utterances. So (b) will be taken to signal good, but less than perfect, access to the relevant information of the whereabouts of the referent of *John* on the day prior to the utterance. (a) on the other hand will be taken to signal that the speaker has as good information as it normally gets about future time about the whereabouts of the referent of *John* on the day following the utterance.

5 Conclusion

I set out to address the question whether there are sound reasons to exclude *will* from the semantics of the other modals on the grounds that *will* is not modal, or, alternatively, to split it into two *wills*, one modal, one non-modal. The morpho-syntactic case is clear, *will* shares all the idiosyncratic features of the other central modal auxiliaries. Exclusion and division has to rely on synchronic semantic arguments. The exclusionist arguments take speaker-subjectivity as the crucial feature of modality and since they simultaneously maintain that the semantics of *will* is centrally volitional or temporally deictic, they also inevitably reach the conclusion that *will* is not modal and thus, it is argued, semantically fundamentally different from the 'real' modal auxiliaries.

Against the exclusionist stand I argued that, first of all, meanings such as 'volition' and 'future-time reference' are not lexico-semantic meanings encoded in *will*. They arise as a result of interpretation of utterances of sentences containing will against assumptions activated in the instance of utterance. I proposed some pertinent assumptions to account for the context sensitivity of sentences containing *will*. A much fuller account of the way assumptions may determine interpretation can be found in a relevance-theoretic framework in Groefsema (1995) and Papafragou (2000), neither of whom, however, treats *will* as a member of the class of modal auxiliaries. An approach based on context sensitivity also gives a very different interpretation of the distributional tests used by Davidsen-Nielsen to identify two different semantic entities expressed by *will*. Different sentence-semantic environments tend to activate different types of assumptions which make the sentences conducive to given types of preferred interpretations.

As far as I am concerned, speaker-subjectivity is a false start in any investigation which claims to deal with the semantics of the modal auxiliaries in general. Both in terms of its morpho-syntax and in terms of its semantics *will* is a central modal auxiliary. Like the other English central modal auxiliaries, *will* operates on the correspondence relation created by tense, which the modal auxiliaries turn into a potential correspondence relation. *Will* signals that the correspondence relation turns out to become verified. The same semantics applies irrespective of whether the overall interpretation of an utterance of a sentence containing *will* is epistemic, deontic or dynamic in traditional modality terms. Whether a given utterance receives an epistemic, deontic or dynamic interpretation depends on the assumptions brought to bear on it (for the contours of an assumption-based framework see Papafragou, 2000).

My overall conclusion has to be that the idiosyncratic morpho-syntax which is shared by the modals reflects the semantics shared by the modals. So any theory that claims to deal with the semantics and pragmatics of the English modal auxiliaries is forced also to include *will*. Because where there is a *will*, there is indeed a modal.

Acknowledgements

I would like to thank Martin Aitken, Niels Davidsen-Nielsen and Henrik Høeg Müller for valuable discussions and constructive criticism of this article.

References

Bache, C. and Davidsen-Nielsen, N. (1997) *Mastering English. An Advanced Grammar for Non-Native and Native Speakers*. Berlin and New York: Mouton de Gruyter.

Coates, J. (1983) *The Semantics of the Modal Auxiliaries*. London and Canberra: Croom Helm.

Davidsen-Nielsen, N. (1988) Has English a future? Remarks on the future tense. *Acta Linguistica Hafniensia* 21: 5–20.

Durst-Andersen, P. (1992) *Mental Grammar. Russian Aspect and Related Issues*. Columbus Ohio: Slavica Publishers.

Durst-Andersen, P. (1995) Imperative frames and modality. *Linguistics and Philosophy* 18: 611–53.

Frawley, W. (1992) *Linguistic Semantics*. New Jersey and London: Lawrence Erlbaum.

Groefsema, M. (1995) Can, may, must and should: A relevance theoretic account. *Journal of Linguistics* 31: 53–79.

Harder, P. (1996) Functional semantics. A theory of meaning, structure and tense in English. Berlin and New York: Mouton de Gruyter.

Harder, P. (1997) Futurity in English: a case for a messy structure. In *Sounds, Structures and Senses. Essays Presented to Niels Davidsen-Nielsen on the Occasion of his Sixtieth Birthday*. C. Bache and A. Klinge (eds) Odense: Odense University Press.

Klinge, A. (1993) The English modal auxiliaries. From lexical semantics to utterance interpretation. *Journal of Linguistics* 29: 315–57.

Leech, G. (1997) *Meaning and the English Verb*. Second edition. London: Longman.

Palmer, F. (1986) *Mood and Modality*. Cambridge: University of Cambridge University Press.

Palmer, F. (1990) *Modality and the English Modals*. Second edition. London and New York: Longman.

Papafragou, A. (2000) *Modality: issues in the semantics-pragmatics interface*. Oxford: Elsevier Science.

von Wright, G. (1951) *An Essay in Modal Logic*. Amsterdam: North Holland.

9 The syntagmatic and paradigmatic patterning of modality in modern German

John Ole Askedal

1 Preliminaries

German modals have been extensively studied from a grammatical, logical, semantic and also from a pragmatic point of view. The present contribution is devoted to modality as a grammatical predicate category, in particular the syntagmatic and paradigmatic patterning of modal constructions in modern German with a view to the grammaticalisation of semantic scope relations. I shall argue that semantic scope and linearity are not wholly isomorphic but that there is evidence for diachronic developments towards semantically more 'natural' linearization.

The modal constructions in question consist of a superordinate, 'governing' (cf. Bech, 1955: 25f.) and a subordinate, 'governed' verb. The governing verbs we shall be dealing with are, first, the six traditional modals *dürfen* 'may, be allowed to', *können* 'can', *mögen* 'may, want, like', *müssen* 'must', *sollen* 'shall' and *wollen* 'will' and, second, certain specific uses of *werden* 'become', *sein* 'be', *haben* 'have', *brauchen* 'need', *scheinen* 'seem', *drohen* 'threaten', *versprechen* 'promise' and a few other verbs with similar semantic and syntactic properties. The latter verbs are often called 'modality verbs' (*Modalitätsverben*) to distinguish them from the six core modals. The main emphasis of the discussion is not, however, on the individual constructions consisting of one governing and one governed verb, but on the syntagmatic interplay of different modal, auxiliary and non-auxiliary constructions in the formation of 'verb chains' (Bech, 1955: 25–30) with a complex hierarchical scope structure. Consider for instance the examples (1a) to (c)[1]:

(1) (a) *Er hat[1] das nicht tun[3] können[2].*
      (perfect of the deontic modal *können* governing the infinitive of a lexical verb)
      He has not been able to do that.

   (b) *Er soll[1] das getan[3] haben[2].*
      (so-called 'perfect infinitive', consisting of the infinitive of the perfect
      auxiliary and the past participle and here depending on the superordinate
      epistemic, *in casu* reportive modal *sollen*)
      He is said to have done that.

   (c) *Er soll[1] das nicht haben[2] tun[4] können[3].*
      (epistemic, reportive modal *sollen* superordinate to the so-called
      'perfect infinitive' of the deontic modal *können* governing the infinitive
      of a lexical verb)
      He is said not to have been able to do that.

In what follows, I shall be concerned with the complex question which verbs may combine in verb chains such as those in (1) and to what extent their linear order concurs with semantic scope relations and what kinds of modal meaning turn up in which positions in verb chains.

Concerning linearity, I adhere to the view that German is basically a verb-final language, i.e., I consider the subordinate clause verb order with the finite verb in final position to be typologically and structurally basic (cf. e.g. Eisenberg, 1995: 381f.; Zifonun et al., 1997: 1498). According to this view, V/2 and V/1 in main clauses are structurally secondary pragmatical markers of main illocutionary functions (basically assertion vs. question). With regard to the semantics of modal verbs and constructions, I shall in the main rely on the by now traditional distinction between deontic ('objective') and epistemic ('subjective') meaning which has for some decades played a prominent part, in one way or other, in most discussions of modality in German (cf. for instance Diewald, 1997: 24ff.; 1999b: 119 et passim) and which is also dealt with in a number of other contributions to this volume (Nuyts, Boye, Herslund, Heltoft). The descriptive and heuristic importance of this distinction lies in its interrelations with differences of syntactic behaviour.

Grammaticalisation enters into the picture insofar as the traditional modals are often conceived of as 'auxiliaries', i.e. verbs with some 'grammatical' function and, concomitantly, specific properties differing from those of common lexical verbs. In this context, the so-called 'modality verbs' mentioned above (e.g. *brauchen, scheinen, drohen* and *versprechen*) are of special interest. There is also the general question of the relation between semantic scope and degree of grammaticalisation, more specifically, whether more grammaticalised verbs have in general broader scope than less grammaticalised verbs. This question is of basic importance in connection with the grammatical productivity of 'notional' categories like modality, temporality and actionality and of specific subcategories like 'deonticity', 'epistemicity' and 'perfect' within the broader categories of modality and temporality. The syntactic active/passive distinction is also relevant in this context.

2   Combinatorial regularities and scope relations

The order of lexicalised semantic predicates is not random. Combinations of higher and lower predicates are formed according to strict rules which define hierarchical syntactic dependency and semantic scope structures[2].

2.1   Maximally superordinate epistemic verbs

Certain verbs governing another, non-finite verb cannot stand in the scope of any other verb-governing verb, which results in the non-occurrence of the infinitive or past participle of these verbs as governed forms. This means that the verbs in question lack periphrastic forms, in particular, they have no perfect (cf. e.g. Hauser-Suida and Hoppe-Beugel, 1972: 71–6) and no future formation with *werden*, cf. for instance (2) to (7):

(2) (a) *Er wird kommen.*
     He'll come.

     (b) **Sie lassen ihn kommen werden.*
          (no embedded infinitive of infinitive-governing *werden*, i.e. no future infinitive)
          They let him be going to come.

(3) (a) *Er mag krank gewesen sein.*
          (epistemic modal *mögen* governing the perfect infinitive of the copular verb *sein*)
          He may have been ill.

     (b) **Er hat krank gewesen sein mögen.*
          (no perfect)
          He has appeared to have been ill.

     (c) **Er wird krank sein mögen.*
          (no future tense with *werden*)
          He is going to appear to be ill.

(4) (a) *Er scheint sich heute gut zu betragen.*
         (modal *scheinen* with the infinitive with the particle *zu*, henceforth:
         zu-infinitive)
         He seems to behave properly today.

     (b) **Er hat sich heute gut zu betragen geschienen.*
          (no perfect)
          He has seemed to behave properly today.

     (c) **Er wird sich heute gut zu betragen scheinen.*
          (no future tense with *werden*)
          He is going to seem to behave properly today.

     (d) **Man forderte ihn auf, sich heute gut zu betragen zu scheinen.*
          (no subordination of infinitive-governing *scheinen* to another verb)
          They admonished him to seem to behave properly today.

(5) (a) *Die Brücke drohte einzustürzen.*
          The bridge threatened to collapse.

     (b) **Die Brücke hat einzustürzen gedroht.*
          (no perfect)
          The bridge has threatened to collapse.

     (c) **Die Brücke wird einzustürzen drohen.* (no future tense with *werden*)
          The bridge is going to threaten to collapse.

(6) (a) *Der neue Forschungsassistent verspricht sich gut zu entwickeln.*
          (modal *versprechen* with the *zu*-infinitive)
          The new research assistant promises to develop well.

     (b) **Vom neuen Forschungsassistenten wird sich gut zu entwickeln versprochen.*
          (no passive in the modal sense intended)
          It is promised by the new research assistant to develop well.

(7) (a) *Er pflegt seinen alten Vater alle vierzehn Tage zu besuchen.*
          (actional iterative *pflegen* with the *zu*-infinitive)
          He usually visits his old father every fortnight.

     (b) **Er bemüht sich, seinen alten Vater alle vierzehn Tage zu besuchen zu
          pflegen.*
          (no subordination of infinitive-governing *pflegen* to another verb)
          He strives to use to visit his old father every fortnight.

Nor can the verbs in question be subordinated to each other, cf. e.g. (8) to (9):

(8) (a) *Er mag das nicht verstanden haben.*
          He may not have understood that.

     (b) *Er scheint das nicht verstanden zu haben.*
          He seems not to have understood that.

     (c) **Er mag das nicht verstanden zu haben scheinen.*
          He may seem not to have understood that.

     (d) **Er scheint das nicht verstanden haben zu mögen.*
          He seems not to have appeared to have understood that.

(9) (a) *Das Haus wird bestimmt einstürzen.*
          The house is certainly going to collapse.

     (b) *Das Haus droht einzustürzen.*
          The house threatens (i.e. appears to be about) to collapse.

     (c) **Das Haus wird einzustürzen drohen.*
               (no future tense of *drohen* 'threaten' in the sense of (9b))
          The house is going to threaten to collapse.

     (d) **Das Haus droht einstürzen zu werden.*
               (cf. the general lack of a 'future infinitive')
          The house threatens to be going to collapse.

What these verbs have in common is modal epistemicity (or some related
semantic category like evidentiality or the like) as expressed by the six traditional modals like *mögen* in (8a). The question of the distinguishability or non-
distinguishability of future and epistemic modal *werden* has been a recurrent
theme in the literature (cf. Saltveit, 1969; Vater, 1975). The epistemic nature of
the use of *scheinen*, *drohen* and *versprechen* in cases like (4a), (5a), (6a), (8b),
(9b) is hardly in doubt (cf. e.g. Askedal, 1997; 1998a; Diewald, 2000). From a
semantic and syntactic point of view, all these verbs form a natural paradigmatic
class of maximally governing elements in German verb chains.

2.2   Periphrastic perfect

Auxiliaries and infinitive-governing verbs not belonging to the paradigmatic
class dealt with in Section 2.1 generally allow for the formation of a periphrastic
perfect[3]. Cf. for instance the perfect constructions in the sentences in (10):

(10) (a)   *Er hat gut arbeiten können.*
      (perfect of deontic modal)
      He has been able to work well.

  (b)   *Er ist geschlagen worden.*
      (perfect of the *werden* passive)
      He has been beaten.

  (c)   *Man hat ihn laufen lassen/(ge)sehen.*
      (perfect of Accusativus Cum Infinitivo (hereafter ACI) construction with
      lassen 'make, let' or perception verbs like *sehen* 'see' with the infinitive)
      They have let/seen him run.

  (d)   *Er hat zu gehorchen gehabt.*
      (perfect of *haben* 'have' in a construction with the *zu*-infinitive having
      necessive modal meaning)
      He has had to obey.

  (e)   *Viele Arbeiten waren noch zu erledigen gewesen.*
      (perfect of *sein* 'be' in a passive construction with the *zu*-infinitive having
      necessive modal meaning)
      A lot of work had still had to be done.

  (f)   *Sie hat ihn aufgefordert, mehr und besser zu arbeiten.*
      She has encouraged him to work more and better.
      (perfect of lexical verb governing the *zu*-infinitive)

Inversely, the perfect infinitive cannot be subordinated to ACI verbs, cf. (11):

(11) (a)   *Das Kind hatte ein Eis gekauft.*
      The child had bought an ice cream.

  (b)   **Sie sah/hörte/ließ das Kind ein Eis gekauft haben.*

2.3   Deontic modal verbs

Deontic modals may have in their scope the passive (12a), ACI verbs (12b) and infinitive-governing lexical verbs (12c), cf.:

(12) (a)   *Das Haus soll jetzt verkauft werden.*
      The house is now to be sold.

  (b)   *Sie können ihn gehen lassen.*
      They can let him go.

  (c)   *Sie will die Kollegen auffordern, mehr und besser zu arbeiten.*
      She will encourage her colleagues to work more and better.

On the other hand, the subordination of deontic modals to other verbs is subject to a number of restrictions. Modals cannot be governed by ACI verbs, cf. (13):

(13)   *Sie sah/hörte das Kind ein Eis kaufen dürfen.
         She saw/heard the child being allowed to buy an ice cream.

Nor can deontic modals be passivised, cf. (14):

(14)   *Schwimmen wird von ihr gekonnt.
         To swim is being mastered by her.

(Nicht) brauchen '(not) need to', wissen 'be able to' and haben 'have to' behave similarly in both respects, cf. (15) to (17):

(15) (a) Er braucht kein zweites Lied zu singen.
          He need not sing another song.

     (b) *Sie hörte ihn kein zweites Lied zu singen brauchen.
          (no subordination to ACI verbs)
          She heard him not need to sing another song.

     (c) *Ein zweites Lied zu singen wird von ihm nicht gebraucht.
          (no passive)
          To sing another song is not needed by him.

(16) (a) Er weiß mit solchen Leuten gut umzugehen.
          He knows how to deal with such people.

     (b) *Man sieht ihn mit solchen Leuten gut umzugehen wissen.
          (no subordination to ACI verbs)
          One sees him not to know how to deal with such people.

     (c) *Von ihm wird mit solchen Leuten gut umzugehen gewußt.
          (no passive)
          It is not known by him how to deal with such people.

(17) (a) Er hat mit schwierigen Leuten umzugehen.
          He has to deal with difficult people.

     (b) *Man sieht ihn mit schwierigen Leuten umzugehen haben.
          (no subordination to ACI verbs)
          One sees him have to deal with difficult people.

     (c) *Von ihm wird mit schwierigen Leuten umzugehen gehabt.
          (no passive)
          It is had by him to deal with difficult people.

(8a) is an example of the subordination of the perfect infinitive to an epistemic modal. This construction is typical of epistemicity, but to a certain extent deontic modals occur in the same superordinate position in relation to the perfect infinitive when the tense meaning of the entire construction is parallel to the corresponding use of *werden* with the perfect infinitive denoting a completed future action, cf. (18):

(18) (a) *Er muß/wird das Buch bis Dienstag gelesen haben.*
　　　　 He must/will have read this book by Tuesday.

On the other hand, the ordinary perfect of a modal with the 'substitute' infinitive is hardly amenable to a future interpretation but rather restricted to past time reference, cf. e.g. (18b) (quoted from Diewald, 1998: 28, who does not, however, comment on the tense meaning of this example):

(18) (b) *Er hat das Buch bis Dienstag lesen müssen.*
　　　　 He had to read the book by Tuesday [last].

2.4　ACI verbs and passive auxiliaries

ACI verbs and passive auxiliaries govern lexical verbs, including infinitive-governing lexical verbs, cf. (19):

(19) (a) *Sie sahen ihn sich bemühen, mehr und besser zu arbeiten.*
　　　　 They saw him trying to work more and better.

　　 (b) *Er wurde aufgefordert, sich zu bemühen, mehr und besser zu arbeiten.*
　　　　 He was encouraged to try to work more and better.

Passive and ACI construction are in general mutually exclusive (Zifonun et al., 1997: 1418, 1801), cf. (20):

(20) (a) **Er wurde davon laufen gehört.*
　　　　 He was heard running away.

　　 (b) **Man sah ihn geprügelt werden.*
　　　　 They saw him being beaten.

　　 (c) **Er wurde geprügelt werden gesehen.*
　　　　 He was seen being beaten.

The passive auxiliary and the ACI verbs thus belong to the same paradigmatic category. In this connection, mention has to be made of two further facts of German grammar. First, the ACI verb *lassen* 'make, let', and to a certain extent even other ACI verbs, occur with an infinitive which is construed passively despite the lack of passive morphology (Zifonun et al., 1997: 1415), cf. e.g. (21) (quoted from Zifonun et al., 1997: 1415f.):

(21) (a) *Lang läßt ihn von einem jungen Mann spielen, der nicht älter ist als Karlos.*
Lang allows him to be played by a young man who is not older than Karlos.

   (b) *Ich habe läuten hören.*
I have heard bells ringing.

Second, the ACI verb *lassen* 'make, let' (but not the subclass of perception verbs of the ACI verbs) is used reflexively with the syntactic alignment and periphrastic tense formation properties of a regular passive auxiliary, cf. (22):

(22) (a) *Der schwere Tisch läßt sich nicht von der Stelle bewegen.*
The heavy table cannot be moved from its position.

   (b) *Der schwere Tisch hat sich nicht von der Stelle bewegen lassen.* (perfect)
The heavy table could not be moved from its position.

   (c) *Der schwere Tisch wird sich nicht von der Stelle bewegen lassen.*
       (*werden* future)
It is not going to be possible to move the heavy table from its position.

The subordination of this *sich lassen* passive to an ACI verb is at best dubious, cf. (22d):

(22) (d) ?**Man sah den schweren Tisch sich von der Stelle bewegen lassen.*
They saw the heavy table being capable of being moved from its position.

On account of its syntactic and semantic properties, *sein* with the *zu*-infinitive is naturally seen as a member of the same paradigm, cf. (23):

(23) (a) *Die Probleme sind nicht zu lösen gewesen.*
       (perfect)
The problems have not been possible to solve.

   (b) *Die Probleme werden sofort zu lösen sein.*
       (*werden* future)
The problems will be possible to solve.

   (c) **Man sah die Probleme nicht zu lösen sein.*
       (no subordination to ACI verbs)
They saw the problems not being capable of being solved.

The periphrastic perfect (23a) and future (23b) are both possible, but subordination to an ACI verb is straightforwardly excluded (23c). Equally impossible is the subordination to a (deontic) modal or to the corresponding necessive non-passive construction with *haben* and the *zu*-infinitive, cf. (24a) to (b):

(24) (a)   *Das Problem darf zu lösen sein.
           It is allowed that the problem is possible to solve.

     (b)   *Die Arbeit hatte zu erledigen zu sein.
           The work had to be possible to solve.

The restrictions applying in (24) are hardly explainable by scope restrictions but rather have to do with the modal semantics of the *sein* and *haben* constructions in question.

2.5   Infinitive-governing lexical verbs

In addition to the infinitive-governing predicates described so far, there exist a great number of purely lexical verbs governing the infinitive. Such verbs trigger a new 'cycle' when they themselves govern a verb belonging to one of the groups described in 2.2–2.4, cf. (25), or another infinitive-governing lexical verb, cf. (26), which shows a combination of both options:

(25) (a)   *Er meint das Buch mal gelesen zu haben.*
               (lexical verb *meinen* with the perfect infinitive)
           He thinks he has at some point read the book.

     (b)   *Die Mannschaft befürchtet, das nächste Mal besiegt zu werden.*
               (lexical verb *befürchten* with the passive infinitive)
           The team fears that it is going to be defeated the next time.

     (c)   *Sie glaubt, noch immer ein bißchen Polnisch sprechen zu können.*
               (lexical verb *glauben* governing the infinitive-governing modal *können*)
           She believes she can still speak a bit of Polish.

(26)   *Sie haben ihn gebeten, die Kollegen auffordern zu wollen, sich von seinem
               Beispiel inspirieren zu lassen, etwas mehr und besser zu arbeiten.*
           They have asked him to be willing to encourage the colleagues to be inspired
               by his example to work more and better.

3   Categorial positions and scope relations in German verb chains

The combinatorial regularities described in the preceding Section 2 and the scope relations deriving from them, are summarised in the chart in (27), which is based on Verb/Last as the basic verb position in German (Zifonun et al., 1997: 1498)[4]:

(27)　　Categorial positions

CP6	CP5	CP4	CP3	CP2	CP1	CP0
						finite morpheme: pres. ind. pret. ind. pres. subj. pret. subj. (imperative)
					future *werden* epistemic modals deontic modals modal *scheinen* modal *drohen* modal *versprechen* actional *pflegen*	
				perfect		
			deontic modals modal *brauchen* modal *wissen* modal *haben*			
		passive *werden* *(sich) lassen* *sehen, hören…* modal-passive *sein*				
	infinitive-governing lexical verb					
governed non-finite verb						

The chart in (27) amounts to a left-branching formula for the morphosyntactic constitution of modern German verb chains comprising two or more verb forms and the semantico-syntactic hierarchy of scope relations associated therewith. It thus provides a general description of grammaticalised scope relations in German verb chains consisting of governed and governing verbal predicates.

It should be noted that the linear order inherent in (27) is not in every detail identical with actualised linear order in spoken or written chains. It does not take into account V/2 and V/1 in main clauses or the preposing of the auxiliary *haben* in certain verb-final chains (cf. e.g. (1c)), nor does it take into consideration the possibility of extraposing a *zu*-infinitive governed by a lexical verb (cf. e.g. (26))[5].

3.1   Functional content and topological properties of the categorial positions

The matrix in (28) shows the distribution of content categories over categorial positions:

(28)   Content categories and categorial positions

	0	1	2	3	4
tense	+	+	+		
epistemic modality		+			
actionality		+			
deontic modality		+		+	+
passive					+
causativity					+

Tense appears in CP0 as finite present and past endings, in CP1 it is represented by the future auxiliary *werden* and in CP2 by the perfect auxiliaries *haben* and *sein*. Epistemic modality is restricted to the superordinate CP1. The core domain of deontic modality is CP3. In addition, deontic modality is an option even in CP1 as a paradigmatic alternative to *werden* with the perfect infinitive. In CP4, deontic modality is parasitic on the passive in the sense that CP4 comprises passive constructions without as well as with modal meaning (*werden* with the passive participle on the one hand, *sich lassen* with the bare infinitive and *sein* with the *zu*-infinitive on the other), but no modal constructions which are not also passive. Finally, causativity, which has grammaticalised means of expression in a great many languages, is represented by *lassen* in CP4.

A fair number, but not all of the predicates in CP1-CP4 in (27) and (28) are traditionally considered to be auxiliaries. The traditional auxiliaries are:

werden as a future (CP1) and a passive (CP4) marker, *haben* and *sein* in the perfect (CP2) and even the modals in their deontic (CP3) and epistemic (CP1) functions. On the other hand, causative-permissive *lassen* 'make, let' and the perception verbs *sehen, hören* etc. in CP4 are semantic predicates which are not in general categorised as auxiliaries in German (or in the other Germanic languages), although they belong to the same CP as the passive auxiliary. In this sense, CP4 constitutes a transitional paradigm between CP1-CP3 as auxiliary paradigms on the one hand and the infinitive-governing lexical verbs in non-auxiliary CP5 on the other.

CP1-CP4 on the one hand and CP5 on the other differ with regard to the distributional properties of the governed non-finite verb form. Non-finite forms governed by verbs belonging to CP1-CP4 cannot be extraposed, i.e. they are part of so-called 'coherent' (Bech, 1955) or 'enclosed' (Folsom, 1966) verb constructions (Askedal, 1989: 3–5, 105), cf. for instance (29)[6]:

(29) (a) *weil er krank zu sein scheint* (CP1). →*weil er scheint, krank zu sein.*
   because he seems to be ill.

 (b) *weil er sehr hart gearbeitet hat* (CP2). → *weil er hat, sehr hart gearbeitet.*
   because he has been working very hard.

 (c) *weil er nicht mehr so viel arbeiten kann* (CP3). → *weil er nicht mehr kann, hart (zu) arbeiten.*
   because he cannot work so hard any more.

 (d) *weil er mit den Leuten gut umzugehen wußte* (CP3). → *weil er wußte, mit den Leuten gut umzugehen.*
   because he knew how to deal with the people.

 (e) *weil er sofort mit der Peitsche geschlagen wurde* (CP4). → *weil er sofort wurde, mit der Peitsche geschlagen.*
   because he was instantly beaten with the whip.

 (f) *weil sie ihn nach zwei Wochen Haft wieder laufen ließen* (CP4). → *weil sie ihn nach zwei Wochen Haft ließen, wieder (zu) laufen.*
   because they let him go again after two weeks of detention.

Extraposability ('non-coherent, unenclosed construction') is a property of infinitives with *zu* governed by verbs belonging to CP5, cf. for instance (30):

(30) *weil er das Buch nicht mehr zu lesen beabsichtigt* (CP5). → *weil er nicht mehr beabsichtigt, das Buch zu lesen.*
   because he does not intend to read that book any more.

The general morphosyntactic rule is that a governed past participle or infinitive without *zu* cannot be extraposed; only the *zu*-infinitive allows for extraposition (the 'coherence rule' 'Kohärenzregel' of Bech, 1955: 68). In other words, all verbs traditionally considered to be grammaticalised auxiliaries in German govern a non-extraposable non-finite verb form, but not all verb constructions showing this topological restriction contain a traditional auxiliary.

3.2   Recursiveness within categorial paradigms

In Section 2.1, it was shown that the verbs belonging to CP1 cannot combine with each other and this was indeed put forward as a reason for assuming that these verbs form a paradigm. However, recursiveness within paradigms is to a certain extent possible on lower CP levels. In this connection, recursiveness means that two (or in theory perhaps even more) predicates belonging to the same CP may be combined within that CP, without any predicate belonging to another CP intervening between the two (or more) predicates.

A case in point is *haben* as a perfect auxiliary belonging to CP2. In South German dialects with loss of simple past tense forms ('Präteritumschwund'; cf. Lindgren, 1957), recursiveness is fully grammaticalised as a means of forming new periphrastic pluperfects with one finite and one non-finite occurrence of *haben*[7]. Cf. (31):

(31)   *Er hat schon die Mauer ausgebessert gehabt, als…*
        He had already repaired the wall when…

In CP3, recursiveness is to a limited extent possible with core modals, cf. (32):

(32) (a) *Petra will die Kinder fotografieren können.*
          Petra wishes to be able to photograph the children.

   (b) *Man muß ja nicht unbedingt zwanzig Sprachen sprechen können.*
        It's not absolutely necessary to be able to speak twenty languages.

   (c) *Er soll nach Hause fahren dürfen – das will ich ja!*
        He has to be permitted to go home – that is what I want!

(Nicht) brauchen also partakes of this recursiveness, cf. (33):

(33)   *Man braucht ja nicht unbedingt zwanzig Sprachen sprechen zu können.*
        One need not be able to speak twenty languages.

Wissen with the *zu*-infinitive is probably not totally ruled out either, cf. (34):

(34)   *Er soll mit solchen Leuten umzugehen wissen. (Sonst kann er sich einen
          anderen Job suchen.)*
        He has to know how to deal with those kind of people. (If not, he can go
          looking for work elsewhere.)

Haben with the *zu*-infinitive does not appear to possess the potential for the
kind of recursiveness illustrated in (32) to (34), cf. (35):

(35)   **Er darf zu gehorchen haben.*
        He is allowed to have to obey.

This perhaps indicates that *haben* with the *zu*-infinitive is less integrated into
the paradigm of deontic modals than *brauchen* and *wissen*.
     CP4 is constituted by the impossibility of combining the passive auxiliary
and ACI verbs. Whether recursiveness is to be assumed in the group of ACI
verbs depends on how one rates the grammaticality of sentences like those in
(36), which are, to say the least, uncommon in actual usage:

(36) (a) *Die Mutter ließ das Kind den Vater eine Violinsonate von Beethoven spielen
             hören.*
          The mother allowed the child to listen to the father playing a violin sonata
             by Beethoven.

     (b) *weil die Mutter das Kind den Vater eine Violinsonate von Beethoven spielen
             hören ließ.*
          because the mother allowed the child to listen to the father playing a violin
             sonata by Beethoven.

Lexical infinitive-governing verbs of CP5 combine freely within the limits of
semantic compatibility and pragmatic comprehensibility, cf. (37):

(37)   *Man hat ihn aufgefordert, die Kollegen zu bitten, sich nun endlich darum zu
          kümmern, das Projekt zu Ende zu führen.*
        They urged him to ask the colleagues to finally see to the completion of the
          project.

In such cases, a new 'verb-chain cycle' is in fact triggered (cf. also (26)). It
is therefore not natural to describe combinations of this kind as instances of
CP-internal recursiveness.
     On the whole, recursiveness within CPs is a fairly marginal phenomenon.
It does not occur on the highest CP level (CP1), but only on lower CP levels
and, in the standard language, it is more likely to be met with in CP3 than in
CP2 or CP4.

4   Perspectives on grammaticalisation

As indicated earlier, the fact that there are several CPs and several predicates belonging to each CP prompts the question whether there are grammaticalisation differences to be observed between and within CPs. In particular, it has been noted that several CPs comprise traditional auxiliaries but also other predicates which are not traditionally considered to be auxiliaries.

4.1   Grammaticalisation differences within and between categorial positions

First, one may ask whether a CP is homogeneous with regard to grammaticalisation, i.e. whether all members of the CP in question have reached the same level of grammaticalisation. This is clearly not in general the case.

Within CP1, *werden* and the epistemic modals are clearly more grammaticalised than the verbs governing the *zu*-infinitive. With regard to valency, *scheinen* still governs an optional dative object, whereas regular auxiliaries are as a rule valency-neutral, cf. (38):

(38)   *Er schien (ihnen) zufrieden zu sein.*
        (To them) he seemed to be content.

On the other hand, if general combinability with lexical verbs in the active and the passive is considered a criterion of (full) grammaticalisation, *scheinen* is more grammaticalised than either *drohen* or *versprechen*, cf. first (39) ((39b) is quoted from Gunkel, 2000: 114):

(39) (a)   *weil wieder gestreikt zu werden scheint.*
            There seems to be a strike again.

     (b)   *??... weil wieder gestreikt zu werden droht.*
            There is a strike threatening again.

Concerning *drohen* and *versprechen*, I have argued elsewhere that the former verb is more highly grammaticalised than the latter in the modal, epistemic use (Askedal, 1997), cf. e.g. (40a) and (c) (from Zifonun et al., 1997: 1282) and (40b) (from Gunkel, 2000: 114), which indicate that *versprechen* is subject to more combinability restrictions than *drohen* and *scheinen*:

(40) (a)   *Ihm droht/scheint [...] widersprochen zu werden.*
            He threatens to be contradicted.

     (b)   **An diese Sache verspricht ernsthaft herangegangen zu werden.*
            This matter promises to be dealt with in a serious manner.

     (c)   *An diese Sache droht/scheint [...] ernsthaft herangegangen zu werden.*
            This matter seems to be dealt with in a serious manner.

Furthermore, according to Gunkel (2000: 115–118, 120), the modal, epistemic use of *drohen* and *versprechen* is subject to specific semantic restrictions pertaining to (non-)intentionality that are not found with *scheinen*. In general, *scheinen* is subject to less lexical and constructional restrictions than *drohen* and, in particular, *versprechen* (cf. also Zifonun et al., 1997: 1282–5)[8].

The perfect auxiliaries in CP2 pose no problems in this regard, but there are obvious grammaticalisation differences within CP3. As is well known, *brauchen* is functionally integrated into the system of modals as the negated counterpart of *müssen* 'have to' (cf. Folsom, 1968). As I have shown elsewhere (Askedal, 1998b), *brauchen* has acquired all important syntactic properties of true modals, but lags behind with regard to morphological, inflectional properties in the standard language. Concerning semantics, an epistemic use is empirically attested but apparently of infrequent occurrence (Askedal, 1998: 62f.), cf. e.g. the sentences in (41), which are authentic examples that require an epistemic reading:

(41) (a) *Es braucht nicht unbedingt ein Irrtum des Computers gewesen zu sein.* (TV)
         It need not have been a computer error.

   (b) *Ebenso brauchte nicht unbedingt sie die Eintrittskarte in Iesolo verloren zu
         haben.* (L. Fortride, *Kennzeichen Rosa.*)
         It didn't have to be her who had lost the ticket in Iesolo.

According to the common view, modals derive semantically from lexical verbs, by first developing a deontic modal meaning and, secondarily, if at all, an epistemic meaning (cf. in general Sweetser, 1990: 49–75; and, concerning German, Diewald, 1999a: 1 et passim). Such developments can be seen as a process of increasing semantic abstraction and, presumably, increasing grammaticalisation. In this perspective, the rare occurrence of the epistemic use of modal *brauchen* indicates that this verb still falls short of the grammaticalisation level of the core modals, where the epistemic use is a common option. The complete absence of an epistemic reading in the case of *wissen* and *haben* in CP3 is an equally clear indication of an even lower degree of grammaticalisation in the case of these verbs.

In CP4, the modally and aspectually neutral *werden* is obviously more highly grammaticalised as a passive auxiliary than modal *sich lassen* and *sein* with the *zu*-infinitive[9]. Concerning the two latter constructions, one may note that, in impersonal passive constructions, *sich lassen* allows for an optional expletive subject *es* which is not possible in constructions with *sein* and the *zu*-infinitive, cf. (42a) vs. (42b):

(42) (a) *weil (es) sich mit solchen Frauen gut plaudern läßt.*
         because it's easy to do small talk with such women.

   (b) *weil (*es) in diesem Jahr mit Neuwahlen zu rechnen ist.*
         because elections are to be expected this year.

With regard to the possibility of an expletive subject, (42a) is thus closer to the productive type of lexical impersonal construction than (42b) and this may be taken as an indication of a somewhat lesser degree of grammaticalisation in the case of (42a).

The other verbs in CP4, i.e. the ACI verbs, are all of them two-place predicates (or three-place predicates, if the accusative and the infinitive are counted as separate arguments rather than one 'small clause') with a lexical valency of their own. The causative-permissive verb *lassen* is semantically closer to 'grammatical' status than the others but is not equally naturally considered a grammaticalised auxiliary on a par with the other verbs we have discussed.

Considering the relationship between CPs, one might perhaps, from a purely theoretical point of view, be tempted to expect broader semantic-syntactic scope to correlate with higher degree of grammaticalisation. As mentioned earlier, this may hold good with regard to the relationship between epistemic and deontic modals (cf. Diewald, 1997: 27–9)[10], but it is far from being a general scope regularity. As shown in the preceding paragraphs, individual CPs comprise verbs on different grammaticalisation levels and for this reason the supposition that any verb occupying a higher CP position (*n*) shows a higher degree of grammaticalisation than any verb belonging to a lower CP (*n* + 1…) cannot be correct. For instance, it is hardly subject to doubt that *werden* as a passive auxiliary in CP4 is more grammaticalised than *haben* or *wissen* as deontic 'modality verbs' in CP3 or *versprechen* as an epistemic 'modality verb' in CP1. Nor would it make much sense to assume that *werden* in CP1 is more grammaticalised than *werden* in CP4 (or vice versa).

4.2   Change of categorial position

Although higher categorial position in the present-day system in (27) does not *per se* imply a higher level of grammaticalisation, there do exist cases where a change of position is involved in the grammaticalisation process. In a historical perspective, one may indeed hypothesize that the scope hierarchy in (27) is to a considerable extent also a grammaticalisation hierarchy. The verbs in CP1-CP3 and the auxiliary-like verbs in CP4 have in fact arisen out of earlier non-auxiliary lexical uses of the verbs in question.

The future auxiliary *werden* in CP1 was originally, according to one traditional view, a copular verb of CP6 with a predicative in the shape of a present participle which through phonological attrition became homonymous with the infinitive (Dal, 1966: 131–2). Similarly, the perfect auxiliaries *haben* and *sein* in CP2 also belonged to CP6. *Haben* was a transitive verb requiring a co-predicative to the object, whereas *sein* behaved syntactically on a par with *werden*, requiring a predicative characterizing the subject (cf. Grønvik, 1986: 16–19 and 30f.).

The epistemic use of the core modals in CP1 is no doubt a further development of the basic deontic meaning in CP3 (cf. Sweetser, 1990 on English and Diewald, 1999a on German). It is commonly assumed that the present-day deontic modals originated from verb lexemes with less abstract meanings.

Haben with the *zu*-infinitive in CP3 clearly derives from transitive *haben* as a CP6 verb. Here, the syntactic dependency relationship between the accusative object and a quasi-attributive *zu*-infinitive in a 'shared object construction' (Ebert, 1976: 113; cf. also Ebert, 1978: 28–30) has been reanalysed as verb-dependence of the infinitive, cf. (43):

(43) (a)   *Er hatte* [NP *eine schwere Aufgabe zu bewältigen*]. →

   (b)   *Er hatte* [NP *eine schwere Aufgabe*] [predicate constituent *zu bewältigen*].
         He had a difficult task to cope with.

The result of this reanalysis is that no accusative object is required for the infinitive to occur, cf. (43c):

(43) (c)   *Er hat unbedingt* [predicate constituent *zu gehorchen*].
         He certainly has to obey.

It seems likely that the deontic modal use of *wissen* 'be able to' has developed along the same lines, cf. (44a) to (b):

(44) (a)   *Er wußte* [NP *eine schöne Geschichte zu berichten*]. →

   (b)   *Er wußte* [NP *eine schöne Geschichte*] [predicate constituent *zu berichten*].
         He knew how to tell a pleasant story.

Again, in consequence of the reanalysis, an infinitive is no longer required, cf. (44c):

(44) (c)   *Er weiß immer gut* [predicate constituent *zu berichten*].
         He always knows how to narrate well.

It is possible that a similar reanalysis process has caused *brauchen* to go from CP6 to CP3 (and, as a secondary option that is fairly marginal in actual usage, further to CP1; cf. (41)), in consequence of a semantic change 'use > need'[11], cf. (45a), (b) to (c):

(45) (a)   *Er braucht (nicht)* [NP *etwas*].
         He needs something./He does not need anything.

   (b)   *Er braucht nicht* [NP *etwas zu unternehmen*]. →

   (c)   *Er braucht nicht* [NP *etwas*] [predicate constituent *zu unternehmen*].
         He does not need to do anything.

And then, without a nominal object in (45d):

(45) (d) *Er braucht nicht* [predicate constituent *zu arbeiten*].
          He does not need to work.

Concerning *pflegen*, it is a curious fact that this verb, when governing a *zu*-infinitive, formerly occurred in the perfect, cf. (46), which, despite the fairly recent example (46b), can no longer be considered current usage:

(46) (a) *Hab ich auch je gepflegt dir also zu thun…* (Luther)
          Have I ever used to do unto you…

     (b) *Cornelie, sich wohl erinnernd, welche Formen Zustimmung bei dem Vater
          anzunehmen gepflegt hatte, verstand augenblicklich.* (I. Seidel)
          Cornelie, who remembered what forms her father's consent used to assume,
          understood immediately.

In connection with (46b), Aldenhoff (1962: 211) makes the interesting remark that 'sämtliche Grammatiker den Ersatzinf. als veraltet [betrachten]' 'all grammarians consider the substitute infinitive obsolete', which implies that, in earlier times, the socalled 'substitute infinitive' was used instead of a participle proper (Aldenhoff, 1962: 211), cf. the examples in (47) (from Merkes, 1895: 124):

(47) (a) *Bischof Albrecht von Mainz hat pflegen zu sagen…* (Luther)
          Bishop Albrecht of Mainz used to say…

     (b) *So hat man unsere Musen zu mahlen pflegen.* (Opitz)
          This is how we used to paint our muses.

     (c) *Wie… er die ziemlich scharfe Frage vordessen an anderen dergleichen
          Personen… hat pflegen zu exequiren.* (C. Müller)
          How he… formerly used to direct the fairly sharp question to other similar
          persons…

If the examples in (46) to (47) can be assumed to be representative of the development of *pflegen* governing the *zu*-infinitive, it would seem that the substitute infinitive was first introduced after the establishment of the perfect construction and then discarded before the perfect went out of use. In any case, the occurrence of the perfect with the substitute infinitive shows beyond doubt that actional *pflegen* once behaved syntactically as a deontic not an epistemic modal, whereas in the contemporary language, where *pflegen* in the perfect is no longer possible, the affinity is with the epistemic modals. In syntagmatic terms, this means that actional *pflegen*, presumably not an easy bedfellow of deontic modals from a semantic point of view, has made a leap from CP3 to CP1.

Scheinen with the *zu*-infinitive most likely owes its present status as a CP1 verb to a reanalysis from copular verb belonging to CP6 to a verb-governing auxiliary (cf. Diewald, 2000: 350–52). This entails a concomitant reanalysis of the infinitive from predicative, functionally on a par with adjectives and nouns in cases like (48), to auxiliary phrase constituent with different syntactic properties in (49)[12], cf.:

(48) (a)   *Der Fall schien problematisch.*
           The case seemed problematic.

  (b)   *Der Fall hatte problematisch geschienen.*
           The case had seemed problematic.

(49) (a)   *Der Fall schien problematisch zu sein.*
           The case seemed to be problematic.

  (b)   **Der Fall hatte problematisch zu sein geschienen.*
           The case had seemed to be problematic.

When *scheinen* is used as a copular verb in CP6, the perfect is possible as in (48b), but when used as a CP1 verb, no perfect occurs in (49b).

In the present language, *drohen* and *versprechen* are CP1 verbs that do not occur in the perfect, cf. (50) to (51):

(50) (a)   *Das Haus droht einzustürzen.*
           The house threatens to collapse.

  (b)   **Das Haus hat einzustürzen gedroht.*
           The house has threatened to collapse.

(51)(a)   *Das Wetter verspricht gut zu werden.*
           The weather promises to be good.

  (b)   **Das Wetter hat gut zu werden versprochen.*
           The weather has promised to be good.

Still, the following example (52) from Goethe shows *drohen* in a topologically 'coherent' ('enclosed') construction in the pluperfect and with a dative object that, contrary to modern usage, appears to be governed by *drohen*:

(52)   *so schied ich mit günstigem Wind von dem Ufer, welches mir lästrygonisch*
           zu werden gedroht hatte. (*Goethe Werke.* Sechster Band. Vermischte
           Schriften ausgewählt von Emil Staiger. Biographisches. Zur Literatur. Zur
           Naturwissenschaft. Sprüche. Frankfurt am Main.)

         with a favourable wind I then parted from the shore which had threatened to
           become laestrygonic.

Examples of this kind indicate that the modern epistemic modal meaning originated as a semantic shift with *drohen* (and, presumably, likewise *versprechen*) as a CP5 verb. The coherent, non-extraposed construction in (52) can presumably be considered as an indication of transition from CP5 to CP3. The present loss of the perfect (and of the future with *werden*) is a sure sign of a further leap to CP1. In any case, a syntactic-semantic split has led to the emergence of a secondary epistemic-modal variant belonging to CP1 with both *drohen* and *versprechen*.

It should be noted that the ACI verbs have as a group remained remarkably stable. The only fairly clear case of grammaticalisation within this group is the development of reflexive *sich lassen* into a dispositional modal addition to the set of passive-marking predicates headed by unmarked *werden*. This development of *(sich) lassen* remains within the paradigmatic confines of CP4.

5   Concluding remarks

The purpose of the present contribution has been to study modality in modern German as part of a system of grammaticalised predicate categories which together form a hierarchical structure of syntactic dependency and semantic scope relations. The present-day system can be described in terms of categorial positions (CPs). To describe the role of modality in this syntactic – syntagmatic and paradigmatic – system, two main modal categories are needed, which I have chosen to call 'deontic(ity)' and 'epistemic(ity)' in accordance with what I perceive to be their prototypical semantic content. Today, the linear distribution of the 'notional' categories of 'deonticity' and 'epistemicity' in CPs seems 'natural' from the point of view of semantic and logical scope, but there is historical evidence that the modern CP distribution of a number of predicates is the result of a gradual grammaticalisation process involving change of CP from lower to higher. In general, grammaticalisation is a measure of categorial content productivity. In a fairly short-term diachronic perspective, modality is such a productive grammatical category in German. Grammaticalisation differences within individual CPs testify to the lexical and grammatical productivity of the modal categories 'deonticity' and 'epistemicity'.

Notes

1   Lower index marks broader and higher index narrower scope.

2   Cf. in particular Bierwisch (1966), Engel (1980, 1994: 104–12). The present description is a further development of views and rules originally set forth in Askedal (1991: 9–12).

3   Hauser-Suida/Hoppe-Beugel (1972: 76–7) enumerate a small number of idiosyncratic exceptions with lexical verbs that are not relevant in this connection.

4   CP = categorial paradigm (or content position); pres. = present; pret. = preterite; ind. = indicative; subj. = subjunctive.

5   I suspect that (28) comes close to what Heltoft (this volume) would call a 'linguistic semantic structure', to be placed between 'semantic (content) structure' and '(surface) expression' in a stratified account of linguistic content and expression structure.

6   Further constructions characterised by non-extraposability of the governed non-finite form are *kommen* 'come' with the past participle (*er kam die Treppe heruntergetrampelt* 'he came tumbling down the stairs') and *bleiben* 'remain' with the bare infinitive (*er blieb draußen stehen* 'he remained outside'). It is evident that neither belongs in the auxiliary domain from a functional point of view.

7   In the opinion of Thieroff (1992: 208–19), this grammaticalisation drift is about to intrude into the standard language, thereby enriching the system of temporal reference with new means of differentiation.

8   Although it can be assumed that *werden* and the epistemic modals are more highly grammaticalised than *scheinen*, one may also refer to the connection between stativity and the modal, epistemic reading observed by Saltveit (1969: 179–81) in connection with the epistemic use of *werden* and the modals as a kind of lexical preference rule (if not a restriction in the proper sense). In contrast, the inherently stative *scheinen* combines freely with stative as well as non-stative infinitives.

9   The passive constructions form grammaticalisation hierarchies of their own, cf. for instance (i) to (iii):

(ia)   *Der Raum wird (von den Bewohnern des Hauses) nicht mehr benutzt.*

(ib)   **Der Raum wird unbenutzt.*

(iia)   *Der Raum ist (*von den Bewohnern des Hauses) nicht mehr benutzt.*

(iib)   *Der Raum ist unbenutzt.*

(iiia)   **Der Raum bleibt (von den Bewohnern des Hauses) nicht mehr benutzt.*

(iiib)   *Der Raum bleibt unbenutzt.*

In the *werden* passive, agents are as a rule optional, but participles with the adjectival negation prefix *un-* cannot be used. In the *sein* passive, there are certain restrictions against agents and adjectival participles with *un-* occur occasionally. The *bleiben* passive is subject to more restrictions than the *sein* passive and participles with *un-* are used regularly in case of negation.

On the passive system as a whole see for instance Askedal (2002). For a discussion of the 'dative/recipient passive' with *bekommen/erhalten/kriegen* and the past participle see for instance Askedal (2001).

10   In this context one may note that Diewald (1997: 25, 27) also assumes some sort of functional relatedness between epistemic modality and mood. This supposition may seem reasonable from a semantic and pragmatic point of view, but it should not be forgotten that epistemic modals may in principle appear both in the indicative and in the subjunctive (even though they predominantly occur in the indicative and *dürfen* only shows up in the subjunctive form *dürfte*). The adjacency of CP1 and CP0 in (27) should only be taken to indicate that the CP1 predicates may only turn up as finite, not as non-finite verb forms, not that CP1 predicates do themselves express mood.

11   For a detailed analysis of the semantic change(s) involved see in particular Scaffidi-Abbate (1973), who does not, however, deal with the possibility of syntactic reanalysis.

12   On the development of *scheinen* see also Willems/van Pottelberge (1998: 490–500).

References

Aldenhoff, J. (1962) Der Ersatzinfinitiv im heutigen Deutschen. In *Revue des Langues Vivantes* 28 (3): 195–217.

Askedal, J. O. (1989) Über den Infinitiv ohne bzw. mit 'zu' im heutigen Deutsch. Klassenbildung regierender Lexeme und Hauptzüge der Distribution (1), (2). In *Deutsch als Fremdsprache* 26 (1, 2): 2–7, 103–6.

Askedal, J. O. (1991) 'Ersatzinfinitiv/Partizipersatz' und Verwandtes. Zum Aufbau des verbalen Schlußfeldes in der modernen deutschen Standardsprache. In *Zeitschrift für germanistische Linguistik* 19 (1): 1–23.

Askedal, J. O. (1997) *drohen* und *versprechen* als sogenannte 'Modalitätsverben' in der deutschen Gegenwartssprache. In *Deutsch als Fremdsprache* 34 (1): 12–19.

Askedal, J. O. (1998a) Satzmustervariation und Hilfsverbproblematik beim deutschen Verb *scheinen*. In K. Donhauser and L. M Eichinger (eds) *Deutsche Grammatik. Thema in Variationen. Festschrift für Hans-Werner Eroms zum 60. Geburtstag.* Germanistische Bibliothek 1. 49–74. Heidelberg: Universitätsverlag C. Winter.

Askedal, J. O. (1998b) *brauchen* mit Infinitiv. Aspekte der Auxiliarisierung. In A. Mádl and G. Dietz (eds) *Jahrbuch der ungarischen Germanistik 1997* 53–68. Budapest: Gesellschaft ungarischer Germanisten; Bonn: Deutscher Akademischer Austauschdienst.

Askedal, J. O. (2001) Grammaticalisation and Persistence in the German
  'Dative/Recipient Passive' with *bekommen/kriegen/erhalten*. In
  Interdisciplinary Journal for Germanic Linguistics and Semiotic Analysis 6
  (1): 107–34.
Askedal, J. O. (2002): Zum deutschen Passiv: Konversenbildung, seman-
  tisch-lexikalische Ausdifferenzierung und Grammatikalisierung. In
  Arbeitsberichte des Germanistischen Instituts der Universität Oslo 19:
  77–92.
Bech, G. (1955) *Studien über das deutsche verbum infinitum.* Vol. 1.
  København: Munksgaard.
Berger, D., Drosdowski, G. et al. (1985) *Duden. Richtiges und gutes Deutsch.
  Wörterbuch der sprachlichen Zweifelsfälle.* Duden, Band 9. Third edition.
  Mannheim, Wien and Zürich: Dudenverlag.
Bierwisch, M. (1966) *Grammatik des deutschen Verbs.* Studia Grammatica II.
  Fourth edition. Berlin: Akademie-Verlag.
Dal, I. (1966) *Kurze deutsche Syntax auf historischer Grundlage.* Third edition.
  Tübingen: Niemeyer.
Diewald, G. (1997) *Grammatikalisierung. Eine Einführung in Sein und Werden
  grammatischer Formen.* Germanistische Arbeitshefte 36. Tübingen:
  Niemeyer.
Diewald, G. (1999a) *Die Modalverben im Deutschen. Grammatikalisierung
  und Polyfunktionalität.* Reihe Germanistische Linguistik 208. Tübingen:
  Niemeyer.
Diewald, G. (1999b) The integration of German modals into the paradigm
  of verbal moods. In C. Beedham (ed.) *Langue and Parole in Synchronic
  and Diachronic Perspective. Selected Proceedings of the XXXIst Annual
  Meeting of the* Societas Linguistica Europaea, *St. Andrews, 1998* 119–29.
  Amsterdam etc.: Pergamon.
Diewald, G. (2000) *Scheinen* als Faktizitätsmarker. In M. Habermann, P. O.
  Müller and B. Naumann (eds)*Wortschatz und Orthographie in Geschichte
  und Gegenwart. Festschrift für Horst Haider Munske zum 65. Geburtstag*
  333–55. Tübingen: Niemeyer.
Ebert, R. P. (1978) *Historische Syntax des Deutschen.* Sammlung Metzler 167.
  Stuttgart: Metzler.
Ebert, R. P. (1986) *Infinitival Complement Constructions in Early New High
  German.* Linguistische Arbeiten 30. Tübingen: Niemeyer.
Eisenberg, P. (1995) German. In E. König and J. van der Auwera (eds) *The
  Germanic Languages* 349–87. London: Routledge.
Engel, U. (1980) Der Verbalkomplex im Deutschen. In M. Dyhr, K. Hyldgaard-
  Jensen and J. Olsen (eds) *Festschrift für Gunnar Bech. Zum 60. Geburtstag
  am 23. März 1980.* Kopenhagener Beiträge zur Germanistischen

Linguistik, Sonderband 1. 123–59. København: Institut for germansk
Filologi, Københavns Universitet.

Engel, U. (1994) *Syntax der deutschen Gegenwartssprache*. Grundlagen der
Germanistik 22. Third edition. Berlin: Erich Schmidt.

Eroms, H.-W. (1992) Die Baugestalt des deutschen Satzes: Hierarchie, Position
und Klammer. In *Germanistentreffen Belgien – Niederlande – Luxembourg
– Deutschland, Köln, 29.10.-03.11.1991*. DAAD Dokumentationen und
Materialien 21. 249–74. Bonn: Deutscher Akademischer Austauschdienst.

Folsom, M. H. (1966) *The Syntax of Substantive and Non-Finite Satellites to
the Finite Verb in German*. Janua Linguarum, Series Practica XXX. The
Hague and Paris: Mouton.

Folsom, M. H. (1968) 'brauchen' im System der Modalverben. In
Muttersprache 78 (6): 321–29.

Grønvik, O. (1986) *Über den Ursprung und die Entwicklung der aktiven
Perfekt- und Plusquamperfektkonstruktionen des Hochdeutschen und
ihre Eigenart innerhalb des germanischen Sprachraumes*. Oslo: Solum;
Paderborn, Wien and Zürich: Ferdinand Schöningh.

Gunkel, L. (2000) Selektion verbaler Komplemente. Zur Syntax der
Halbmodal- und Phasenverben. In R. Thieroff, M. Tamrat, N. Fuhrhopp
and O. Teuber, (eds) *Deutsche Grammatik in Theorie und Praxis* 112–21.
Tübingen: Niemeyer.

Hagège, C. (1993) *The Language Builder. An essay on the human signature
in linguistic morphogenesis*. Amsterdam studies in the theory and history
of linguistic science, Series IV. Current issues in linguistic theory 94.
Amsterdam and Philadelphia: John Benjamins.

Hauser-Suida, U. and Hoppe-Beugel, G. (1972) *Die Vergangenheitstempora
in der geschriebenen Sprache der Gegenwart. Untersuchungen an aus-
gewählten Texten*. Heutiges Deutsch I/4. München: Hueber; Düsseldorf:
Schwann.

Heine, B., Claudi, U. and Hünnemeyer, F. (1991) *Grammaticalisation. A
Conceptual Framework*. Chicago and London: The University of Chicago
Press.

Hopper, P. J. and Traugott, E. C. (1993) *Grammaticalisation*. Cambridge,
England: Cambridge University Press.

Lindgren, K. B. (1957) *Über den oberdeutschen Präteritumschwund*. Annales
Academiæ scientiarum fennicæ. Ser. B 112,1. Helsinki: Academia scientiarum fennica.

Merkes, P. W. (1895) *Der neuhochdeutsche Infinitiv als Teil einer umschrie-
benen Zeitform. Historisch-grammatische Betrachtungen*. Inaugural-
Dissertation zur Erlangung der philosophischen Doktorwürde an der
Universität Göttingen. Leipzig.

Saltveit, L. (1969) Das Verhältnis Tempus–Modus, Zeitinhalt–Modalität
im Deutschen. In U. Engel, P. Grebe and H. Rupp (eds) *Festschrift für*

Hugo Moser zum 60. Geburtstag am 19. Juni 1969 172–81. Düsseldorf: Schwann.

Scaffidi-Abbate, A. (1973) 'Brauchen' mit folgendem Infinitiv. In *Muttersprache* 83 (1): 1–45.

Sweetser, E. E. (1990*) From Etymology to Pragmatics. Metaphorical and Cultural Aspects of Semantic Structure*. Cambridge Studies in Linguistics 54. Cambridge, England: Cambridge University Press.

Thieroff, R. (1992) *Das finite Verb im Deutschen. Tempus – Modus – Distanz*. Studien zur deutschen Grammatik 40. Tübingen: Narr.

Vater, H. (1975) Werden als Modalverb. In J. Calbert and H. Vater *Aspekte der Modalität* 71–148. Tübingen: Narr.

Willems, K. and van Pottelberge, J. (1998) *Geschichte und Systematik des adverbalen Dativs im Deutschen. Eine funktional-linguistische Analyse des morphologischen Kasus*. Studia Linguistica Germanica 49. Berlin and New York: Walter de Gruyter.

Zifonun, G., Hoffmann, L., Strecker, B. et al. (1997) *Grammatik der deutschen Sprache*. Schriften des Instituts für deutsche Sprache 7.1–7.3. Berlin and New York: Walter de Gruyter.

10 Mood and modality in Russian, Danish, and Bulgarian. Determinant categories and their expanding role*

Per Durst-Andersen

1 Introducing linguistic supertypes

It is the aim of this chapter to attempt to demonstrate that an analysis of the mood system of a particular language may benefit from taking its starting point in an analysis of the entire linguistic system. If one applies an atomistic approach by focusing solely on the single members of the mood system, the inevitable consequence will be that the potential mood and modality functions carried out by other verbal categories will be ignored and therefore also the interrelationship between the mood system and the modality system of the language in question. One could in fact argue that not only should verbal categories such as tense, aspect and voice be included in an holistic analysis, but also nominal categories such as case and definiteness because due to isomorphism nominal categories may reproduce the grammatical function of verbal categories.

In this connection, I would like to draw attention to the Georgian language that exhibits a special case of harmony between the verbal categories of tense, aspect and mood, on the one hand and the nominal category of case, on the other. Case distinctions are not governed by the semantic role or the syntactic function carried by the NP, but are subordinated to a principle of harmony. The subject function as well as the direct object function can be signalled both by the nominative and the dative case. The nominative case is used whenever the existentiator is the figure of a stable picture or the actor is the figure of an unstable picture being received by the speaker. The nominative case is connected to the speaker-related notion of direct experience – it reflects objective reality. The dative case is used whenever the existentiator is the figure of a stable image or the actor is the figure of an unstable image created by the speaker himself, be it on the basis of deduction or abduction. The dative case is connected to the speaker-related notion of indirect experience – it reflects subjective reality. In other words, it appears that two different case forms have taken over functions which are carried out by the categories of mood and modality in other languages (for a detailed description of the above-mentioned harmony, see Harris, 1982; Hewitt, 1995; Holisky, 1981; Durst-Andersen, 1995).

In the present chapter I shall restrict myself to including in my analysis all verbal categories found in Bulgarian, Russian and Danish. I will perform the linguistic analysis within my own framework of linguistic supertypes which is an attempt to typologise the entire system of individual languages into three supertypes, viz. speaker-oriented, reality-oriented and hearer-oriented languages (cf. Durst-Andersen, 1996a and 1997). The theory is cognitively based and argues that people have three different mental representations of, for instance, one and the same event, i.e. a state caused by an activity:

i)   The visual experience of the event;
ii)   the mental model of an event;
iii)   the stored copy of the event (it may be stored in the past world store or in the present world store).

These three different representations correspond to three different levels, each with its own function:

i)   Identification;
ii)   assimilation;
iii)   storing.

From a strictly pragmatic point of view, all languages, of course, express the speaker's feelings and attitudes, take the hearer into consideration and refer to situations and objects in our world. But speaking of the grammatical structure, the idea is that any language has to make a fundamental semiotic choice between three possibilities of anchoring the utterance:

i)   It may verbalise the first level where the event is identified on a visual basis;
ii)   it may verbalise the second level where the event is assimilated according to a mental model; or
iii)   it may verbalise the third level where the event is stored.

Irrespective of choice, the utterance will always refer to exactly the same event, but what is said about the event referred to will be different and expressed by different verbal forms: The directly or indirectly experienced event will be expressed by a mood form – the category of mood forms the basis of speaker-oriented languages; the pure reference to the event via a mental model will be expressed by an aspectual form – the category of aspect constitutes the basis of reality-oriented languages; and the form with an index to either the past or the present world store will be a tense form – the category of tense makes up the basis of hearer-oriented languages.

Each supertype is characterised by a certain way of thinking which is anchored in what with Klimov's term (cf. Klimov, 1977; 1983) I call a determinant category, be that mood, aspect or tense. A determinant category will not only determine the structure of the entire linguistic system thereby creating isomorphic relations and harmony (cf. the above-mentioned relations in Georgian), but will also expand and take over functions normally expressed by other categories. In that way a speaker-oriented language easily becomes a language (e.g. Bulgarian or Georgian), where mood forms will be prominent, a hearer-oriented language (e.g. Danish or English) easily develops a system which is dominated by tense forms and a reality-oriented language (e.g. Russian or French) easily takes the shape of a language where aspect takes part in the formation of any finite or non-finite form.

These findings are supported by independent evidence from an investigation carried out by the Indian typologist D. N. S. Bhat (Bhat, 1999). After having analysed the TAM-system of several genetically unrelated Indian languages he found that they could be divided according to their relative prominence of tense, aspect or mood – however, without getting into a deeper analysis of the substituting functions of the prominent categories of particular languages. In the following I shall try to do what Bhat failed to do. Note that I shall use the term determinant category when speaking of tense, aspect or mood as a category in its entirety. I shall retain Bhat's term *prominent* for that member of the determinant category that not only forms its cognitive basis, but also has the leading role. Thus the simple past/aorist form is the prominent member of the determinant category of tense in hearer-oriented languages, the perfective form is the prominent member of the determinant category of aspect in reality-oriented languages and the direct experience form is the prominent member of the determinant category of mood in speaker-oriented languages. The prominent member will correspond to what from a functional point of view is called the marked member. However, we need a new term because we normally associate the unmarked member with substituting functions within its own domain. Here we observe that the marked member may fulfil substituting functions outside its own domain.

In the following sections I shall examine the TAM-system of Russian, Danish and Bulgarian and against this background show that each determinant category has expanded across its own boundaries and has moved into new positions thereby taking over domains from other verbal categories. In other words, I want to show how tense as the determinant category of Danish has taken over various mood and modality functions, how aspect as the determinant category of Russian has acquired clear modality functions in its infinitive and imperative forms as well as in the present tense forms and, finally, how mood as the determinant category of Bulgarian has gained considerably more power, not only by repeating the structure of the oblique mood system within the indicative mood itself, but also by reinterpreting the three old tense forms, viz. the aorist, the perfect and the imperfect forms, as modality forms. Bulgarian is a case of special interest because it offers extremely good pieces of evidence for the claim that what functions as the determinant and therefore the central category in one language may function as a peripheral category in another. Bulgarian distinguishes sharply between perfective and imperfective verbs as Russian does and the Bulgarian system seems to operate in exactly the same way as does the Russian one (cf. Mikkelsen, 2002). In Bulgarian, however, aspect only performs an *assisting* role in the make up of the utterance – in contradistinction to the central role of Russian aspect.

2   Short presentation of the grammatical systems of Russian, Danish and Bulgarian

2.1   Russian as a reality–based language

From a well equipped tense system consisting of the present tense form, the imperfect form, the perfect form, the pluperfect form I and II and the aorist form, Russian developed an aspectual system where all action verbs (or complex verbs) form purely aspectual pairs (e.g. *dat'* (pf)/*davat'* (ipf) 'give'), whereas all non-action verbs (or simplex verbs), i.e. state and activity verbs, are imperfectives and do not form pairs with any other verb, but may derive various perfective as well as imperfective Aktionsarten (e.g. *stojat'* (ipf) 'stand' and *rabotat'* (ipf) 'work'). As a determinant category, aspect changed the lexicalisation patterns found in Old Russian (see Durst-Andersen, 2004) and forced a reinterpretation of the direct cases so that the genitive became their oblique counterpart *per se* – in every way aspect was the driving force behind the creation of a very neat system. The result of this process is that the Russian sentence (not the utterance) is completely designed to be a means to carry the internal and external structure of simple and complex situations in reality. It should be noted that the category of animacy vs. inanimacy (potentially active vs. not potentially active) is the nominal equivalent to the verbal category of aspect. As we will witness below, it is not possible to find a finite or non-finite form in which the aspectual opposition does not take place.

2.1.1   The direct mood system

The direct mood system consists solely of the indicative mood which itself consists of perfective and imperfective present tense forms (e.g. *dast* (pf) 'he'll give' vs. *daet* (ipf) 'he is giving, gives') as well as of perfective and imperfective preterite tense forms (e.g. *dal* (pf) 'he gave' vs. *daval* (ipf) 'he gave, was giving'). The perfective aspect presents the action as an event by asserting the state description and presupposing the activity description, whereas the imperfective aspect presents the action as a non-event, primarily as a process, by asserting the activity description and treating the state description as a standard implicature. In other words, Russian treats an action as a two-sided entity consisting of an activity and a state. This explains why the nominative and the accusative function as direct cases: the nominative refers to the figure of the unstable picture created by the activity situation of an action thus at the same time acting as an index of the underlying subject of an activity description, while the accusative refers to the figure of the stable picture created by the state situation of an action thus at the same time acting as an index of the underlying subject of a state description. It would take us too far if we were to give a detailed description of each category in Russian. Therefore I prefer to give a metaphorical explanation of the *hierarchical organisation* of the Russian TAM-system (see Figure 1).

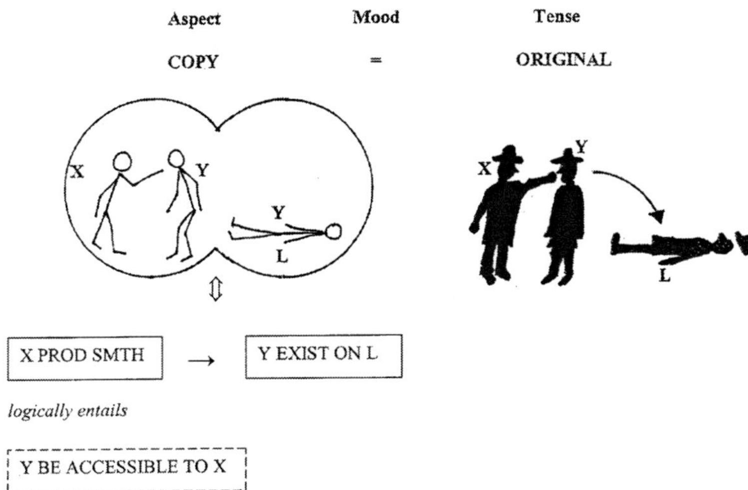

Figure 1: Visualising the Russian utterance *On sbil* (pf/pret/ind) *ego s nog* 'He knocked him out'

Aspect operates on the lexical-grammatical structure of verbs and by so doing it creates a copy of reality: the perfective aspect creates a copy of an event, i.e. a state caused by an activity and the imperfective aspect creates a copy of a process, i.e. an activity intending to cause a state. In our example the perfective aspect creates a copy of an activity where X hits Y which causes a state where Y exists horizontally on the ground (see Figure 1). Tense operates on the output structure of aspect and by so doing places the original in reality: the present tense localises the activity referred to at the moment of speech, while the preterite tense localises the activity referred to before the moment of speech. In our example we are dealing with the preterite tense which has localised the real activity of hitting before the moment of speech – it is thus a past event (see Figure 1). Mood operates on the output structure of tense and by so doing places a relation of equality or a relation of non-equality between the copy created by aspect and the original localised by tense. In the case of the indicative mood (see Figure 1), we are dealing with the relation of equality. This means that according to the speaker there is or was an original. This is tantamount to saying that we are concerned with a true statement. (For a detailed account of the established hierarchy and its manifestations in the morphological structure of Russian verbs, see Durst-Andersen, 1992.)

2.1.2   The oblique mood system

The oblique mood system consists of two different forms, i.e. the subjunctive mood (signalled by *by* + a preterite form of perfective or imperfective verbs, e.g. *dal by* vs. *daval by*) and the imperative mood (signalled by *-Ø* of a perfective or an imperfective verb, e.g. *daj* vs. *davaj*). Both forms are united by their placing a sign of non-equality between the copy and the original. In the case of the Russian subjunctive mood, this relation is understood as a matter of fact that

> (a)   cannot be changed:
> e.g. *Esli on prišel by, ja byl by rad.*
> If he had come, I would have been happy.
>
> or
>
> (b)   can be changed:
> e.g. *Prišel by on!*
> I wish he would come!

In the first case we are dealing with so-called counterfactual meaning and in the latter case we are dealing with the meaning of desire. These two functions are not separated in Russian, but are separated in Bulgarian with interesting consequences, as we shall see. The imperative mood treats this relation as a matter of fact that

> (c)   should be changed:
> e.g. *Pridi k nam!*
> Come to us!

In other words, the hearer is asked by the speaker to create an original on the basis of the copy shown to him.

It is interesting to note that the direct cases function like the direct mood, that the genitive functions like the subjunctive mood and the vocative functions like the imperative mood. This stresses the important point I want to make, namely that the entire linguistic system of Russian is designed to carry situations in reality: aspect tells us whether we are dealing with a copy of an event or a process; tense takes care of the original event or process; mood points out whether we are concerned with an original or just a copy and if it is a copy, whether the original is possible (it is a desire), impossible (it is purely hypothetical) or necessary (it is a request) (see also Durst-Andersen, 1996b).

2.2   Danish as a hearer–oriented language

In hearer-oriented languages the sentence is designed to be a means to carry the information intended for the hearer by the speaker. This means that there must be an important distinction between old and new information. The determinant category is tense or more specifically the distinction between the present perfect and the imperfect. The article system is anchored in the notion of familiarity vs. unfamiliarity and thus functions as the nominal equivalent to tense. It has been shown by Klinge (2002) that the determining function of the category of tense has extremely concrete manifestations in Danish and in English. He convincingly demonstrates why Danish and English should not be called V2-languages, but T2-languages: It is not the verb as such, but the tense marker that determines the word order structure of sentences. His conclusion is that *do* in English has the function of allowing the bound tense marker to escape the lexical verb in order to mark general illocutionary functions through its syntactic position. In other words, it is not only on the level of content that the Danish category of tense determines the functions of other categories – Danish tense also determines various sentence paradigms.

The core verbal system of Danish consists solely of tense forms, a present tense subsystem and a past tense subsystem – you will not find a single aspectual form or a single mood form apart from the mood traditionally called the indicative in this system.

2.2.1   *The present tense subsystem*

The present tense subsystem consists of the present tense form (e.g. *siger* 'says') and the present perfect tense form (e.g. *har sagt* 'has said'). The present tense form and the present perfect tense form are used to give a situation description as well as a characterisation of the subject. These two pragmatic functions can be distinguished by stress in the case of the present tense form if it is needed.

Thus *Han taler húrtigt* with the main stress on the adverb will give a situation description (corresponding to the English *ing*-form *He is talking fast*), while *Han táler hurtigt* with the main stress on the verb will give a characterisation of the subject (corresponding to English *He speaks fast*). When the present perfect form performs its situation description function, it gives what I prefer to call a *news-flash* (e.g. *Jeg har sagt det til hende* 'I have told her about it'), which is opposed to the *flashback function* of the imperfect form (see below). The present perfect form, however, is also used to give a characterisation of the subject – we need to bear in mind that the characterisation function is the only function of state and activity verbs, e.g. *Han har været 10 år i hæren* 'He has been 10 years in the Army' and *Jeg har arbejdet hårdt i dag* 'I have worked hard today'. From the point of view of semantics, both forms can be said to verbalise the present world store: the present tense form verbalises present qualities of situations or persons; the present perfect tense form verbalises situational and mental consequences of past situations, be they actions, activities or states. But from the point of view of pragmatics, there are use restrictions: the present perfect form can only be used if the speaker presumes that the hearer does not have a file similar to his own. In other words, the use of the present perfect form requires that the form is carrying new information to the hearer.

2.2.2   The past tense subsystem

The past tense subsystem consists of the imperfect form (e.g. *sagde* 'said') and the pluperfect form (e.g. *havde sagt* 'had said'). The imperfect form in Danish has taken over the functions of the old aorist (corresponding to *passé simple* in French) and the old imperfect (corresponding to *imparfait* in French), which has given it a whole range of different functions. Its main function is the flashback function where the imperfect form tells a story. In this function it is opposed to the present perfect form which gives a news-flash. In other words, the function of the imperfect can be compared to a motion picture in which events are presented as an indivisible whole in opposition to the function of the present perfect which should be compared to a still picture of the consequent state of a past action. The imperfect form, however, also performs a descriptive function. In this function it takes care of both situation descriptions (e.g. *Mens vi talte sammen,...*' While we were talking together,...') and characterisations of the subject (e.g. *Da han var ung, talte han altid langsomt* 'When he was young, he always spoke slowly'). The pluperfect form performs the same functions, but deals with backgrounded events instead of foregrounded events and with descriptions that constitute preconditions for events (for a detailed account of the Danish tense system, see Harder, 1996 and Durst-Andersen, 2000a).

2.2.3   The peripheral verbal system

The peripheral verbal system involves the aspectual and modal distinctions that the core system lacks. It consists of the so-called *s*-passive (e.g. *siges* 'it is said') and the so-called *blive*-passive (e.g. *bliver sagt* 'it is said', lit. 'it becomes said'), i.e. a voice distinction (see also Heltoft and Herslund, this volume).

- When the *s*-passive is combined with a modal verb, it automatically gets a deontic reading (cf. *Han må fyres* 'He must be fired (and I will do it)'). When it is used without a modal verb, it always involves presentation of knowledge – in other words, it fulfils a characterisation function (e.g. *Der tales mange sprog i Danmark* 'Many languages are spoken in Denmark').

- When the *blive*-passive is combined with a modal verb, it automatically gets an epistemic reading (e.g. *Han må blive fyret* 'He is bound to get fired (I predict)'). When it is used without a modal verb, it always involves presentation of experience – in other words, it gives a situation description (e.g. *Der bliver talt mange sprog i Danmark* 'Many languages are being spoken in Denmark').

As should be evident from this short presentation, Danish has neither a traditional mood category nor a traditional aspectual category. Danish has only tense forms and voice forms at its disposal. As a hearer-oriented language, Danish can be said not only to verbalise the level of mental stores, either the present or the past world store, but also to grammaticalise the so-called appeal function of language (cf. Bühler, 1933) by constantly forcing the hearer to open a new file when the speaker uses either the present perfect form or the indefinite article, or to look for a file already stored when the speaker uses either the imperfect form or the definite article.

2.3   Bulgarian as a speaker–oriented language

Together with Macedonian, Bulgarian is the only Slavic language that has increased the number of verbal forms, presumably at the expense of the loss of all case forms in the noun. Like all Slavic languages Bulgarian developed an aspectual system consisting of perfective and imperfective forms, but it did not skip the old aorist, the perfect, the imperfect and the pluperfect forms. They have been reinterpreted, however, as modal forms – as we shall see in 3.3. Besides that, Bulgarian developed a renarrative system within the indicative mood. As to the nominal system, Bulgarian dropped all case forms and created a so-called article system, which differs in structure, however, from the well-known article systems in Germanic languages.

The verbal system consists of five moods: the indicative mood, the subjunctive mood, the conditional mood, the imperative mood and, finally, the 'fantasy world' mood. The four last mentioned members belong to what I shall call the oblique mood system – in that respect the indicative mood is their non-oblique counterpart:

- The indicative mood consists of two submoods, i.e. a direct experience mood signalled by Ø where the speaker commits himself to the truth or falsity of the propositional content involved and an indirect experience mood signalled by *bil* where the speaker refrains from doing so (see, however, below in Section 3.3, where they will be discussed in detail). All verbs are either perfective or imperfective and all action verbs are paired – the perfective and the imperfective forms only together name the concept of an action. All perfective and imperfective verbs have a tremendous number of what at first sight seem to be tense forms, but later appears to be a combination of tense and mood forms. There are three synthetic forms, viz. present tense forms, imperfect tense forms and the aorist forms and six analytic forms, viz. the present perfect tense forms, pluperfect tense forms and four different future forms which are irrelevant from our point of view. This yields 18 different tense-aspect-mood forms if we restrict ourselves to the direct experience submood forms. As pointed out by several linguists (see e.g. Stojanov, 1977; Maslov, 1982; Andrejčin, 1978; Mikkelsen, 2002), Bulgarian only operates with two absolute tenses, namely forms referring to present time which include the present, the present perfect and two future forms and forms referring to past time which include the imperfect, the pluperfect, two future tense forms and the aorist.

- The subjunctive mood (signalled by the particle *da* + a finite form) expresses desire, but is also used in connection with what I call '*imagined world*'. It should be stressed that this form often acts as a substitute for an infinitive form, which does not exist in Bulgarian – as a speaker-oriented language Bulgarian cannot make use of a form whose content cannot be experienced by any of our human senses. The function of the Bulgarian subjunctive mood is identical to what was mentioned as the second function of the Russian subjunctive mood.

- The conditional mood (signalled by the particle *bi* + the primary *l*-participle) performs the function of counterfactual meaning. Its function is thus identical to what was mentioned as the first function of the Russian subjunctive mood.

- The imperative mood consists of perfective forms, e.g. *napiši!* 'write!' and imperfective forms, e.g. *piši!* 'write!', which, presumably, fulfil the same modal functions as Russian aspect does in the imperative as well as in the infinitive (cf. Section 3.1).

- 'Fantasy world' mood (signalled by the pure stem, e.g. *podsluš! 'listen!'*) is used in comics as a kind of superimposed description. This mood form is completely free of aspectual and temporal marking which makes it rather special (for a detailed description, see Hauge, 1994).

As a speaker-oriented language, the Bulgarian language can be said not only to verbalise the level of identification of our human mind – for instance, by distinguishing whether the entire event or process is seen by the speaker or not – but also to grammaticalise the so-called expressive function of language (cf. Bühler, 1933), for instance, by making the speaker impose his own attitudes on what is experienced by other people. The Bulgarian sentence is in every way designed to be a means to carry the speaker's experiences in the broadest sense of this word. This also concerns the specific Bulgarian article system – the nominal equivalent to the determinant category of mood.

3 Mood and modality functions taken over by the determinant categories

In the following subsections I shall attempt to demonstrate that the determinant categories in Russian, Danish and Bulgarian have expanded into new areas by gaining potential or real ground from other verbal categories. This means that the determinant categories substitute for other verbal categories and occupy positions that are not characteristic of these categories. In other words, we will witness how Russian aspect and Danish tense have taken over modal functions, how tense forms in Bulgarian have taken over modal functions and how its oblique mood system has repeated itself within the indicative mood thus capturing a new position.

3.1 The modality functions taken over by the Russian perfective and imperfective forms

3.1.1 Introductory remarks

As already noted above, the category of aspect can in no way be avoided in Russian. Not only should the speaker choose between two aspectual forms in the present and past tenses, but also in all non-finite forms, for instance, both in the imperative and in the infinitive. In these two cases the general aspectual meaning of the perfective and imperfective aspects has been cancelled (presumably because they do not seem to make sense any more when speaking of a single action) and has been replaced by modal meanings (for a detailed account of the modality functions of the two aspectual forms, see Durst-Andersen, 1995). We find, however, signs of these connections already in the present tense.

3.1.2   The present tense

In the present tense of all action verbs we find clearly distinct modal functions
of the perfective and imperfective aspects:

(1) (a) *On podnimaet 100 kg.*
         He lift.PRES.IPF 100 kg
         He can lift 100 kg.

     (b) *On podnimet 100 kg.*
         he lift.PRES.PF 100 kg
         He can lift 100 kg.

In (1a) we are concerned with a person who has the ability to lift 100 kg,
whereas in (1b) we are dealing with a person who is capable of lifting 100 kg
if he makes a try. It is true that (1a) talks about present time, involves multiple
actions and is a characterisation of the person in question ('He is a person who
has the quality of lifting 100 kg'). It is true that (1b) talks about the future,
involves a single action and contains a prediction of a future consequence if
certain conditions hold ('If he produces an activity, then the 100 kg will be
above his head'). As should be apparent, there are many differences between
(1a) and (1b) and all of them can be accounted for because they directly derive
from their respective aspectual meanings: the imperfective aspect asserts the
activity description and treats the state description as a standard implicature,
denotes single and multiple actions and describes situations or characterises
persons; the perfective aspects asserts the state description while presupposing
the activity description, denotes only a single action and can only describe a
situation. The important thing is, however, that the two aspectual forms in (1)
have become associated with different modal meanings where the imperfective
aspect denotes *ability* and the perfective aspect denotes *possibility*. In other
words, (1a) and (1b) have been coupled to different modal meanings thereby
superseding all the non-modal ones.

3.1.3   The infinitive form

The epistemic vs. non-epistemic distinction that plays a crucial role in English is
of no relevance to Russian. This appears from the fact that epistemic meanings
are expressed by lexicalised units like *dolžno byt'* '(it) must be' and *možet byt'*
'(it) may be', etc., which function as sentence adverbials (always followed by a
comma). However, Russian distinguishes two types of non-epistemic modality,
which is done by the two aspects. Non-epistemic modality deals with various
types of knowledge, viz. with laws of society (deontic modality) and with laws

of nature (alethic modality). Deontic modality includes the deontic modes permission, prohibition, obligation and non-obligation. Alethic modality is concerned with (physical) possibility and impossibility as well as with (internal) necessity and non-necessity (cf. von Wright, 1951; 1968). Although distinct types, deontic and alethic modality enter into a common class, because they are concerned with non-belief, i.e. knowledge in the broad sense of the word. This class is in opposition to epistemic modality, which relates to lack of knowledge, i.e. beliefs (what could be called laws of the human mind, i.e. rational laws or laws of reason). Whereas epistemic modality operates on Hare's so-called *tropic part* of the utterance (e.g. *I hereby say that it is* possibly *true that...*, non-epistemic modality operates on his so-called *phrastic part* (e.g. *I hereby say it is true that it is* possible *for X to produce an activity...*) (cf. Hare, 1949; 1970). This means that deontic and alethic modality share the same scope, but must have different domains – they must operate on different structures. In view of the fact that the perfective and imperfective aspect represent different statement models (cf. Durst-Andersen, 1992; 1994), it is not surprising that they have been connected to the two different types of non-epistemic modality – the imperfective aspect has been coupled to deontic modality and the perfective aspect to alethic modality. In this connection it is interesting to note that von Wright, the originator of deontic logic, only connects deontic modes to what he called actions, symbolised *H* and alethic modes to what he called states of affairs, symbolised *p*. This corresponds, in fact, to the assertive potential of the imperfective and perfective aspects: the imperfective aspect asserts an activity description while the perfective aspect asserts a state description. Let us now turn to data:

(2) (a) *Uže 8 časov – vstavat'!*
   already 8 hours – stand.up. INF.IPF
   It's already 8 o'clock – get up!

  (b) **Uže 8 časov – vstat'!*
   already 8 hours – stand.up.INF.PF

  (c) *Vstat'! – Uže 8 časov.*
   stand.up.INF.PF – already 8 hours
   Get up! – It's already 8 o'clock.

In (2a) the imperfective infinitive itself expresses obligation – *Uže 8 časov* 'it's already 8 o'clock' functions as a deontic source: 8 o'clock makes it necessary for the person to get up. In other words, the imperfective not only denotes a deontic mode, but it also expresses a deontic performative. That we are dealing with a deontic source appears clearly from the fact that it is totally impossible to ask *Počemu?* 'Why?'. This question is ungrammatical because the question has already been given an answer, i.e. 'It's 8 o'clock'. (2b) with the perfective counterpart is ungrammatical because the perfective aspect cannot be used in connection with deontic sources, i.e. sources that prescribe a state – be it by permitting, prohibiting, or obligating a state, or canceling an obligatory state. The perfective aspect can only be used descriptively, as in (2c) where it expresses necessity. Here it will be possible to ask the question why, because there can be no cause-effect relationship between the perfective statement involved in *Vstat'* and the temporal statement in *Uže 8 časov.*

The fact that the Russian perfective and imperfective aspects are intimately connected with alethic and deontic modality, respectively, is also apparent from (3a) and (3b):

(3)   (a)   *Ne sadit'sja v étom rjadu!*
            not sit.down.INF.IMP in this row
            You mustn't sit in this row!

      (b)   *V étom rjadu ne sest'! Vse mesta zanjaty.*
            In this row not sit.down.INF.PF! all seats occupied.
            You cannot sit in this row. All seats are occupied.

In (3b) the negated perfective infinitive itself conveys impossibility: it is stated that it is not possible to sit in a certain row, simply because all chairs are occupied. In (3a) the negated imperfective infinitive itself conveys that it is prohibited for somebody to sit in a certain row because, for instance, his ticket is for another row. Again we observe that the perfective aspect denotes alethic modality and the imperfective aspect deontic modality. This observation can also be made in the imperative mood, as we shall see below.

3.1.4   The imperative mood

In Section 2.1 we briefly mentioned the meaning of the imperative mood as a member of the oblique mood subsystem of Russian. It was stated that the imperative shares the relation of non-equality between the copy and the original with the subjunctive mood, but differs from it by involving the relation of necessity, instead of possibility/impossibility, between the copy and the original. In other words, in connection with the imperative mood the hearer is asked by the speaker to create an original on the basis of the copy. This is another way of putting Searle's description of the imperative as a form, which has world-to-word direction of fit (cf. Searle, 1983: 5). It was also argued that the function of aspect was to create a copy of reality: the perfective aspect creates a copy of an event defined as a state caused by an activity, while the imperfective aspect creates a copy of a non-event, primarily a process, defined as an activity intending to cause a change of state. It goes without saying that the copy-function of aspect must be cancelled if the hypothesis of the different modal functions of the two aspects should hold. This is exactly what turns out to be true. It appears that irrespective of aspectual form the function of any positive imperative of an action verb is to make the hearer change the world by creating an event and that the function of any negated imperative form is to leave the world unchanged either by being totally passive or by doing something to prevent a change. Hence it follows that there should be no choice of aspect with respect to the positive and the negated imperative if we were dealing with ordinary grammar. But we are not. The two aspectual forms have acquired modal functions – the perfective aspect denotes alethic modality and the imperfective aspect denotes deontic modality. But the question, of course, remains: What is the overall function of aspect in connection with the imperative?

Let me illustrate what unites and what differentiates the two aspectual forms on the basis of a well-known and trivial fact about aspectual use in the Russian imperative: prototypically, a host will use the imperfective aspect (see (4a)) if he wants a guest to sit down, while a doctor will use the perfective aspect if he wants his patient to sit down during an examination (see (4b)).

(4) (a) *Sadites'*!
       sit.down.IMP.IPF
       Sit down! (lit.)

When the host sees that his guest is standing and he wants him to be seated, he will know that the reason why the guest is standing is not that he does not want to be seated in a comfortable chair, but that he is waiting for the signal which tells him that he is now allowed to sit down – simply because accepting an invitation implies the acceptance of participating in all subevents, the rules of which are known to him. The rule that seems to govern all other rules says that the guest should not enter into a new subevent before the host has allowed him to do so. Therefore I suggest that when the host utters (4a) he simultaneously permits the guest to sit down. Thus he asks the guest to sit down against the background of a specific *state prescription*, viz. a permitted state, one of the deontic modes. This performative element is absent in the perfective example (b):

(4) (b) *Sjad'te*!
       Sit.down.IMP.PF
       Sit down! (lit.)

In the doctor-patient setting we are not dealing with an invitation at all. The patient will never be invited; he, in fact, invites himself and is entitled to do so, since he, either directly or indirectly, pays for his 'visit' to the doctor. In other words, when the patient is standing, he is waiting for the doctor's signal that tells him which of the possible states the doctor wants him to realise: should he sit down, lie down, or take off his clothes. He himself does not care and will do what the doctor wants him to do if it is within the limits of a doctor's examination. Therefore I suggest that when the doctor utters (4b) he asks the patient to sit down against the background of a *state description*, viz. a possible state, one of the alethic modes. To put it in other words: the function of aspect in the imperative mood is to satisfy the hearer's preconditions for complying with the speaker's request. In issuing permission in (4a) the speaker thus satisfies what he considers to be the hearer's preconditions for complying with his request to sit down – in (4b) it is enough to describe that the desired state is possible.

In the case of a negated imperative form the perfective and imperfective aspects fulfill the same modal functions:

(5) (a) *Ne padaj*!
          Not fall.down.IMP.IPF
          You mustn't fall!

     (b) *Ne upadi* (pf)!
          Not fall.down.IMP.PF
          Mind you don't fall!

The function of a negated imperative is to leave the world unchanged. In the case of (5a) and (5b) there is a risk that the hearer will be on the ground and both forms are united by the function of preventing the hearer from being in that position. In (5a) this is done by issuing prohibition, i.e. the speaker thinks that in giving the hearer a prohibition he satisfies the hearer's preconditions for complying with his request to leave the world unchanged – without this prohibition he does not believe that his request will be complied with by the hearer. In (5b) the speaker is not acting upon the hearer. By describing the state 'You can be on the ground' if you do not do anything to prevent it, he believes that he satisfies the hearer's preconditions for complying with his request to leave the world unchanged – in his own best interest, of course. It is interesting to note that the perfective aspect that presupposes an activity description forces the negation to fall on the state description. In other words, the hearer is asked to do something so that the possible state is not realised (for a detailed account of the imperative mood in Russian compared to English and Danish, see Durst-Andersen, 1995).

3.2   The mood and modality functions taken over by the Danish tense forms

3.2.1   Introductory remarks

Whereas in the case of Russian it was clear that the category of aspect had taken over modality and not mood functions, it is not easy to decide in Danish, because the category of tense is the only grammatical category of the verb if we disregard the imperative mood. As we shall see below, the expansive function of the category of tense has been so intense that all tense forms in Danish have taken over modal functions.

3.2.2   The pluperfect form as counterfactual

Although the pluperfect form normally denotes temporally backgrounded events and characterisations that hold prior to the point of reference, it also has a modal meaning. Just as in English, the Danish pluperfect tense form is used to denote so-called counterfactual meaning. This meaning can be conveyed by the pluperfect form alone without *hvis... så*; 'if... then:

(6)   *Havde du   spurgt hende, havde hun svaret.*
        had   you asked her,   had   she   answered
        If you had asked her, she would have answered.

This is the only way to express counterfactual meaning in Danish. Note that the pluperfect form occurs in both the protasis and the apodosis.

3.2.3   The imagined world function of the imperfect tense form

If we disregard the so-called *imperfectum ludi* (see (7)), no one has paid serious attention to what I shall call the imagined world function of the imperfect tense form:

(7)   *Og så tog   du ind tilbyen og købte   en   dukke.*
        and then took you in to city   and bought a   doll
        And then you went down town and bought a doll.

The *imperfectum ludi* is a specific variety of the imagined world function, which is restricted in use, because it is only used by small children and only when they are playing together. The imperfect form in fact substitutes real events in the sense that the imperfect form is only applied by children when their playing cannot go further in the real world – it may be blocked by the specific location or by lacking a certain person. Under these circumstances children insert an imagined world instead of the real world. The imagined world function is very frequent in use and is, for instance, triggered by all words that have the meaning of imagination:

(8)   *Kan man   i dag   **forestille sig** en   kulturel   begivenhed,   som   folk*
        can one today   imagine   a   cultural   event   that   people

        ville *stå   i   kø   for*
        would stand   in   line for
        Is it possible today to imagine a cultural event that people would stand in
            line for?

It is exactly the imperfect form *ville* 'would' that shows that we are dealing with imagination. We are asked by the speaker to use our imagination and look for some conditions that might create big queues. If the speaker had used *vil* 'will', he would have asked the hearer to look at the real world surrounding us. The split between a real situation description and an imagined world description is apparent in (9a) and (9b):

(9) (a) *Jeg tror,   at   der   **vil** være   mange   i   køen.*
        I   think, that there   will be   many   in the line
        I think that many people will be standing in the line.

    (b) *Jeg tror,   at   der   **ville** være   mange   i   køen.*
        I   think, that there   would be   many   in the line
        I think that many people would be standing in the line.

In (9a) we are talking about a specific queue in a future world and we are finding ourselves in the middle of that queue. It is a real situation description – a description of the objective reality. In (9b) we have no access to the real world – we are located inside an imagined world. It is not a situation description, but a description of the speaker's own imagination – a description of a subjective reality. This distinction between being in a real world and being in an imagined world can in many ways be said to resemble the textual distinction between fact and fiction.

3.2.4   The cancelled future world function of the imperfect tense form

The imagined world function of the imperfect form has a specific manifestation that bears a resemblance to the counterfactual meaning of the pluperfect form. That is why I decided to put this function in a specific subparagraph. Compare the following two utterances:

(10) (a) *Sagde du   det   til hende, **vil**   hun blive   vanvittig.*
         Said   you it   to her,   would she become   mad
         If you tell her, she'll go mad.

(b) *Sagde du det til hende,* **ville** *hun blive   vanvittig.*
    Said you it to her,   would   she become   mad
    If you told her (but I know you won't), she would go mad.

In both (10a) and (10b) the condition (protasis) is expressed by the imperfect form, but its consequence (apodosis) is expressed by different forms which seems to be the reason why the final products are different. In (10b) where the consequence is expressed by an imperfect form thus preserving the harmony as we observed in the counterfactual meaning of the pluperfect form, we get the meaning of a cancelled future world. In short, the speaker imagines a future world in which the hearer tells something to a female person. The speaker already knows that the hearer has dropped the idea so that the consequence can never be realised – it remains in the imagined world. In (10a) where the consequence is expressed by the present tense form we also get an imagined world reading, but the meaning of a cancelled future action is totally absent. In other words, it seems as if Danish has created a future world corresponding to the unreal past world expressed by the pluperfect tense form. In the counter-factual meaning in (6) we are dealing with what could be named *retrospective imagination*: the condition concerns an imagined world of the past world, which makes the condition and its consequence belong to non-reality. In (10a) and (10b) we are dealing with what might be called *prospective imagination*. In both cases we are concerned with an imagined world of the future world, but the use of different tense forms in the apodosis makes the entire utterance meaning different. I shall argue that (10b) deals with unreal prospective imagination, whereas (10a) deals with real prospective imagination.

3.2.5   The present perfect tense form as evidential

The present perfect tense form has also acquired a modal meaning called the modal perfect meaning. This modal meaning is not found in the English present perfect, but it is widespread in the Balkan area – it is, for instance, found in Turkish, Macedonian, Bulgarian and Georgian under the heading of indirect experience. Let us take a look at its modal function and let us contrast it with the imperfect form:

(11) (a) *Tyven   er gået ind ad   døren,   men er forsvundet*
        the burglar is   gone   into through the door, but is   disappeared
        gennem vinduet.
        through the window
        The burglar, I assume, entered through the door, but left through the window.

(b) *Tyven   gik   ind ad   vinduet,   men   forsvandt   ud*
   the burglar went into through the window,   but   disappeared out
   gennem døren
   through the door
   I saw the burglar entering through the window and leaving through the door.

Let us stipulate that some very expensive painting has been stolen from a museum and that the scene of crime has already been investigated by the inspector. Having carried out his investigation the inspector might utter (11a). By doing so he refers to a series of events, but he shows the hearer that he bases his utterance on indirect evidence, for instance, on footprints. If we stipulate that a person utters (11b) immediately after having heard (11a), there is only one possible reading of (11b), namely that the person reports what he saw with his own eyes. In that way, the Danish imperfect and perfect forms enter into a new modal opposition, viz. that of direct vs. indirect experience. This modal opposition can be said to resemble the distinction in the peripheral system between the so-called *s*-passive and the so-called *blive*-passive (see Section 2.2).

3.3   The two submoods of the Bulgarian indicative mood

3.3.1 Introductory remarks

Mikkelsen (2002) presents an extremely interesting analysis of the Bulgarian TAM-system on the basis of the cognitive part of my own theory of linguistic supertypes (cf. Durst-Andersen, 1992; 2000a). His holistic analysis gives new and important insight into the fundamental principles of Bulgarian grammar and – crucially – it makes sense, not only from a synchronic point of view, but also from a diachronic viewpoint. The theory to be presented below is the result of a linguistic reanalysis of Mikkelsen (2002) – it builds on his insights and incorporates his results, but the theory constitutes an attempt to make the different pieces come together.

   I take my starting point in Mikkelsen (2002) and Gerdžikov (1984), but I want to emphasise that I have chosen to divide the indicative mood system into two submoods. Thus I do not consider the so-called renarrative mood system to be opposed to the indicative mood as such. We are concerned with two subsystems which share the modal meaning of the indicative, but differ from one another by basing the modal meaning of the indicative on different types of evidence:

- Direct experience, which is signalled by *zero*, i.e. Ø, consists of three forms, viz. the perfect form, the imperfect form and the aorist form. Originally, they were tense forms, but gradually they have turned into mood forms. As members of the indicative mood all three forms place a sign of equality between the copy shown by the aspectual form and the original localised in reality by the tense form. As members of the direct experience submood they all lay the responsibility for the relation of equality with the speaker. In other words, when using these forms the speaker commits himself to the truth of the propositional content involved because he has direct evidence for it. His specific choice of form is determined by the type of situation to which he was an eyewitness or of which he had other forms of direct experience.

- Indirect experience, which is signalled by *bil* '(lit.) was', consists of three forms, viz. the renarrative form, the inveritative form and the conclusive form. Normally, the particle *bil* is omitted, since there is no possibility of misunderstanding – except for one case, namely in the case of the perfect form. Hence *bil* is always present in the perfect forms of indirect evidence, i.e. the renarrative proper and the conclusive (the perfect form does not form an inveritativus). As members of the indicative mood, they all signal a relation of equality between the copy shown by the aspectual form and the original placed in reality by the tense form. As members of the indirect experience submood, they all lay the responsibility for the relation of equality with another speaker or with reality itself. In other words, in using an indirect experience form the speaker refrains from committing himself to the truth of the propositional content involved in the statement. He deliberately puts the responsibility for the statement outside himself, but, as will be demonstrated below, this is not tantamount to saying that he does not make any commitment at all to the utterance. The three forms differ from one another by expressing different attitudes towards the propositional content of the utterance.

3.3.2   The direct experience mood

As already mentioned above, the direct experience submood consists of three modalities represented by the aorist, the perfect and imperfect forms of perfective and imperfective verbs. Because the perfective and imperfective aspects assign truth values to the propositional content involved, thereby creating correspondences to situations in reality in the shape of events and processes, they have a crucial role in the make up of an utterance. They pair, so to say, propositional models with situational models. Since a statement can be said to consist of a pairing of a certain proposition with a certain situation, it follows that the two aspects actually represent different *statement models* (see Durst-Andersen, 1992; 1994). The perfective aspect asserts the state description q and presupposes the activity description p and by doing that it presents an action as an event, i.e. as a state caused by an activity. The perfective statement model reflects the two-faced nature:

(12)   X produces an activity p and p is sufficient for state q

In my model '*p is sufficient for q*' is actually meant to represent the relation of causation between the activity situation and the state situation as well as the logical relation of strict implication between the two propositions which says that the truth of q is implied by the truth of p by necessity (the logical relation of strict implication is thus the logical correspondent to the relation of causation). The imperfective aspect asserts the activity description p and leaves the state description q as a standard implicature, i.e. it is for the hearer to decide whether q is true or false. By doing that it is capable of representing all non-events, which all necessarily imply a process. In that way the imperfective model becomes a standard model for all imperfective utterances. The imperfective standard statement model has the following form:

(13)   X produces an activity p and it is intended that p is sufficient for the state q

In this model '*it is intended*' (either by X or by the World) also serves two functions. On the one hand, it blocks the truth-value assignment to q (therefore it is for the hearer to decide whether q is true or false) and, on the other hand, it makes reference to an activity that has a state as its goal, i.e. it refers to a process without implying anything about the attainment of that goal.

By using Hare's tripartition of an utterance, viz. the neustic component, the tropic component and the phrastic component, we can say that the perfective and imperfective statement models represent the phrastic component (cf. Hare, 1949; 1970). If we restrict ourselves to the declarative sentence form, we get *I hereby say* in the neustic component. Because we are concerned with the indicative mood, we get *It is true* in the tropic component, i.e. Hare's name for the utterance equivalent to the grammatical category of mood:

Neustic	Tropic	Phrastic
I hereby say	*it is true*	*he produced an activity...*
Sentence form	Mood	Propositional content

Since the choice between direct vs. indirect experience is a choice within the indicative mood, the two submoods must constitute a choice between two varieties of the tropic component *it is true*. I argue that the direct mood form involves *according to me it is true*, whereas the indirect mood form has either *according to somebody else* or *according to something it is true*. We are now in a position to take a closer look at the three modalities of the direct experience mood. Let us start with the aorist form.

The aorist form as expressing direct evidence of the entire event

I shall take as my starting point a simple utterance and use this utterance as a model for my entire presentation in order to prevent confusion:

(14)   *Stojan pročète*   *knigata.*
         Stojan read.PF.AORIST.DIR.EXP   book
         Stojan read the book.

As should be more or less clear from (14), the English translation cannot bring out the aspectual and modal meanings of the Bulgarian utterance. In order to be able to localise the exact contribution that each category makes to the utterance, I suggest paraphrasing (14) according to the *declarative superstructure* introduced above, where the perfective aspect enters into the phrastic part and the direct experience mood into the tropic part:

(14')   I hereby say that according to me it is the case that Stojan produced an
         activity that was sufficient for the fact that the book existed for him as an
         experience and I base my saying so on my seeing/experiencing the activity
         as well as the state.

As is apparent, the function of the aorist form is twofold: first, as a member of the direct mood subsystem of the indicative mood it shows that the speaker takes the entire responsibility for the statement; secondly it adds the speaker's reason for doing so, namely that he directly experienced both the activity and the state. In other words, he might have seen Stojan involved in a particular reading activity and afterwards he might have experienced that he actually knows the content of the book in question. This means that the entire original past action (or event) was directly experienced by the speaker (i.e. *p*-and-*q*) – the total event was recorded by the speaker himself. Since the function of the aorist in, for instance, Old Russian and Modern French (in the shape of *passé simple*) is to present an event in its totality, i.e. it fulfils a flashback function where the hearer is watching a motion picture, it seems as if the Bulgarian aorist has preserved its scope properties from the time it functioned as a tense form, but that at a certain moment of time it dropped the temporal function and instead gained a modal function. As a tense form it presented the activity and the state in its totality as a film, i.e. as a flashback – as a modal form it says that both the activity as well as the state are directly experienced by the speaker. From being a member of a hearer-oriented category where something was presented by the speaker in such a way that the hearer saw a motion picture, it has become a member of a speaker-oriented category where the hearer is told the exact reason why the speaker commits himself to the truth of the propositional content involved.

The perfect form as expressing direct experience of the consequent state

I shall use the same utterance as in (14) to show the exact difference between the aorist and the perfect:

(15)   *Stojan e pročel*   knigata.
          Stojan read.PF.PERF.DIR.EXP   book
          Stojan has read the book.

Once again we have to paraphrase the utterance in order to be able to appreciate the exact contribution from each single category:

(15')   I hereby say that according to me it is the case that Stojan produced an
           activity that was sufficient for the fact that the book existed for him as an
           experience and I base my saying so on my experiencing the state.

The function of the perfect form is also twofold. First, as a member of the indicative mood it shows that the speaker takes the entire responsibility for the statement. Secondly, it adds the speaker's reason for doing so, namely that he directly experienced the state. In other words, he might have experienced from talking to Stojan that he has a profound knowledge of the book in question. Since, however, the speaker takes the responsibility for a statement that represents an event and not only a state, he, in fact, presents an *argument*. He directly experienced the state 'Stojan knows the content of the book' and because of that he takes this as a fact that needs an explanation. In using the perfective aspect, which presents an action as an event, he matches the fact with a rule that can explain it. In other words, he concludes that 'Stojan produced a reading-activity that caused the state' on the basis of the premiss 'Stojan knows the content of the book'. This is an *abductive* inference, i.e. an inference to best explanation (see Deutscher, 2002, who mentions this type as belonging to the late writings of Peirce). What we see here is a neat collaboration of aspect and mood, which, of course, makes the decoding of the utterance very easy for the hearer.

If we take a look at the temporal function of the perfect in, for instance, British English, Danish and Modern Written French (in the shape of *passé composé*), it appears that the perfect is used to present a past event as a present state which was left because of a past action carried out. Compared to the aorist form it fulfills a news-flash function where the hearer is shown a still picture of the consequent state. From this perspective, it seems as if the Modern Bulgarian perfect has preserved its scope properties from the time it functioned as a perfect tense form but changed domain. As a tense form it presented the present state as something that was left because of a past action. As a modal form it says that the consequent state is directly experienced by the speaker – with the conventional implicature (if the verb is perfective) that this state results from the activity named by the verb. From being a member of a hearer-oriented category where something was presented in such a way that the hearer saw a still picture, it has become a member of a speaker-oriented category where the hearer is given the argument for the speaker's commitment to the truth of the entire statement involved in the utterance: the fact that q is true (I experienced the state directly) is explained by X's production of p.

The imperfect as expressing direct experience of the activity involved

Let us look at the imperfect that corresponds to the two previously examined utterances – I stress that it can only occur in subordinate clauses:

(16)   (*kagato*) *Stojan pročeteše*   *knigata* (*šteše da doje pri nas*).
         Stojan read.PF.IMPERF.DIR.EXP   book
         (When) Stojan read the book (he would come to us).

If we insert this utterance in our declarative superstructure we get the following:

(16')   I hereby say that according to me it is the case that Stojan produced an
         activity that was sufficient for the fact that the book existed for him as an
         experience and I base my saying so on my experiencing the activity.

The function of the imperfect form is, of course, also twofold: first, as a member of the indicative mood it shows that the speaker takes the entire responsibility for the statement. Secondly, it adds the speaker's reason for doing so, namely that he directly experienced the activity. In other words, he might have seen Stojan reading the book referred to, either once or several times, but he has no direct evidence for the state. Since, however, the speaker commits himself to the entire statement that represents an event, he again presents an argument, but this time it does not form an abduction, but instead a deduction. Seeing Stojan reading, he inferred that Stojan produced the reading-activity with the purpose that he should acquire the content of the book. This is his first premiss that constitutes the fact. He now applies the rule that 'All actions will turn out as events by their very implementation if we are dealing with non-attainments in a normal world', which functions as the second premiss and he concludes that the state must be true. This is a deductive inference, which can only be applied when we are concerned with actions like reading where there are no obstacles to be overcome in all normal worlds. In the case of attainments, where there are natural obstacles to be surmounted (for instance, the action of convincing), the conclusion is not so easily arrived at.

Since the function of the imperfect in, for instance, Old Russian and Modern Written French (in the shape of *imparfait*) is to present an action as an ongoing process (it presents an unstable picture to the hearer), it seems as if the Modern Bulgarian imperfect has preserved its scope properties from the time it functioned as a tense form and has been subject to a shift in domain. As a tense form it presented the past action as an unstable picture involving an activity. As a modal form it says that the activity was directly experienced by the speaker – with the conventional implicature (if it is a perfective verb) that the process automatically instantiated as an event. From being a member of a hearer-oriented category where something was presented by the speaker in such a way that the hearer saw an unstable picture, it has become a member of a speaker-oriented category where the hearer is given the exact argument for the speaker's commitment to the truth of the entire statement, i.e. it is necessary that if p is true (I experienced the activity directly), then q is also true. Again we observe the neat collaboration between aspect and mood, which makes it easy for the hearer to reconstruct the argument.

3.3.3   The indirect experience mood

As already mentioned above, the indirect experience mood also consists of three members, viz. the renarrative form, the inveritative form and the conclusive form. All forms are signalled by *bil*, which shows that the speaker refrains from committing himself to the truth of the propositional content involved and instead places the responsibility for it outside himself. However, the really interesting thing is that the speaker simultaneously commits himself to the external commitment, for instance, made by another speaker. In other words, each of the three indirect mood forms contains the speaker's own evaluation of the relation of equality placed by somebody else or by reality itself. In that way, the utterance involves two responsible voices, the voice of the cited speaker and the voice of the actual speaker.

The renarrative form

We shall start with the renarrative form, because it is the most simple of the three members of the indirect experience mood:

(17)   *Stojan pročel (Ø)*   *knigata.*
       Stojan read.PF.AORIST.RENAR book
       Stojan read the book (it is said).

If we fit (17) into the declarative superstructure, we get the following paraphrase:

(17')   I hereby say that according to somebody else it is the case that Stojan
         produced an activity that was sufficient for the fact that the book existed
         for him as an experience – according to me: $\Diamond(p$-and-$q)$.

As should be clear from the paraphrase, the renarrative form takes care of
hearsay, but in contradistinction to the inveritative form to be examined just
below the renarrative form involves the speaker's positive evaluation of the
propositional content of the statement: it is judged by the speaker to be possible.
In other words, in using the renarrative form the speaker not only quotes another
speaker, but at the same time makes his own contribution to this utterance
by adding his own positive evaluation of the propositional content involved.
Metaphorically speaking, the speaker can be said to superimpose his own
voice on the 'music' played by the copied speaker. This superimposition, in
fact, states the actual speaker's own precondition for the hearer to believe in
the truth of the cited speaker's statement. The fact that the renarrative form
expresses possibility reminds us of the Bulgarian subjunctive mood where
there is a relation of non-equality between the copy and the original, but – and
this is the important thing – the original *can* come into existence. I shall argue
that the renarrative form of the 'oblique' part of the indicative mood system
repeats the function of the subjunctive mood expressed by *da* + a finite form
of the verb.

The inveritative form

The direct counterpart to the renarrative form is the inveritative form:

(18)   *Stojan bil pročel*   *knigata.*
         Stojan INVER read.PF.AORIST book
         Stojan read the book (but I don't believe it).

The paraphrase of (18) sounds as follows:

(18')   I hereby say that according to somebody else it is the case that Stojan
         produced an activity that was sufficient for the fact that the book existed
         for him as an experience – according to me: $\neg\Diamond(p$-and-$q)$.

It should be clear that the inveritative form is the negative counterpart to the
renarrative form. In other words, the two forms are identical as to the external commitment function, but differ as to the exact contribution made by the
speaker. In (17) the speaker added that according to him it is possible that the
event referred to has taken place. In (18) he adds that according to him it is
impossible – according to him it is not trustworthy relative to the speaker: the
event referred to could not have taken place. This reminds us of the conditional

mood of the oblique mood system where there is a relation of non-equality between the copy and the original, but the original *cannot* come into existence, because we are dealing with an imagined world in retrospect – the past cannot be repeated. Once again we notice that the inveritative form of the 'oblique' part of the indicative mood seems to repeat the function carried out by the conditional form of the oblique mood system, expressed by *by* + the primary l-participle of the verb.

The conclusive form

The conclusive form stands in opposition to the two other members of the indirect mood system by not being a hearsay form, i.e. it does not refer to a statement of an external speaker, but instead to the external reality itself:

(19)   *Stojan e pročel   knigata.*
        Stojan read.pf.aorist.concl book
        Stojan read the book (which is the only possible thing to conclude).

This utterance can be paraphrased in the following way:

(19')   I hereby say that according to something in reality it is the case that Stojan
         produced an activity that was sufficient for the fact that the book existed
         for him as an experience – according to me: $\neg\Diamond\neg(p\text{-and-}q)$.

In the case of the conclusive form the speaker lays the responsibility for the statement in reality itself and at the same time he adds that the event must have taken place. While the two other members involved the notion of possibility, the conclusive form involves the notion of necessity. The modal function of the conclusive reminds us of the imperative mood where there is a relation of non-equality between the copy and the original, but the original *should* come into existence.

3.3.4   On the relation between the oblique mood system and the indirect experience submood

We have just seen an intimate correlation between the oblique mood system consisting of the subjunctive, the conditional and the imperative mood and the indirect experience subsystem of the indicative mood system consisting of the renarrative, the inveritative and the conclusive members. The two systems differ from one another by putting different relations between the copy shown by the aspectual form (i.e. the perfective or the imperfective form) and the original localised in reality by the tense form: where the oblique mood system puts a relation of non-equality between the copy and the original, which means that there is/was no original, the indirect experience submood system puts the relation of equality between the copy and the original. This relation, however, is not placed by the speaker of the utterance, but by an outsider which is cited. Apart from that, it seems as if there exist diagrammatic relations: both the subjunctive and the renarrative denote possibility; both the conditional and the inveritative denote impossibility; and both the imperative and the conclusive denote necessity. This creates the hypothesis that what could be called the external oblique mood system has repeated itself within the internal oblique mood system of the indicative mood. The indirect experience mood subsystem can be regarded as a copy of the original oblique system. In both systems the speaker himself makes his own additional commitment in modal terms. In other words, he assigns a modal truth to the propositional content of the utterance – he could not have assigned an absolute truth, because absolute truth is restricted to direct experience in Bulgarian.

4   Conclusion

I have just attempted to demonstrate that what functions as a determinant category in language not only forces other categories to be in harmony with it, but also expands into new areas by taking over potential or real functions from other verbal categories. This especially concerns mood and modality functions:

- In Danish it was shown that all members of the category of tense have taken over modal functions – at present, tense is the only verbal category in Danish.
- In Russian it was demonstrated that the category of aspect has taken over modality functions – the perfective aspect denotes alethic modality, while the imperfective aspect denotes deontic modality.
- In Bulgarian it was argued that old tense forms have been reinterpreted as modal forms and that the oblique mood system has repeated itself within the indicative mood giving rise to a subdivision of the indicative mood system.

After having examined the TAM-system of three very different languages with special emphasis on the mood and modality functions carried out by its different members I shall try to describe my understanding of the notions of mood and modality. I shall use Hare's three components and in fact let him give an offer of an explanation. Categories that operate on the tropic component by assigning the relation of equality or non-equality between the copy and the original (which manifest themselves as 'it is true' and 'it is not true') belong to the category of mood. Hence the indicative mood and all oblique mood forms like the subjunctive, the conditional and the imperative will all be members of the mood system of a language. All these members are basically concerned with absolute truth although the various oblique mood forms also involve modalities – this is, however, on another level. Categories that operate on the phrastic component or which specify the relation of equality in modal terms belong to the category of modality. This means that some categories, for instance, the categories of direct vs. indirect experience in Bulgarian, involve both mood and modality. They not only assign an absolute truth in the form of plus or minus, but simultaneously also a modal truth in the shape of possible, impossible or necessary.

Acknowledgements

I would like to express my gratitude to K. R. Hauge, Jørn Qvonje, Marina Pantcheva and H. K. Mikkelsen for valuable comments concerning the Bulgarian language.

References

Andrejèin, L. D. (1978) Osnova bălgarska gramatika. Sofija: Nauka i izkustvo.

Bhat, D. N. S. (1999) *The Prominence of Tense, Aspect and Mood*. Amsterdam/ Philadelphia: John Benjamins.

Bühler, K. (1965) [1934] *Sprachtheorie. Die Darstellungsfunktion der Sprache*. Stuttgart: Gustav Fischer Verlag.

Comrie, B. (1981) *Language Universals and Linguistic Typology*. Oxford: Blackwell.

Deutscher, G. (2002) On the misuse of the notion of 'abduction' in linguistics. *Journal of Linguistics* 38: 469–85.

Durst-Andersen, P. (1992) *Mental Grammar. Russian Aspect and Related Issues*. Colombus, Ohio: Slavica.

Durst-Andersen, P. (1994) Russian aspect as different statement models. In C. Bache et al. (ed.) *Tense – Aspect – Action* 81–112. Berlin, New York: Mouton de Gruyter.

Durst-Andersen, P. (1995) Imperative frames and modality. Direct vs. indirect speech acts in English, Danish and Russian. *Linguistics and Philosophy* 18: 611–53.

Durst-Andersen, P. (1996a) Towards a multifunctional grammar. Language, mind and reality in a grammatical description. *Hermes* 17: 75–102.

Durst-Andersen, P. (1996b) Russian case as mood. Journal of Slavic Linguistics 4: 177–273.

Durst-Andersen, P. (1997) Towards a theory of linguistic supertypes: Speaker-based, hearer-based and reality-based languages. In B. Palek (ed.) *Proceedings of LP'96* 125–152. Prague: Charles University Press.

Durst-Andersen, P. (2000a) En kognitiv analyse af perfektum og imperfektum i dansk. *NyS* 26–27: 131–64.

Durst-Andersen, P. (2000b) The English progressive as picture description. *ALH* 32: 45–103.

Durst-Andersen, P. (2002) Situationssyntaks vs. Propositionssyntaks. En semiotisk-baseret typologi på tværs af eksisterende typer. In P. Durst-Andersen (ed.) *Sprog og typer i kontrast* in *Copenhagen Working Papers* in LSP 3–2002: 25–55. Copenhagen: CBS.

Durst-Andersen, P. (2005) Fra oldrussisk til moderne russisk. Leksikaliseringsmønstre og syntaktiseringsmekanismer. In L. Heltoft et al. (eds) *Grammatikalisering og struktur* 57–84. Copenhagen: Museum Tusculanum.

Gecadze, I. O. and Gajdarova, F. A. (1982) O vyraženii sub'ektno-ob'ektnych otnošenij v iberijsko-kavkazskich jazykach. In E. D. Kacnel'son (ed.) Kategorija sub'ekta i ob'ekta v jazykach razliènych tipov 154–88. Leningrad: Nauka.

Gerdžikov, G. (1984) *Preizkazvaneto na glagolnoto dejstvie v* bălgarskija ezik. Sofija: Nauka I izkustvo.

Givón, T. (1979) *On Understanding Grammar*. New York: Academic Press.

Givón, T. (1984) *Syntax. A Functional-typological Introduction*. Vol. I. Amsterdam: John Benjamins.

Harder, P. (1996) *Functional Semantics. A Theory of Meaning, Structure and Tense in English*. New York – Berlin: Mouton de Gruyter.

Hare, R. M. (1949) Imperative sentences. *Mind* 58: 21–39.

Hare, R. M. (1970) Meaning and speech acts. *Philosophical Review* 79: 3–24.

Harris, A. C. (1982) Georgian and the unaccusative hypothesis. *Language* 58: 290–306.

Hauge, K. R. (1994) Verbal interjection in Bulgarian child language and comic strips. In *Oslo Contributions to the 13th Meeting of Nordic Slavists* 17–28. Oslo: Universitetet i Oslo.

Hewitt, B. G. (1995) *Georgian. A Structural Reference Grammar*. Amsterdam/ Philadelphia: John Benjamins.

Holisky, D. A. (1981) Aspect theory and Georgian aspect. In P. Tedeschi and A. Zaenen (eds) *Tense and aspect* (=Syntax and Semantics, 14) 127–44. New York: Academic Press.

Hult, A. MS. Material til verbets morfologiska kategorier i de centrale balkanspråk jämförda med de nordslaviska språken, särskildt ryska.

Klimov, G. A. (1977) *Tipologija jazykov aktivnogo stroja*. Moskva: Nauka.

Klimov, G. A. (1983) *Principy kontensivnoj tipologii*. Moskva: Nauka.

Klimov, G. A. and Alekseev, M. E. (1980) *Tipologija kavkazskich jazykov*. Moskva: Nauka.

Klinge, A. (2002) Tense as a determinant category in English and Danish. In P. Durst-Andersen (ed.) *Sprog og typer i kontrast* in *Copenhagen Working Papers* in LSP, 3–2002 91–115. Copenhagen: CBS.

MacDonald, L. (1990) *A Grammar of Tauya*. Berlin/New York: Mouton de Gruyter.

Malone, T. (1988) The origin and development of Tuynca evidentials. *IJAL* 54: 119–40.

Mikkelsen, H. K. (2002) Det bulgarske TAM-system som type betragtet. In P. Durst-Andersen (ed.) *Sprog og typer i kontrast* in *Copenhagen Working Papers* in LSP 3–2002: 116–50. Copenhagen: CBS.

Mithun, M. (1999) *The Languages of Native North Amerika*. Cambridge: Cambridge University Press.

Searle, J. R. (1983) *Intentionality. An Essay in the Philosophy of Mind*. Cambridge: Cambridge University Press.

Stojanov, S. (1977) *Gramatika na bălgarskija knižoven ezik*. Sofija: Nauka i izkustvo.

Willett, T. (1988) A cross-linguistic survey of the grammaticization of evidentiality. *Studies in Language* 12: 1–97.

von Wright, G. H. (1951) *An Essay in Modal Logic*. Amsterdam: North-Holland.

von Wright, G. H. (1968) *An Essay in Deontic Logic and the General Theory of Action*. Amsterdam: North-Holland.

11 Modal polyfunctionality and Standard Average European[1]

*Johan van der Auwera and Andreas Ammann,
with Saskia Kindt*

1 Introduction

With 'modal polyfunctionality' we refer to the fact that modal expressions can have various meanings or, more generally, functions. Consider (1a) to (b) and (2a) to (b).

(1) (a) You may keep the change.
    (b) You may be mistaken if you think this will be easy.

(2) (a) You must leave the premises immediately.
    (b) You must be joking!

The uses of *may* in (1a) and *must* in (2a) express permission and obligation, respectively. Such readings are next to impossible in (1b) – because one normally does not permit anyone to be mistaken – and in (2b) – because it is equally odd to oblige someone to be joking. This kind of polyfunctionality is not only found in English, but it seems to be typical of several other European languages, to the extent even that one could consider it as a feature of 'Standard Average European'. This is the key question of the chapter: is modal polyfunctionality a 'Europeanism' or not?

In Section 2 the notion of 'Standard Average European' will be clarified. In Section 3 we further elucidate the notion of 'modal polyfunctionality'. Section 4 brings the two notions together and our tentative answer to the basic question of the chapter will be positive: there are indeed indications for considering modal polyfunctionality to be typical of Europe. In Section 5 we discuss how languages can lose modal polyfunctionality. In Section 6 we find more support for a contact hypothesis in some facts about the borrowing of modal markers and we sketch the possibility of yet another feature of modality that may be typically European, its 'verbiness'. Section 7 is the conclusion.

2   Standard Average European

The term 'Standard Average European' (SAE) is due to Benjamin Lee Whorf. In 1939, in a paper that was first published in 1941, but became more accessible in the reprint of 1956, Whorf discussed the linguistic expression of time, space and matter in Hopi and compared it to the corresponding strategies found in western European languages:

> Since, with respect to the traits compared, there is little difference between English, French, German, or other European languages with the *possible* (but doubtful) exception of Balto-Slavic and non-Indo-European, I have lumped these languages into one group called SAE (Whorf, 1956 [1941]: 138).

Whorf was not really interested in pursuing work on Standard Average European, however, nor in what one would nowadays call 'areal typology'. He was not really the first to consider the possibility of a *Sprachbund* in Western Europe either – perhaps the linguist to be credited for this is Beckmann (1934). And as to the term, it probably was not meant in a very serious way – neither was his earlier (1956 [1937]: 87) 'general Indo-European'. In this day and age, however, both the insight and the term are becoming accepted, in large measure due to a project funded by the European Science Foundation, the EUROTYP project (1990–1995) (see e. g. van der Auwera, 1998).

The state of the art of the research on Standard Average European is described by Haspelmath (2001). Just like any other *Sprachbund*, Standard Average European needs to be identified in terms of grammatical properties and in terms of languages that are or were adjacent and belong to different families or at least branches. For Standard Average European, the languages involved comprise at least continental West Germanic and Gallo-Romance, often also other Germanic and Romance as well as other adjacent Indo-European and non-Indo-European languages. Features include the presence of both definite and indefinite articles (3a), relative pronouns (3b), 'have'-perfects (3c), participial passives (3d) and the non-pro-drop character (also illustrated with (3c)).

(3) (a) *die Frau, ein Mann*   German
          la femme, un homme   French
          the woman, a man

     (b) *das Wort, das du suchst*   German
          le mot que tu cherches   French
          the word that you are looking for

     (c) *Sie hat gearbeitet.*   German
          Elle a travaillé.   French
          She has worked.

(d) *Kennedy wurde ermordet.*   German
     Kennedy fut tué.   French
     Kennedy was murdered.

If we take just these five features and restrict ourselves, for illustration only, to Irish, Icelandic, German, French, Spanish, Russian, German and Hungarian, we arrive at Table 1 – data all based on Haspelmath (2001).

	Ir	Ice	Ger	Fre	Spa	Rus	Hng
Def + Indef articles	No	No	Yes	Yes	Yes	No	No
'have'-perfects	No	Yes	Yes	Yes	Yes	No	No
Relative pronouns	No	Yes	Yes	Yes	Yes	Yes	Yes
Participial passives	Yes	Yes	Yes	Yes	Yes	Yes	Yes
Non-pro-drop	No	Yes	Yes	Yes	No	No	No

Table 1: Some features characterising Standard Average European

Table 1 illustrates that with respect to the five features tabulated, German and French are Standard Average European, Spanish and Icelandic a little bit less so, but for a different reason, Russian is better than Irish and non-Indo-European Hungarian scores better than Irish. Note that we do not require any of the above features to be unique to Standard Average European. One does find definite and indefinite articles outside of Europe (Lyons, 1999) and even the non-pro-drop feature, which is at least rare outside of Europe, is nevertheless not unique to it. Siewierska (1999: 239) lists the Sko language Vanimo, spoken in Papua New Guinea and the Oceanic languages Aneityum and Labu as non-pro-drop languages and we could add the Oceanic languages Kele (Ross, 2002a: 142) and Yabem (Ross, 2002b: 291).

3   Modal polyfunctionality

The term 'modal polyfunctionality' is to refer to the fact that modal verbs or, better, modal markers may have more than one function. More specifically, we will call the modal marker 'polyfunctional' if it allows both a so-called 'epistemic' and what we will call a 'situational' interpretation.[2] We have shown this with data from English in (1) and (2). But English is not at all alone in having polyfunctional modals. This can be illustrated with (4) (for an explanation of abbreviations, see list of abbreviations after the notes).

(4) (a) Norwegian (Bokmål) (Eide, 2002: 18)
Jon kan være på kontoret.
Jon can be on office. DEF
Jon may be in his office.

(b) Polish (Ewa Schalley, p. c.)
On może teraz skoczyć do wody.
he can. 3SG now jump. INF. PFV to water. GEN
He may jump into the water now. or
He may be jumping into the water now.

Let us concentrate on the Norwegian example. In one of the interpretations of (4a) we take the speaker to believe that it is possible that Jon is in his office. This is the 'epistemic' reading. The terminology is fairly conventional, with 'epistemic' deriving from the Greek word for 'knowledge'. The epistemic use indeed refers to the speaker's knowledge, his degree of certainty about or commitment to the truth of the proposition 'Jon is in the office'. With epistemic possibility, the degree is intermediate. The speaker is by no means certain. It is compatible with the speaker's beliefs that Jon is in his office, but it is equally compatible that he is not. But then there is another reading, the non-epistemic one. In this reading (4a) expresses that Jon has permission to be in his office. This permission derives from a person, possibly just the speaker, or a group of persons, possibly society as a whole, which has codified its permissions – as well as obligations – in conventions and laws (see 5).

(5) Women may wear hats in church.

Instead of negatively characterising this possibility as 'non-epistemic', we like to call this reading 'situational' (van der Auwera and Ammann in print c) – another term found in the literature is 'root' (Coates, 1983). The reading is situational because the possibility is a component of the situation referred to by the sentence. It thus contrasts with the epistemic reading, in which the modality is not within the situation, but rather concerns the speaker's degree of confidence as to whether or not the situation obtains. Of course, for many sentences, there may only be one reading. This has already been illustrated with English (1a) to (b) and again with (5). The fact remains that by itself English *may* is polyfunctional.

For the purposes of this chapter the term 'polyfunctionality' will only refer to the contrast between the epistemic and the situational functions. This is not the whole story, however. At least there are subtypes of situational possibility and markers may or may not be vague between the subtypes. The situational subtype illustrated so far, that of permission, is commonly called 'deontic'.

In (6) the possibility is also in the situation, but it concerns an ability rather than a permission.

(6) (a) Norwegian (Bokmål) (Eide, 2002: 25)
     Marit kan svømme.
     Marit can swim
     Marit can swim.

     (b) Polish (Ewa Schalley, p. c.)
     Magda może czytać.
     Magda   can. 3SG read. INF. IPFV
     Magda can read.

The possibility is situational, but not deontic. One can call it 'dynamic' (Palmer, 1986/20012) or 'dispositional' (Eide, 2002). We prefer 'participant-internal' (van der Auwera and Plungian, 1998), because it contrasts with 'participant-external', which we take as a superordinate term for 'deontic'. The subclassification of possibility is not, however, important for this chapter. It suffices to make clear that the examples in (6a) to (b) are no less situational than the ones in (4a) to (b) and (5).

With necessity the distinctions are fully parallel.

(7)   Norwegian (Bokmål) (Eide, 2002: 8)
     Jon må   være på kontoret.
     Jon must be   on office. DEF
     Jon must be in his office.

The deontic reading refers to an obligation for Jon to be his office. The epistemic one, often also called 'inferential', refers to a conclusion the speaker is making. Relative to the speaker's evidence, it follows – it is necessary – that Jon is in his office. Compared to epistemic possibility, we are now dealing with a higher degree of certainty and with a probability rather than a mere possibility.

Note also that we are fully aware of the fact that the distinction between possibility and necessity is not really an either-or matter. We are in fact dealing with a cline and there may well be more points on any modal cline for any language than just one simple possibility point and another simple necessity point. For German epistemic modality, for instance, we may well be dealing with a scale like (8).

(8)   *könnte > kann / mag > sollte > müsste / dürfte > wird > muss*

The meanings of modal verbs interact in complex ways and a scale such as (8) probably does not reflect the usage of every speaker of German. Nevertheless, it is usually easy to identify markers as belonging either to the possibility family, like *könnte, kann* and *mag*, or the necessity family, like *müsste, dürfte, wird* and *muss*. Towards the middle it may be more difficult, like with *sollte,* the subjunctive form of a weak necessity modal.

We are also aware of the fact that some markers are vague between necessity and possibility. In Danish, for instance, *må* can function for both permission and obligation.

(9)   Danish (Davidsen-Nielsen, 1990: 187)
        Nu må   du fortælle.
        now may/must   you tell
        Now you may/must tell a story.

This vagueness could be called 'polyfunctionality' too, but we do not study this phenomenon in this chapter. Markers like Danish *må* will count both for necessity and for possibility.

We have deliberately used the terms 'function' and 'polyfunctionality'. It is not important for our purposes to decide on whether or not we are dealing with a modal *kunne* in (4a) that has one meaning, necessarily a little abstract and vague and two or more uses or functions, or rather with a polysemous *kunne,* with two or more meanings. In the literature on modal verbs, both monosemy and polysemy accounts find their supporters. For English, Perkins (1983) is a good example of a strong monosemy thesis, as compared with Palmer (1979) for a polysemy thesis. It is also common to find mixed accounts. Modals tend to have many more functions than just two or three and then authors may consider a monosemy analysis appropriate for some and a polysemy account for others. For the Old Japanese verbal suffix *-beshi,* for instance, Narrog (2002: 126–7) points out that the average analysis posits five to six meanings, with an extreme going to twenty-two meanings, but he defends polysemy for only two meanings and derives all other readings through vagueness or implicature.

Modal polyfunctionality is not a surprising phenomenon. There is a large body of work demonstrating that the epistemic function is a natural and cross-linguistically widely attested development of the situational one, which may furthermore involve an increase in degree of grammaticalisation. This scenario is represented in the form of a small semantic map[3] in (10).

(10)

(10) 'says' that both situational modality and epistemic modality occupy a place in semantic space – the two ellipses. The functions are very close to each other

– they are connected with a line. This line is actually an arrow, meaning that if a language develops one function out of the other, it is situational modality that leads to epistemic modality and not the other way round[4].

Cross-linguistic studies supporting the claim represented in (10) and referring to much of the language-specific work are Bybee, Perkins and Pagliuca (1994) and van der Auwera and Plungian (1998), with the former focusing on the grammaticalisation facts and the latter on the semantics. The examples in (11) to (12) supply two non-European illustrations of the polyfunctionality. They also show that the polyfunctionality is not only a feature of verbs/auxiliaries as in Norwegian and Polish, but also of suffixes (West Greenlandic) and particles (Ainu).

(11)   West Greenlandic (Fortescue, 1984: 292, 294)

   (a) *Inna-jaa-ssa-atit.*
       go. to. bed-early-NEC-IND. 2SG
       You must go to bed early.

   (b) *Kǿbenhavni-mii-ssa-aq.*
       Copenhagen-be. in-NEC-IND. 3SG
       She must be in Copenhagen.

(12)   Ainu (Refsing, 1986: 204, Tamura, 2000: 118)

   (a) *A   kor   nispa,   hokure kuni   a   cisehe   orun   e   hosipi.*
       I   ATTR husband hurry NEC   we   house. of ALL   you return
       My husband, you must hurry and return to our house.

   (b) *Tapan   hekaci   poro   yakun,   isanispa ne   an   kuni*
       this   youth   be. big   if   doctor   as/into   be   NEC
       p   ne.
       thing   become
       When this child grows up, (s)he should become a doctor.

Some languages use the same markers for situational and epistemic functions, but with a different syntactic pattern. In Irish, modal verbs combine with a verbal noun when the reading is situational, but with a finite complement when it is epistemic (Ó Siadhail, 1989: 289). In Maltese, the expressions of epistemic modality trigger the presence of the copula *jkun*, comparable to English 'may be (the case)' or 'must be (the case)' (Borg and Azzopardi-Alexander, 1997: 241). The modal verb itself as well as the copula are always in the third person singular masculine form, as shown in (13a) for epistemic possibility. In (13b), an expression of situational possibility, the modal verb *seta'* is inflected for person and there is no copula.

(13)   Maltese (Borg and Azzopardi-Alexander, 1997: 241, 240)
   (a) *Jista'   jkun   li   qieghed   hemm*
       can. 3SG. M   be. 3SG. M   that located. M. SG   there
       It may be the case that he's there.

   (b) *Tistghu   toqoghdu   bil-qieghda.*
       can. 2pl   stay. 2pl   with. the-sitting
       You can/may sit down.

So the patterns which Maltese uses for situational and epistemic possibility are not identical. But the markers that express the modal notions are the same for both situational and epistemic modality in Maltese (*seta´* 'can' and *ghandu* 'must'), as well as in Irish. Therefore we include such cases as instances of polyfunctionality.

Finally, we will consider a language to exhibit modal polyfunctionality for either necessity or possibility if there is at least one marker for necessity or possibility, as the case may be, that exhibits the polyfunctionality. In other words, we by no means require the whole set of markers or even a majority to be polyfunctional.

4 Modal polyfunctionality in Standard Average European

In van der Auwera and Ammann (in print b), we investigated modality on the basis of a more or less representative sample of 284 languages, itself based on the 200 language sample that was set as a goal for the overall *World Atlas of Language Structures* (Dryer, Haspelmath, Gil and Comrie in print). We addressed the issue of modal polyfunctionality and claimed that the overlap of expressions for both possibility and necessity seemed most typical of Europe, though we did not then link up this finding with the Standard Average European hypothesis.

The actual number of languages on which we based the observation was 205 languages, with a remaining 79 languages for which we considered the evidence to be inconclusive. The latter set comprised almost exclusively non-European languages, thus giving the sample a European bias. For this reason, we have expanded the 205 language set with non-European languages. At this stage the number of additional languages is 37, thus reaching a total set of 241 languages. There is a bibliographical bias now: we have chosen languages with good descriptions and available experts or both. But even then, as we will see, for 15 languages of the overall set of 241 languages we could only reach a partial hypothesis. Moreover, on the basis of our experience with the repeated checking of the data, we expect to have underrepresented the polyfunctionality. Especially in languages in which the marking of situational modality is not (highly) grammaticalised, the existence of the epistemic reading may have escaped the grammarian's attention. But the opposite danger is also present: on the basis of the input from mostly English (but also French, German and Russian) native speakers and/or linguists may have felt forced to contrive artificial interpretations.

For the 241 languages we again investigated whether the language allows polyfunctionality for both possibility and necessity. As compared to van der Auwera and Ammann (in print b), we have more languages and we also have more categories. We earlier distinguished between three categories: no modal polyfunctionality, full modal polyfunctionality (necessity and possibility) and partial modal polyfunctionality (either necessity or possibility but not both). In this study we split up the third category. And we also include languages for which we have conclusive information only for possibility or necessity if they do display this polyfunctionality in this one domain. These languages are now in the category of 'necessity only' or 'possibility only', but they may be promoted to 'necessity and possibility' on the basis of more information. The four categories are mapped in the map in Appendix 1.

Type		Number of languages
	necessity and possibility	49
The language shows modal polyfunctionality for	necessity only	26 (+?4)
	possibility only	28 (+?11)
	neither necessity nor possibility	123

Table 2: Do languages show modal polyfunctionality?

On the basis of these figures and maps, we draw the following conclusions:

i) polyfunctionality for either or both necessity and possibility occurs on all continents;
ii) there is no indication that either possibility or necessity is more likely to be expressed with polyfunctional markers;
iii) polyfunctionality for both necessity and possibility is much more restricted and is most conspicuous for Europe

The first conclusion was to be expected. The processes through which epistemic modality functions may arrive from situational ones are semantic and universal, as described by Bybee, Perkins and Plagliuca (1994) and van der Auwera and Plungian (1998). The second conclusion was not exactly expected, but at least it makes sense. Given that the process is a semantic one, we indeed cannot imagine anything in the semantics of necessity or possibility that would ease the polyfunctionality. The third conclusion reinforces the hypothesis in van der Auwera and Ammann (in print b): modal polyfunctionality for both possibility and necessity is typical of Europe: the majority of the additional languages do not exhibit the full polyfunctionality omnipresent in Europe.

Let us have a more careful look at the languages mapped for modal poly-functionality with regard to both possibility and necessity. We list them by phylum, using the classification of Grimes (2000), the 14th edition of the *Ethnologue*[5].

Afro-Asiatic	Amharic, Arabic (Cairene Egyptian), Hausa, Hebrew, Maltese
Altaic	Turkish, Tuvin
Austronesian	Kumak, Tagalog
Daic	Thai
Dravidian	Kannada, Malayalam, Tamil, Telugu
Eskimo-Aleut	Greenlandic (West)
Indo-European	Afrikaans, Danish, Dutch, English, Faroese, French, German, Greek, Irish, Italian, Kashmiri, Latvian, Lithuanian, Macedonian, Persian, Polish, Portuguese, Rumanian, Russian, Serbian/Croatian, Slovenian, Spanish, Swedish
Isolate	Basque
Na-Denne	Navajo
Niger-Congo	Moore, Fon, Yoruba
Nilo-Saharan	Zarma
North Caucasian	Bagvalal
Sepik-Ramu	Yimas
Sino-Tibetan	Chinese (Mandarin)
South Caucasian	Georgian
Uralic	Finnish

Table 3: Languages with modal polyfunctionality for necessity and possibility

The phylum for which the largest number of languages with modal polyfunc-tionality for both possibility and necessity is documented is Indo-European. As a first comment, it is important to stress that the actual number of languages is itself not important, because the sample still has a European bias. Secondly, genetic affiliation is a significant part of the explanation, but it is not the whole story, except for much of Romance, in which the polyfunctionality goes back to Latin *posse* and *debēre* (Lewis and Short, 1879/1975: 1403f.; Bolkestein, 1980: 120–33, 146). Note that Indo-Iranian does not seem to join in as a group and of course, if we are dealing with a Western *Sprachbund*, it should not. At least, Armenian, Marathi, Maithili, Panjanbi and Hindi were investigated and not found to exhibit the double polyfunctionality. We hasten to add though that many more Indo-Iranian languages should be investigated and with at least Persian clearly showing the double polyfunctionality it is possible that the Western area is part of a much larger area. We also have to add that there are exceptions in Western Europe, like Catalan, Icelandic and Welsh, but we will discuss them later on and show that they actually were 'well-behaved' modal polyfunctional languages at an earlier stage. Furthermore, even though a language family like Germanic may have most of its languages polyfunctional, the development from situational to epistemic functions has taken place in historical times (e. g. Goossens, 1985; 2000 on English, or Nuyts, 1996 on Dutch) and this is too late to blame it all on any ancestral language. In Romance the modal polyfunctionality remained stable over many centuries almost throughout, even in Rumanian, which replaced its ancestral *debēre* with a South Slavic *a trebui*. Such a long history of uninterrupted modal polyfunctionality may be the exception rather than the rule in Europe and thus blaming only Latin for the polyfunctionality is not good enough. Thirdly, we also find non-Indo-European languages exhibiting the double polyfunctionality and at least some of them are known to have been influenced by Western Indo-European languages, viz. Basque, Maltese and even West Greenlandic (Fortescue, 1984: 293). Finnish belongs here too and it is of particular interest that Northern Saami, which was in the sample as well, shows absolutely no modal polyfunctionality (Sammallahti, 1998: 85; Bartens, 1989: 295–96, 421). This evidence suggests that the concentration of modal polyfunctionality in Europe has an areal dimension. Whether or not an areal influence could have played a role for other languages close to Europe, viz. Cairene Egyptian Arabic, Hebrew or Turkish is a matter that demands more study. With respect to Turkish, for instance, it is interesting to see that of the three other Turkic languages in the sample neither Uzbek nor South Azerbaijani show any polyfunctionality, but then faraway Tuvin is like Turkish.

Note that a language does not have to be geographically close to Europe or a European language area. What matters more is cultural distance. The case of Tagalog might be instructive. It has full polyfunctionality. It is clear that the language has undergone influence from Spanish and one of the many loans in Tagalog from Spanish is *puwede* 'can'. Even for Chinese, European influence on the modals, most specifically on the epistemic function, has been suspected (Wang, 1943/1985: 352; 1944/1991: 102 – reference due to Li, 2003: 238).

A last point to remind ourselves of is that there is absolutely no need to explain all of the double modal polyfunctionality through contact convergence starting from Europe. For one thing, as the spread of polyfunctionality for just possibility or just necessity clearly shows (see the map in Appendix 1), the potential for modal polyfunctionality is universal. For another thing, if modal polyfunctionality could have spread through convergence in Europe, it could have spread elsewhere as well. And finally, modal polyfunctionality is still to some extent a family matter, characterising the Romance, Germanic and Slavic languages. These languages are European, but there could just as well be non-European languages that fell for modal polyfunctionality. Dravidian languages of Southern India might be such a family.

5   How to lose modal polyfunctionality?

Since possibility and necessity are closely related, one could be tempted into thinking that if a language has a polyfunctional modal (or several) in one domain, it will also have polyfunctional modals in the other. But this is not the case. Tables 4 and 5 in Appendix 2 list some 20-odd languages that are polyfunctional only for possibility and about as many for necessity. This asymmetry can be shown even in English. *Must* can be used for situational and epistemic necessity as in (14a) and (14b). But *can* does not show the same degree of polyfunctionality: (14c) is awkward or just wrong (one expects *may* or *could* instead), whereas (14d), the negation, is acceptable. But if we bring in negation, then we find epistemic *mustn't* to be strange (14e), at least in British English (Tottie, 1985: 109).

(14) (a)   You must leave now.
    (b)   You must be joking.
    (c)   He can be joking.
    (d)   Those two can't be twins!
    (e)   That bike is yellow, so it must not be Jane's.

There are two possible reasons why a language lacks the polyfunctionality. One is that the situational marker simply never developed any epistemic uses and the epistemic markers derive from other domains (like the expression of a future or the grammaticalisation of a 'think' verb or 'seem' or 'be' construction – see van der Auwera and Plungian, 1998 and van der Auwera and Ammann in print a). The other is that the language had polyfunctional possibility and necessity modals at an earlier stage, but a later process of grammaticalisation 'pushed' one of the older markers out of the situational domain. The new marker is situational and the old one retains only the epistemic functions. Phenomena of this kind have been described already by Kuryłowicz (1964). When a new expression enters the language, it does not always oust an older one. The older competitor may be used alongside the new expression, or it may be relegated to uses that were peripheral before. Epistemic modal functions could be peripheral in just this sense.

An example of this scenario comes from Catalan. In earlier stages, the modality expressions in Catalan were 'well-behaved' for a Romance language and hence it had a symmetrical system. There was one central marker for possibility (continuing the Latin verb *posse*) and one for necessity (continuing the Latin verb *debēre*) and both were polyfunctional. But this no longer holds for Modern Catalan. *Deure* < Latin *debēre* 'must, should' is considered a Castilianism in situational uses. By now it is only accepted by the prescriptive grammar of Catalan when it encodes epistemic necessity (Hualde, 1992: 325) and for situational necessity one uses *haver de* 'have of'. Things are similar with *deber (de)* in the prescriptive grammar of Spanish, which recommends to use *deber* without *de* if the reading is situational and with *de* if it is epistemic, but in Spanish most speakers do not bother to make this distinction (Silva-Corvalán, 1995: 87). In Spanish, a newly grammaticalised necessity expression, *tener que*, which compares to English 'have to' (literally 'have that'), has also moved into the epistemic realm lately (Silva-Corvalán, 1995: 90). So we see two opposing trends in Ibero-Romance. The development in Spanish preserves and even strengthens the identity of situational and epistemic necessity expressions. By contrast, the history of Catalan shows how a symmetrical system can become asymmetrical through the grammaticalisation of a new marker that has stripped an earlier marker of its situational function, but has not acquired an epistemic one itself. Compare (15a) to (b) from Catalan with (16a) to (b) from Spanish.

(15)   Catalan (Hualde, 1992: 325)
   (a) *Heu*   *de fer-ho*   *aviat.*
      have. 2PL   of   do. INF-it   soon
      You (pl.) have to do it soon.

   (b) *Deu*   *haver*   *arribat ja.*
      must. 3SG   have. INF   arrived   already
      He must have arrived already.

(16)   Spanish
   (a) *Debéis*   *hacerlo*   *pronto.*
      must. 2pl   do. INF. it   soon
      You (pl.) have to do it soon.

   (b) *Debe*   *haber*   *llegado ya.*
      must. 3sg   have. INF   arrived   already
      He must have arrived already.

For Icelandic, a similar kind of scenario would seem plausible: for possibility there is polyfunctionality, but for necessity there is a division of labour between epistemic *hljóta* and situational *verdha*. But the epistemic verb probably had a situational use before, given that it derives from and still also functions as a main verb meaning 'get' (see van der Auwera and Plungian, 1998: 103–4 on Swedish, and Enfield 2001; 2002 on South-East Asia). The story of Welsh is slightly different. It is polyfunctional in the field of necessity, with the marker *rhaid* (King, 1993: 212). It has an epistemic possibility marker *efallai* and a situational possibility marker *gallu*. However, the two are etymologically related, but the relationship has become opaque and *efallai* should be considered an adverb (Fife, 1990: 279; King, 1993: 261). Thus, Welsh differs from its sister language Irish, mentioned above at the end of Section 3[6]. So in Welsh, different from Catalan or Icelandic, the situational source element of the epistemic marker is still in place, but there has been a clear formal split. For Welsh, we can no longer talk about the two functions of one form, but rather about the single functions of two forms. What Welsh, Catalan and probably also Icelandic share, however, is that they once did exhibit the Euro-typical modal polyfunctionality. For outside of Europe, historical sources are often absent, of course, but it is our hunch that for many of the non-European languages lacking the said polyfunctionality, the reason is different: it is not that they had it and then lost it, they never had it. This hunch is hereby offered as a task for future research.

6   Other evidence

There is no way that our cross-linguistic survey can show to what extent the massive modal polyfunctionality we find in Europe is the result of contact interference. For this, more fine-grained comparative work is necessary, synchronic but especially diachronic. But even at this stage, it is useful to point out that modal markers seems to be borrowed easily, worldwide[7] and also in Europe, which, if anything, should be in favor of the assumption that modality could be a feature of a *Sprachbund*. The German modals, in particular, are a 'success story' (Hansen, 2000: 77). German modals traveled into Swedish (the modal *måste* 'must', Birkmann, 1987: 301, 380) and Hungarian (the particle *muszaj* < *muss sein* 'must be', Hansen, 2000: 9), but especially into Slavic – a journey well described by Hansen (2000). West and East Slavic languages borrowed *müssen* 'must, have to' from German and less frequently *dürfen*, which means 'may' in Modern German, but used to be an expression of necessity. In Russian, *musit'* was later lost from the standard language and survives only in the dialects (Hansen, 2000: 83). The South Slavic languages did not borrow a necessity modal from German directly, but probably split off a necessity verb from the older possibility verb, a process which spread southeastward from Slovenian (Hansen, 2000: 85–6) and never reached Bulgarian. Hansen explains the success of *müssen* in Slavonic in the following way: when speakers of Slavic languages came into contact with speakers of German, their languages only had verbal auxiliaries for volition and possibility. This was the situation in Old Church Slavonic, where the necessity expressions also had lexical uses and were impersonal (Hansen, 2000: 89). Through language contact with German, which had auxiliarised *müssen* as an auxiliary expressing necessity, the West Slavic languages as well as Ukrainian and Belorussian borrowed this modal directly, whereas Slovenian and Serbian/Croatian calqued it. By the time the borrowed verb reached Russian, the non-verbal, impersonal *dolžen* had already become fixed as a necessity expression, so *musit'* did not have as much of a gap in the system to fill (Hansen, 2000: 90)[8].

More than 30 years ago, Porák (1968) also studied East and West Slavic modal systems with a focus on borrowed items but with an additional focus on the nature of the modal expressions. According to Porák, Czech and Russian can be seen as two extremes. In Czech, modal expressions are usually verbs inflected for person. The uses of modal infinitives and modal adverbs are receding. By contrast, Russian resorts more to modal infinitives and impersonal expressions and it does not have a modal verb for necessity. In this language, the agent can still be marked for dative case in some expressions of modality, which is no longer possible in Czech (Porák, 1968: 101). Polish, Slovak and Moravian dialects of Czech are intermediate: like Standard Czech, their modal systems contain a necessity verb borrowed from German, but modal infinitives and expressions that are not inflected for person are more common than in Standard Czech (Porák, 1968: 100–1). The distribution is that of an areal cline. The archaic side is Russian and the modernising one is Czech and the driving force is 'Europäisierung' through German and possibly even medieval Latin. So we see that European modals had already set a linguist thinking about a contact hypothesis long before our present awareness of the reality of a Standard Average European *Sprachbund*. And Porák's old observation that the more European East and West Slavic languages use inflected verbs for modality is a pointer for future research. In van der Auwera and Ammann (in print a) we also noted – but our study was restricted to epistemic possibility – that Europe uses verbs for this domain more frequently than any other region in the world, despite a universal tendency for bound markers like clitics or affixes (Bybee, 1985: 168), particles or adverbs (van der Auwera and Ammann in print a). The verbiness of modality may well be another feature of Standard Average European, connecting well with the European verbiness of at least one other domain, viz. possession, as expressed by a 'have' verb.

Conclusion

In this chapter we hope to have shown that modal polyfunctionality for both necessity and possibility is not spread evenly in the families and regions of the world. It is clear that the said polyfunctionality is typical for at least 'western' Indo-European and for Europe. To that extent there is evidence for considering modal polyfunctionality for necessity and possibility as part of the make-up of Standard Average European, but there is a need for more and more detailed research, synchronic (esp. on Semitic, Finno-Ugric, Turkic and Indo-Iranian) and diachronic. We also claimed that modal polyfunctionality is a universal potentiality, which can realise itself independently for possibility and for necessity. We also commented on the decline of polyfunctionality and we have shown that modal markers seem to be borrowed easily. We ended on a comment on the verbiness of European modal markers, particularly the ones that express epistemic modality and we raised the question whether this too could be a feature of Standard Average European.

Notes

1   This chapter continues the work reported on in van der Auwera and Ammann (in print a, b, c). The ideas were presented at Wayne State University (Michigan Linguistic Society Nov 2002) and at LACITO (*Langues et Civilisations à Tradition Orale*, Paris June 2003). Most of the sources and experts consulted are listed in Dryer, Haspelmath, Gil and Comrie (in print). For the 'additional languages' we want to express our gratitude to the following colleagues: Mahamane L. Abdoulaye (Kanuri, Zarma), Azeb Amha (Amharic, Male, Wolaytta), Erik Andvik (Tshangla), Isabelle Bril (Kumak), Mary Ann Corbière (Ottawa), Yavar Dehghan (South Azerbaijani), Magdi Fouad (Egyptian Arabic), Nilson Gabas Jr. (Karo), Louise Anna Hercus (Wirangu), Dmitry Idiatov (Toura), Stephanie Inglis (Micmac), Alan Jones (Mekeo), Malika Kaheroui (Tachelhit Berber), Behrooz Mahmoodi-Bakhtiari (Persian) Andrej Malchukov (Even), Martha Ratliff (Hmong), Madeleine Somte (Ngam), Mark Van de Velde (Eton), Jean-Christophe Verstraete (Umbindhamu) and Marie-Thérèse Zerbo (Moore). We dedicate this chapter to the memory of our companion-in-languages Ludo Lejeune.

2   A point on terminology: for some linguists a marker can be called 'modal' only if it exhibits the situational – epistemic polyfunctionality (Thráinsson and Vikner, 1995: 53; Eide, 2002: 17–18; for a slightly wider notion of 'polyfunctionality' see Hansen, 2000: 87). This is not our conception and if it turns out that polyfunctionality is specifically European, then a definition that requires polyfunctionality is not a good candidate as a universal category. Our conception shows some affinity with that of Nuyts (this volume) in that we share his concern to keep in mind that situational and epistemic modality are different domains, a point which we stress through showing that their similarity by no means forces an

identical coding. Yet, different from Nuyts, we see no reason to abandon the term 'modality' as a superordinate term.

3   On 'semantic maps' in general, see Haspelmath (2003). A more comprehensive semantic map for modality is offered by van der Auwera and Plungian (1998).

4   The unidirectionality is not entirely uncontested. Thus Willie (1996: 345f) claims that the use of a combination of the Navajo markers meaning *t'áá* 'just' and *'aaníí* 'true' or *'íiyisíí* 'true' for deontic necessity is a secondary function and that the primary use of the construction is 'it is true', i. e. epistemic. With the same goal of showing that there can be counterexamples to the unidirectionality thesis, Livnat (2002: 110–113) describes uses of the adverb *ʔulay* 'perhaps' in contexts where its usage mitigates or aggravates deontic illocutionary force. In theory, if situational (in this case deontic) necessity and epistemic necessity are distinct, but similar concepts and if the transition from one domain to the other is a process of analogy (and nothing else), one would expect to find processes of language change going both ways in roughly the same amounts in the languages of the world. But this is not the case. Instead, there is an overwhelming (even if maybe not absolute) directionality: from situational to epistemic functions.

5   In Appendix 2 we provide similar tables for the other categories (Tables 4–6). Note that Table 6 contains a language that is not listed in Grimes (2000[14]): Karo, spoken in Brazil. 'It is genetically affiliated with the Ramarama branch of the Tupi family, one of the largest families of languages in South America. Karo is supposedly the sole language of its branch' (Gabas, 1999: viii).

6   The Welsh facts conform to a worldwide tendency for verbs to be used more frequently for situational than epistemic functions (Bybee, 1985: 168; van der Auwera and Ammann in print a, in print c). As verbs become epistemic, they can be turned into affixes or adverbs (like *efallai*).

7   For example, Chamorro has borrowed at least four modal markers from Spanish (Topping, 1973/1980[3]: 152–4, 265). *Puede* 'perhaps', *kasi* 'probably, perhaps' and *tieneki* 'surely, certainly', like most of the 'sentence-modifiers' in Chamorro, derive from Spanish (*puede* 'can, may', *casi* 'almost, nearly', *tiene que* 'has to'). The obligation marker *debidi* < *debe de* is of Spanish origin as well. Modal expressions of Arabic origin are found in 14 languages in our sample: Bagirmi, Bambara, Gujari, Hausa, Hunzib, Indonesian, Lezgian, Maba, Mehri, Persian, Swahili, Berber (Tamazight), Turkish and Uzbek. Russian has exported the necessity marker *nado* to Evenki, Ket and Udihe. A necessity expression *musti/mesti* has diffused throughout East Asia and several West African languages express necessity with *doolè* or similar words. In his grammar of Miya, Schuh (1998: 363) identifies *dóolèe* as a borrowing from Hausa. He points out that this goes for many of the 'complement taking expressions' in Miya (including modal ones) 'and other languages in this area which have been heavily influenced by Hausa' (1998: 362[8]). We owe the reference to this passage to Mahamane L. Abdoulaye.

8   This is a bit of a weak point about Hansen's description and explanation of the areal phenomenon of Slavic necessity modals. In what sense should *dolžen* have been more firmly established in the Russian modal system and why would this fact have blocked the integration of *musit'* into Standard Russian? Modern Rus-

sian is not unlike Old Church Slavonic: it has several expressions of necessity which are not (or at least not clearly) verbs. Hansen (2001: 187–9) mentions the competing marker *nado* – which, like *dolžen*, is not a verb, but also not marginal. Such strategies were also available for expressions of necessity at the time the West Slavic languages first borrowed *müssen* and yet, the borrowed modal was incorporated into the modal system. If a modal auxiliary of German origin offered any structural advantages to the speakers of Polish and Czech, why could the speakers of Russian do without it?

Abbreviations

The following is a list of abbreviations used in the article:

1	first person
2	second person
3	third person
ALL	allative
ATTR	attributive
DEF	definite article
GEN	genitive
IND	indicative
INF	infinitive
IPFV	imperfective
M	masculine
NEC	necessity
IND	indicative
PFV	perfective
PL	plural
SG	singular

Appendix 1

Modal polyfunctionality in 241 languages

Key to map opposite

◉	Necessity and possibility	◆	Possibility only
○	Necessity only	☐	Neither necessity nor possibility

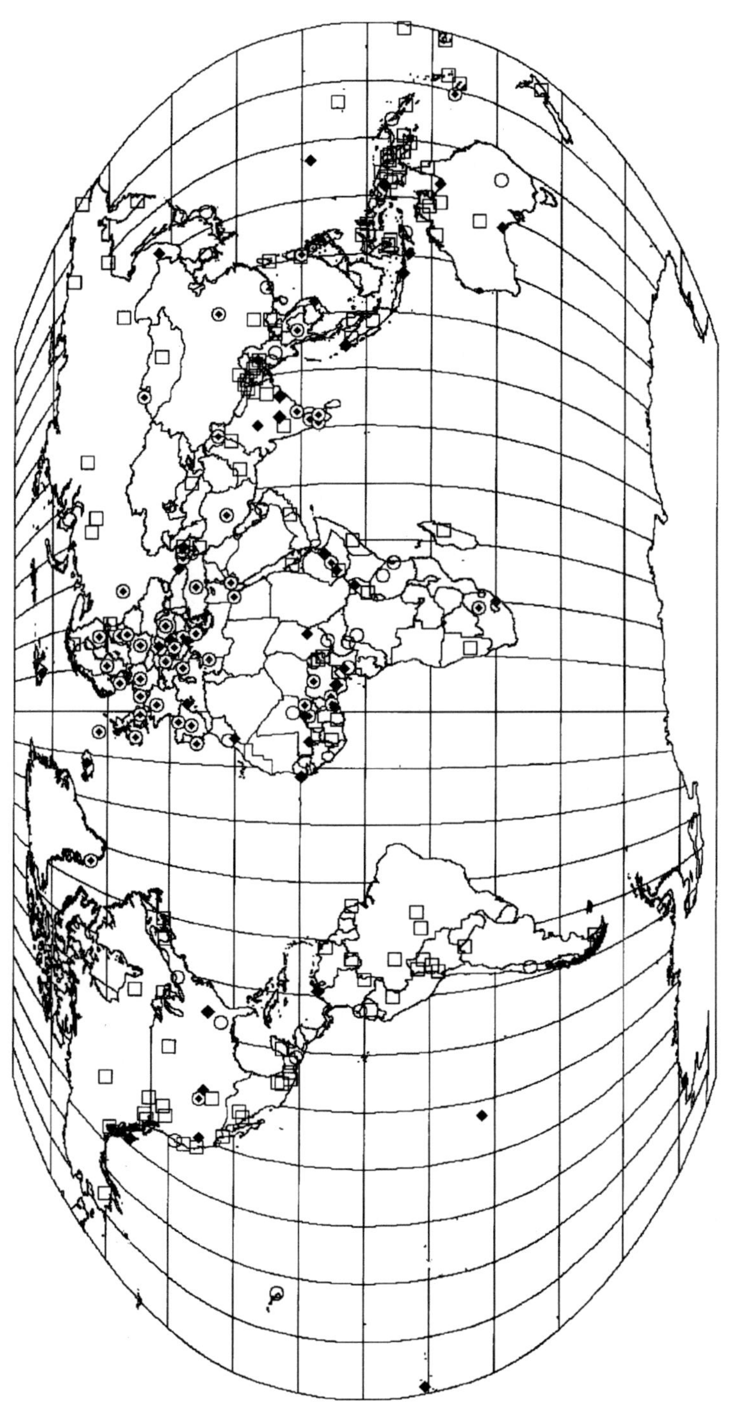

Appendix 2

Afro-Asiatic	Berber (Tachelhit),[Oromo (Harar)], Wolaytta
Australian	Kayardild, Wirangu
Austronesian	[Aceh], [Balinese], Futunan (East), Kambera, Rapanui
Altaic	Udihe
Austro-Asiatic	Vietnamese
Austronesian	Chamorro
Chibchan	[Ica]
Dravidian	[Kui], [Kolami]
Indo-European	Albanian, Catalan, Hindi, Icelandic, Romani (Vlach)
Isolate	[Yuchi]
Kiowa Tanoan	Kiowa
Na-Dene	[Haida]
Niger-Congo	Bafia, Bambara, Ewe, [Igbo], Koromfe, [Wolof (Dakar)], Zulu
Nilo-Saharan	Lango, Maba
Penutian	Miwok (Southern Sierra)
North Caucasian	Abkhaz, Lak
Sino-Tibetan	Naga (Tangkhul)
Trans-New Guinea	[Dani (Lower Grand Valley)]
Uralic	Hungarian

Table 4: Languages with modal polyfunctionality for possibility, but not necessity (no square brachets) and languages with modal polyfunctionality for possibility and inconclusive information on necessity (in square brackets)

Afro-Asiatic	Arabic (Gulf), Arabic (Moroccan), Iraqw
Araucanian	Mapuche
Australian	Ngiyambaa
Austronesian	Hawaiian, [Teop], Tetun
Barbacoan	Awa Pit
Indo-European	Armenian (Eastern), Welsh
Iroquoian	Oneida
Isolates	Ainu, Korean
Japanese	Japanese
Mayan	Jakaltek

Muskogean	Koasati
Niger-Congo	Eton, Fula/Pulaar, Kanuri, Swahili, Ngam
Nilo-Saharan	Lingala, [Songhay (Koyraboro Senni)], Sango
Penutian	Coos (Hanis)
Sino-Tibetan	[Bawm], Burmese, Chinese (Yue)
Uralic	[Nenets]

Table 5: Languages with modal polyfunctionality for necessity, but not possibility (no square brackets) and languages with modal polyfunctionality for necessity and inconclusive information on possibility (in square brackets)

Afro-Asiatic	Hdi, Kera, Male, Mehri, Tigri, Somali
Algic	Cree (Plains), Ottawa, Micmac, Passamaquoddy-Malisseet, Yurok
Altaic	Azerbaijani (South), Even, Evenki, Khalka, Uzbek
Arawakan	Paumari
Austro-Asiatic	Kammu, Khasi, Mundari, Semelai
Austronesian	Batak (Karo), Dehu, Fijian, Indonesian, Kapampangan, Kilivila/Kiriwana, Malagasy, Maori, Mekeo, Mokilese, Muna, Paiwan, Ratahan, Taba/East Makin, Tukang Besi, Tuvaluan, Ura
Australian	Mangarari, Maranungku, Nunggubuyu, Pitjantjara, Umbindhamu, Ungarinjin, Wambaya
Aymaran	Aymara
Chon	Ona/Selknam
Chukotko-Kamchatkan	Chukchi
Creole	Ndyuka
Dravidian	Brahui
East Papuan	Lavukaleve
Eskimo-Aleut	Yup´ik
Hmong-Mien	Hmong Dao, Hmong Njua, Iu Mien
Hokan	Diegueño, Pomo (Southeastern)
Indo-European	Maithili, Marathi, Punjabi

Isolates	Cayuvava, Kutenai, Nivkh, Trumai, Warao, Yukaghir
Keres	Acoma
Khoisan	Khoekhoe
Mataco-Guaicuru	Mataco
Mayan	Maya (Itza)
Mixe-Zoque	Zoque (Copainalá)
Mosetenan	Tsimané/Mosetén
Na-Dene	Slave, Tlingit
Niger-Congo	Akan, Mundang, Nkore-Kiga, Supyire, Toura, Vengo
North Caucasian	Hunzib, Lezgian
Oto-Manguean	Mixteco (Chalcatongo), Otomí (Mezquital), Zapoteco (Yatzachi)
Panoan	Shipibo-Konibo
Penutian	Nez Perce, Umatilla
Quechuan	Quechua (Imbabura)
Salishan	Lillooet, Squamish
Sino-Tibetan	Dzongkha, Garo, Ladakhi, Lepcha, Meithei (Manipuri), Naga (Mao), Tshangla, Yamphu
Siouan	Lakota
Tacanan	Araona
Trans-New Guinea	Amele, Asmat, Awara, Daga, Ekari, Imonda, Kapau, Kobon, Marind, Una, Usan
Tucanoan	Barasano
Tupi	Karo
Uralic	Khanti, Mansi/Vogul, Saami (Northern), Votic
Uto-Aztecan	Nahuatl (Tetelcingo), Pima Bajo, Yaqui
Yanomam	Sanuma
Yenisei Ostyak	Ket

Table 6: Languages with no attested modal polyfunctionality

References

Bartens, H.-H. (1989) *Lehrbuch der saamischen (lappischen) Sprache.* Hamburg: Buske.

Beckmann, N. (1934) *Västeuropeisk syntax: Några nybildningar i nordiska och andra västeuropeiska språk.* Göteborgs högskolas Årsskrift XL 4. Göteborg: Elanders.

Birkmann, T. (1987) *Präteritopräsentia: Morphologische Entwicklungen einer Sonderklasse in den altgermanischen. Sprachen* Linguistische Arbeiten 188. Tübingen: Niemeyer.

Bolkestein, A. M. (1980) *Problems in the Description of Modal Verbs: an investigation of Latin.* PhD Dissertation. University of Amsterdam. Assen: Van Gorcum.

Borg, A. and Azzopardi-Alexander, M. (1997) *Maltese.* Routledge Descriptive Grammars. London and New York: Routledge.

Bybee, J. (1985) *Morphology: a study of the relation between meaning and form.* Typological Studies in Language 9. Amsterdam: Benjamins.

Bybee, J., Perkins, R. and Pagliuca, W. (1994) *The Evolution of Grammar: tense, aspect and modality in the languages of the world.* Chicago: University of Chicago Press.

Coates, J. (1983) *The Semantics of the Modal Auxiliaries.* London: Croom Helm.

Davidsen-Nielsen, N. (1990) *Tense and Mood in English. A Comparison with Danish.* Berlin: Mouton de Gruyter.

Dryer, M., Haspelmath, M., Gil, D. and Comrie, B. (eds) (in print) *World Atlas of Language Structures.* Oxford: Oxford University Press.

Eide, K. E. (2002) *Norwegian modals.* Doctoral dissertation. Norwegian University of Science and Technology, Trondheim.

Enfield, N. J. (2001) On genetic and areal linguistics in mainland South-East Asia: parallel polyfunctionality of 'acquire'. In A. Y. Aikenvald and R. M. W. Dixon (eds) *Areal Diffusion and Genetic Inheritance. Problems in Comparative Linguistics* 255–90. Oxford: Oxford Unversity Press.

Enfield, N. J. (2002) *Linguistic Epidemiology: semantics and grammar of language contact in mainland South-East Asia.* Curzon Asiatic Linguistics. London and New York: Routledge.

Fife, J. (1990) *The Semantics of the Welsh Verb: a cognitive approach.* Cardiff: University of Wales Press.

Fortescue, M. (1984) *West Greenlandic.* Croom Helm Descriptive Grammars. London, Sydney and Dover, NH: Croom Helm.

Gabas, N. Jr. (1999) *A Grammar of Karo, Tupí (Brazil).* Doctoral dissertation University of California, Santa Barbara.

Goossens, L. (1985) *The Auxiliarization of the English Modals.* Working Papers in Functional Grammar 7. Amsterdam: Universiteit.

Goossens, L. (2000) Patterns of meaning extension, 'parallel chaining', subjectification and modal shifts, In A. Barcelona (ed.) *Metaphor and Metonymy at the Crossroads* 149–69. Berlin: Mouton de Gruyter.

Grimes, B. F. (ed.) (2000) *Ethnologue*. Dallas: SIL International.

Hansen, B. (2000) The German modal verb 'müssen' and the Slavonic languages: the reconstruction of a success story. *Scando-Slavica* 46: 77–93.

Hansen, B. (2001) *Das slavische Modalauxiliar: Semantik und Grammatikalisierung im Russischen, Polnischen, Serbischen/Kroatischen und Altkirchenslavischen.* Slavolinguistica 2. Munich: Sagner.

Haspelmath, M. (2001) The European linguistic area: Standard Average European. In M. Haspelmath, E. König, W. Oesterreicher and W. Raible (eds) *Language Typology and Language Universals: Sprachtypologie und sprachliche Universalien: la typologie des langues et les universaux linguistiques. An International Handbook: ein internationales Handbuch: manuel international* 1492–510. Berlin and New York: Walter de Gruyter.

Haspelmath, M. (2003) The geometry of grammatical meaning: semantic maps and cross-linguistic comparison. In M. Tomasello (ed.) *The new psychology of language: Cognitive and functional approaces to language structure. Vol.* 2. 211–42. Mahwah, New Jersey: Lawrence Erlbaum.

Hualde, I. (1992) *Catalan.* Routledge Descriptive Grammars. London and New York: Routledge.

King, G. (1993) *Modern Welsh: a comprehensive grammar.* London and New York: Routledge.

Kuryłowicz, J. (1964) *The Inflectional Categories of Indo-European.* Heidelberg: Winter.

Lewis, C. T. and Short, C. (1879/1975) *A Latin Dictionary: founded on Andrew's edition of Freund's Latin Dictionary. Revised, Enlarged and in Great Part Rewritten.* Reprint. Oxford: Oxford University Press.

Li, R. (2003) *Modality in English and Chinese: a typological perspective.* Doctoral dissertation. University of Antwerp.

Livnat, Z. (2002) From epistemic to deontic modality: evidence from Hebrew. *Folia Linguistica Historica* 23: 107–14.

Lyons, C. (1999) *Definiteness.* Cambridge: Cambridge University Press.

Narrog, H. (2002) Polysemy and indeterminacy in modal markers: the case of Japanese beshi. *Journal of East Asian Linguistics* 11: 123–67.

Nuyts, J. (1996) Das modale Hilfsverb *kunnen* und das System der epistemischen Modalität im Niederländischen: Überlegungen zur Synchronie und Diachronie. *Leuvense Bijdragen* 85: 33–54.

Nuyts, J. This volume. The modal confusion. On terminology and the concepts behind it.

Ó Siadhail, M. (1989) *Modern Irish: grammatical structure and dialectal variation.* Cambridge Studies in Linguistics, Supplementary Volume 1989: 1. Cambridge: Cambridge University Press.

Palmer, F. (1979) *Modality and the English modals.* London: Longman.

Palmer, F. (1986/2001) *Mood and Modality*. Cambridge: Cambridge University Press.

Perkins, M. R. (1983) *Modal Expressions in English*. London: Pinter.

Porák, J. (1968) Modalverben im Tschechischen und Deutschen. In *Deutsch-tschechische Beziehungen im Bereich der Sprache und Kultur*, B. Havránek and R. Fischer (eds) 97–101. Abhandlungen der sächsischen Akademie der Wissenschaften zu Leipzig. Philologisch-historische Klasse 59. Berlin: Akademie-Verlag.

Refsing, K. (1986) *The Ainu Language*: *the morphology and syntax of the Shizunai dialect*. Aarhus: Aarhus University Press.

Ross, M. (2002a) Kele. In J. Lynch, M. Ross and T. Crowley (eds) *The Oceanic Languages* 123–47. Curzon Language Family Series. Richmond: Curzon.

Ross, M. (2002b) Jabêm. In J. Lynch, M. Ross and T. Crowley (eds) *The Oceanic Languages*. 270–96. Curzon Language Family Series. Richmond: Curzon.

Sammallahti, P. (1998) Saamic. In D. Abondolo (ed.) *The Uralic Languages* 43–95. Routledge Language Family Descriptions. London and New York: Routledge.

Schuh, R. (1998) *A Grammar of Miya*. University of California Publications in Linguistics 130. Berkeley, Los Angeles and London: University of California Press.

Siewierska, A. (1999) From anaphoric pronoun to grammatical agreement marker: why objects don't make it. *Folia Linguistica* 33: 225–51.

Silva-Corvalán, C. (1995) Contextual conditions for the interpretation of poder and deber in Spanish. In J. Bybee and S. Fleischman (eds) *Modality in Grammar and Discourse* 67–105. Typological Studies in Language 32. Amsterdam and Philadelphia: John Benjamins.

Tamura, S. (2000) *The Ainu Language*. ICHEL Linguistic Studies 2. Tokyo: Sanseido.

Thráinsson, H. and Vikner, S. (1995) Modals and double modals in the Scandinavian languages. *Working Papers in Scandinavian Syntax* 55: 51–88.

Topping, D. M. with the assistance of Dungca, B. C. (1973/1980) *Chamorro Reference Grammar.* Honolulu: University Press of Hawaii.

Tottie, G. (1985) The negation of epistemic necessity in present-day British and American English. *English World-Wide* 6: 87–116.

van der Auwera, J. with Ó Baoill, D. P. (ed.) (1998) *Adverbial Constructions in the Languages of Europe*. Berlin and New York: Mouton de Gruyter.

van der Auwera, J. and Ammann, A. (in print a) Epistemic possibility. M. Dryer, M. Haspelmath, D. Gil and B. Comrie (eds) In *World Atlas of Language Structures*. Oxford: Oxford University Press.

van der Auwera, J. and Ammann, A. (in print b) Overlap between situational and epistemic modal marking. In M. Dryer, M. Haspelmath, D. Gil and B. Comrie (eds) *World Atlas of Language Structures*. Oxford: Oxford University Press.

van der Auwera, J. and Ammann, A. (in print c) Situational possibility. In M. Dryer, M. Haspelmath, D. Gil and B. Comrie (eds) *World Atlas of Language Structures*. Oxford: Oxford University Press.

van der Auwera, J. and Plungian, V. (1998) Modality's semantic map. *Linguistic Typology* 2: 79–124.

Wang, L. (1943) *Zhongguo Xiandai Yufa*. Modern Chinese Grammar. Shanghai: Commercial Press. Reprinted in 1985. Beijing: Commercial Press.

Wang, L. (1944) *Zhongguo Yufa Lilun*. Theory of Chinese Grammar. Shanghai: Commercial Press. Reprinted in 1991. Jinan: Shandong Education Press.

Whorf, B. L. (1941) The relation between habitual thought and behavior to language. In L. Spier (ed.) *Language, Culture and Personality*: *essays in memory of Edward Sapir* 75–93. Menasha, Wis.: Sapir Memorial Publication Fund. Reprinted in J. B. Carroll (ed.) (1956) *Language, Thought and Reality*: *selected writings of Benjamin Lee Whorf* 134–59. Cambridge, Mass.: The MIT Press.

Whorf, B. L. (1945) Grammatical categories. *Language* 21: 1–11. Reprinted in J. B. Carroll (ed.) (1956) *Language, Thought and Reality*: *selected writings of Benjamin Lee Whorf* 87–101. Cambridge, Mass.: The MIT Press.

Willie, M. (1996) On the expression of modality in Navajo. In S. Midgette, E. Jelinek, K. Rice and L. Saxon *Athabascan Language Studies. Essays in Honor of Robert W. Young* 331–46. Albuquerque: University of New Mexico Press.

Index

CPSIA information can be obtained at www.ICGtesting.com
Printed in the USA
BVOW011744040612

291743BV00003B/27/P